Why Smart People Do Dumb Things

Mortimer R. Feinberg, Ph.D.,
AND
John J. Tarrant

A Fireside Book
Published by Simon & Schuster
New York·London·Toronto·Sydney·Tokyo·Singapore

FIRESIDE
Rockefeller Center
1230 Avenue of the Americas
New York, New York 10020

Copyright © 1995 by Mortimer Feinberg and John J. Tarrant

Designed by Diane Stevenson/Snap-Haus
Manufactured in the United States of America

3 5 7 9 10 8 6 4 2

Library of Congress Cataloging-in-Publication Data
Feinberg, Mortimer R.
Why smart people do dumb things / Mortimer R. Feinberg and John J. Tarrant.
p. cm.
"A Fireside book."
Includes index.
1. Decision-making. 2. Intellect. 3. Stupidity. 4. Errors—Psychological
aspects. 5. Cognitive therapy—Popular works. 6. Conduct of life. I. Tarrant, John J.
II. Title.
BF448.F45 1995
153.4'6—dc20   94-32599
CIP

ISBN: 0-671-89258-4

To Rachel Kara Feinberg and Joshua Adam Feinberg,
that they may know what to avoid,
and to Gracie and Woody,
who *always* get it.

Contents

Acknowledgments

More people gave us valuable stories, ideas and insights than we are able to name here. We are deeply grateful to them all.

Our special thanks to General Meir Amit, David Asman, Dennis C. Bottorff, Robert A.M. Coppenrath, Carl Dargene, Martin Edelston, Malcolm Elvey, Dr. Harvey B. Feinberg, Dr. Stuart Feinberg, Dr. Todd Feinberg, Milton Gould, Jonathan Green, Frank Grizlecki, Hamid D. Jafar, Ahsan Ullah Khan, Conrad Kiechel, Judge Gerald Klein, John Lytle, Lorian Marlantes, John F. McGlynn, Stacey Slaughter Miller, Sheldon O. Newman, Scott Northcutt, Mark F. Price, M.A. (Oxon), M.B.A., Wallace Rasmussen, Erhard Rittinghaus, Gerald R. Roche, John Safer, the Honorable David B. Saxe, Mahlon Scott, Robert C. Seaver, Brendon Sexton, Dr. Steven M. Sliwa, Peter Small, Gracia Smith, Dr. Paul M. Steinberg, Tomio Taki, Cal Turner, Jr., Ed Uhl, Gus Van Sant, Richard A. Voell, Jim Wesley, Dr. Mary Wolfe, Sir Brian Wolfson, and R. Lyman Wood.

Anita Diamant guided us to the right publisher.

Kara Leverte gave us ideas for subject matter along with her superb editorial skills.

And of course we acknowledge all those, famous and unsung, who appear in these pages as smart people who have done very dumb things. We thank them all, and we wish them well.

Introduction:

So What's the Problem?

If you are of above average intelligence—and if you have mastered the use of high intelligence to solve problems and achieve goals—it is the premise of this book that *you are at risk because of the strength of your cognitive equipment.*

The risk is that, at a critical moment, your intellect will betray you into a blunder so devastating that everyone will wonder, "How could he/she have been so dumb?"

Disaster can take one of a number of forms. You suddenly say or do something that damages a relationship, ruins a career, destroys a dream. You deliberately pursue a course that will wreck you on the rocks of personal calamity, while people of lesser intelligence wonder what you're doing. You "push the envelope" so hard that the envelope breaks and you tumble to destruction. You lose touch with ordinary people and the real world to such a degree that rivals and events conspire to humiliate and defeat you.

In each of these cases, the catastrophe is *self-induced.* You don't fail because you weren't smart enough, but because you were *too* smart. Your brains have betrayed you.

Strong intellect is an obvious advantage in life. We know this from observation and experience. The proposition is supported by considerable research, beginning with the landmark studies of Lewis M. Terman of Stanford University. In 1921 Terman—who developed the Stanford-Binet intelligence test and introduced the term *intelligence quotient* (IQ)—selected 1,500 gifted children from two to fourteen years old. He studied this group (in comparison with a control group) for thirty-five years. The persons of high intelligence were healthier, more emotionally stable, and more productive, and had a lower divorce and suicide rate than those of lesser mental equipment. Overall, as subsequent studies corroborate, bright people enjoy greater success in life than those who are less bright.

If you're smart you have a distinct edge in life's competitive arena. That's the bright side.

The dark is that one can be sabotaged by one's own intellect.

Diagnosis, Prevention, Recovery

This book is a program that will help you deal with the danger of stumbling over your own brain at a critical point in your life.

First, we will explore self-induced misfortunes among the rich, the famous, and the powerful. In effect, we will use the Lords of the Earth as our laboratory animals. (We've tracked more men than women, simply because up till now, men have had the greater opportunities to louse themselves up in the eyes of the world.)

Then we'll examine the ways in which similar calamities befall intelligent individuals at critical stages of their careers and personal lives.

We will sort these episodes into classifications and propose a theory intended to explain why they happen. Our explorations will make extensive use of case histories of bizarre self-inflicted cognitive wounds.

Finally we offer a menu of tools, exercises, growth techniques, and self-insight devices, designed to

- **Measure your vulnerability**
- **Predict the way in which your intelligence is most likely to betray you**
- **Build your immunity**
- **Help you recover from a serious misstep**
- **Enable you to help someone else before it's too late**

Risk increases with IQ and status. The smarter you are, and the more you've accomplished, the greater the risk. You may fall into one of five categories of persons at whom this book is aimed:

- *You don't believe you're at risk.* Let us challenge that comfortable assumption. You may still feel invulnerable after you've finished the book, but at least you may have enjoyed reading about the embarrassments of other bright people.

- *It hasn't happened to you yet but you suspect it could happen.* We'll work together to see that it doesn't happen.

- *You've already had the unhappy experience of being betrayed by your own brainpower.* Then you know how bad it can be. We offer a way to keep it from happening again.

- *You see someone else in danger, and you want to help.* Become an intellectual lifeguard by using these principles and recommendations.

- *You need to prevent intellectual self-destruction in the men and women who work for you.* This can be the most important benefit of the principles and prescriptions set forth in this book. You'll find questions you can use in job interviews to gauge vulnerabilities. You'll find case histories that may resemble the cases of some of your key people. And you'll find recommendations for managing bright people so that they don't turn their intellectual guns against themselves or the enterprise.

It's All in Your Mind. Self-inflicted intellectual damage is a serious topic. Serious topics need not be treated ponderously and solemnly. We present our findings, our analyses, and our recommendations in a form that is, we hope, stimulating, interesting, effective—even entertaining.

Since the problem is created by the superior intellect, its solution lies within the superior intellect. This book lays out guidelines by which you can channel your intelligence so that it continues to serve your best interests instead of, at some cataclysmic moment, betraying you.

Part I.

IN SEARCH OF A VIRUS

We start by looking at the empirical data: case histories of calamity. We examine a variety of idiotic acts by people who are smart enough to know better. Many of these bizarre doings seem inexplicable; our job is to find an explanation.

You'll join us in the laboratory of human stupidity. You'll work through this material with us. We'll analyze our case histories, asking, "What caused a smart person to act in this dumb way?" We'll then seek to extract useful principles—and to apply those principles to the situations we all confront in our business and personal lives.

Self-destructive use of intelligence is serious but not fatal. You can keep it from happening, and you can recover from it. But you cannot be immune from it. As you'll see, it strikes when least expected—and makes the most brilliant of mortals look like dummies.

Smart people—when alerted to a potential problem—can use their intelligence to prevent the problem from becoming a reality.

We have work to do, so let's begin.

Chapter 1.

SMART SCREWUPS
ANONYMOUS IS
IN SESSION

"**M**y name is Ed," says the gentleman with the scraggly beard, "and I'm a smart screwup. What I did . . ."

We're at a meeting of Smart Screwups Anonymous (SSA)—known informally by its members as ASS-Backwards. This is the support group for persons of high intelligence who commit inexplicably stupid blunders. Some of those at this meeting are well known; you'll recognize them. Others you don't know. (For your convenience we identify them briefly at the end of the chapter.) They all share the same problem. They have loused up their lives by doing idiotic things that people as smart as they are should not have done.

We'll be meeting many of them later, getting more details about their weird lapses of intellect. What we're trying to do is figure out why.

But, shhh. Ed is going on.

"Let's not mince words. When you need a manager for a high-profile political campaign, I'm the best you can get. Maybe Carville is in my class, but nobody else. But back there in ninety-three it looked like my reputation was going down the tubes. My candidate was forty points behind a guy we were supposed to beat easily. But on election day we pulled it out.

"I was back on top of the world! So what did I do? I told a bunch of reporters we won by bribing black ministers not to push to get out the vote. I'm a smart guy. How could I do such a dumb thing?"[1]

They Say "We" Blew It

"Tell me about it," interrupts the formidable lady with the British accent. "You may address me as Your Ladyship. We do not suffer fools gladly. Indeed it has always been our policy to make the fools do the suffering. One of the unfortunate attributes of democracy is that the fools can strike back. They become exercised about the most ridiculous things—for example, they have had the audacity to criticize us for referring to ourselves as we, which in their benighted state they claim is a prerogative of Her Majesty. And then there is the plague of the cabinet. Unfortunately in our country even the greatest leaders are burdened by a cabinet, which of course consists of idiots and pygmies. When we were in power we always made sure to remind them that that's what they are—idiots and pygmies. We referred to the opposition as 'dead parrots,' but somehow they learned to fly. When we needed their support to remain in office we told them again what we thought of them, but that, nevertheless, we would consent to continue as their leader. Pygmies they may have been, but they did have the power to end our career, and perhaps we overlooked that. . . ."[2]

"You can't think of everything," says the round-faced bespectacled fellow clad in prison garb. "My name is Stew, and, boy, am I a smart screwup! What a deal I had! The biggest and best store of its kind in the world! Shoppers and tourists from all over! Tom Peters wrote about me as a model of excellence. Paul Newman posed with his arm around me. I was Mr. Entrepreneur.

"When you're Mr. Entrepreneur you go after every buck, right? We had this computer whiz design a program so we could skim some of every day's take, avoid the taxes. Maybe it didn't amount to that much more in our pockets, given the profits we were making, but, why not?

"Of course looking back now maybe it wasn't that smart to try to fly to the Caribbean with $75,000 in cash. And maybe it wasn't all that bright to let the computer guy go, knowing what he knew about the setup. . . ."[3]

Stew finishes telling his sad story. His successor announces, "I'm Mary, and I am a smart screwup. I teach first grade. I take that responsibility seriously, and I try to find ways to prepare my students for life. Even in first grade children should know about race relations. We had two black students in the class. So I used them to dramatize slavery. One child was 'sold.' The other was chained to a post to show how slaves were beaten. It seemed like a good idea at the time. But the school board, the parents, and the whole town went crazy."[4]

I Thought They Liked It!

The next speaker, though somewhat careworn, bears himself with the vestiges of authority. "You can call me Bob, and I guess you'd have to say I am a smart screwup. I was smart enough to carve out a tremendous reputation as a progressive, a caring legislator, a leader on issues like equal opportunities for women. So, here and there, I would give some of the gals around me a little hug, a little kiss, a little pat on the fanny? Then when they came after me about it, those hypocrites on the ethics committee, I said to them, 'Here, you want proof of my innocence? Look at my diaries.' Inasmuch as the diaries had other stuff in there that was very damning, you'd have to say what I did was dumb. . . ."[5]

Next comes Leona, an imperious figure: "When you're on top, who cares about all those little people? All they're good for is paying taxes. I did what I wanted, and said what I wanted. . . ."[6]

An intense young man says, "I'm Paul, and you can put me down as a smart screwup. I'm smart. First in my class, recruited like crazy by a dozen firms, fast-tracked right toward the top. When I got to senior management level I used the same skills that had paid off for me all my life. Like the skill to make your critics look like assholes—whether there's anything to what they're saying or not. After all they don't call it the War Room for nothing. When they snipe at you, you snipe back. What I overlooked was that these were not seminar room debates any longer, we were playing for keeps, and sometimes the guy who criticizes your plan just might be right. I debated instead of listening. I decimated all my critics, got my plan approved. My big chance. When the plan fell apart along with my career I realized I was too damn smart for my own good. I should have listened."[7]

Our Cover-up Was Different from Their Cover-up

"You would have thought," says the next speaker, "that somebody who worked on the House Judiciary Committee investigation into Watergate would have learned that in Washington the cardinal sin is not the original act but the cover-up. I'm Hillary, by the way, and I'm here on merit. We had a little no-account situation out there in Little Rock. Nobody cared about it, nobody understood it, and anyway it all happened long ago in another place. So what did we do? A lot of smart people got together and tried to manage the media, which was like trying to manage the way a tiger eats a raw steak. Result? White-Watergate!"[8]

"You should always go with your instincts—or at least that's what I used to think. By the way, I'm Stephen, and I'm proud to stand here and tell you I'm a smart screwup, maybe the smartest screwup you ever saw. The great thing about being smart is you can go along with your most outrageous instincts and get away with it, because everybody knows you're brilliant. That's why I hired the male stripper—you know, the hunk I got to take off his clothes in front of my boss and a whole bunch of stuffed shirts from business and government. Brought my skyrocketing career to a sudden halt, at least at the time. . . ."[9]

"Like a lot of women," says Evelyn, "I was smarter than my husband but I thought it was my role in life to soft-pedal that fact, be a good soldier, keep the marriage going at all costs. So I went along with things I knew were dumb. When the marriage fell apart anyway I was so damn mad I thought, "I'll show him. Who needs to think about things like retirement, making sure I get a decent share of the pension. . . ."[10]

A man with patent-leather hair smiles out at the room. "I'm Sol, et cetera, et cetera. I could always do everything I wanted better than anybody else. Outthink everybody else, outpolitic everybody else, outmaneuver everybody else. Chief judge, maybe governor next, who knew how far I'd go?

"One other thing. I could outlove anyone else. A man of my attainment, I feel things deeper and express them better. Joy was the love of my life. How could she give the brush-off to somebody like me? So of course I had to take measures, like sending condoms to her daughter and making threatening phone calls. Naturally I used my head to keep from getting caught. I called under a fake name, went around to different phone booths, wore a beard. . . ."[11]

"Why did you let this woman twist you around her finger?" The older man glares at Sol. "You wanted her, you should have *taken* her! It was your right! Superior individuals have every right. . . ."

This outburst comes from Doctor Jules, whose ideas about what superior people are entitled to have become well known to the rest of the group.[12] When order is restored, a young woman stands.

"My name is Angela, and I am an SS. I fought hard to make it big in my field. When the headhunter took me to lunch I knew this was it. But I played it just right, hard to get. They gave me the job, which with bonus was worth half a mil plus going in, and the sky was the limit. Plus the perks, which I assure you I battled to get. Status is important. You need to establish your credibility. They like went white at the lips when I insisted on an original Schnabel in my office, but they needed me, these old establishment types. They knew they needed the kind of fresh thinking I could bring them. So they went along with the guaranteed skiing vacations in the Alps and the cabin cruiser for get-away-from-it-all meetings with my key people. So why wouldn't they go along with the car? Granted, it's an old company, stuffy, they weren't used to the idea of a stretch limo always available to me; true, their chairman drove himself around in a Ford Fairlane. But they went along with everything else, why wouldn't they go along with this?

"And why, I ask myself now, did I have to push so damn hard for something that didn't matter all that much to me?" Angela sits, shaking her head.[13]

"Bobby Ray is my name," says the wiry man with the upright posture and the skeletal face. "A lifetime of service to my country, an unblemished record, the unanimous praises of the entire Washington press corps—and then disgrace! No one had ever questioned my brilliance and my ability. Then they had the audacity to ask me the kinds of questions they would ask any run-of-the-mill politician looking for a job. And the things they said about me, I could not believe it, these were the kinds of things that get said about other people. Not about me."[14]

"Who gives a damn what the media say about you? I didn't. I challenged those reporters who were following me around. I said, 'Take your best shot. You think I'm involved in Monkey Business? Prove it!' Well, they did. I'm Gary, and I could have been president if not for a picture in the *National Enquirer*, and I guess that makes me a smart screwup."[15]

"Intimidation. Intimidation is key. When you intimidate you can get away with anything. They were all scared of me. Who would have the guts to challenge my numbers, huh? They bought my numbers and they paid me unreal bonuses. But then somebody must have looked at the bottom line. . . ."[16]

Next is Chuck. "We got this terrific idea to make more money out of the 1992 Olympics. Along with NBC, my cable company would run real-time pay-per-view coverage. We gave it a catchy name—Triplecast. Of course we tested the idea. You don't think we'd go into something as expensive as this without testing, do you? The thing is, the testing didn't give us the answers we wanted. Turned out only one percent of the potential market said they would positively be Triplecast subscribers. Should have junked the idea then. But we liked it so much, and had put in so much work on it. It was a masterpiece. And, taking a second look at the research, if you added the Maybes to the Certains you got a respectable figure. So that's what we did. But when we ran the Triplecast, all the Maybes turned into Nos. The only ones that bought were the original one percent. We all took a bath."[17]

"I am Ann, and I run a big university, with campuses spread across the state. I wanted to consolidate certain academic programs to avoid overlap in the disciplines. Well. There are a great many demands on my time. I couldn't afford to take the time to convince the deans that they should give up some of their turf. Perhaps I should have put more emphasis on persuasion. However, there are only so many hours in the day. There are demands on my time. I serve on many corporate boards. This supplements my income, and I also receive grants from these companies for special university programs. Some people seem to think I spent too much time on my outside activities. Now it seems that I am in trouble with certain university board members. These things should be settled within our own community, they are not the business of outsiders. But a prominent newspaper wrote a negative article about my consulting!"[18]

The next speaker says, in a resonant voice, "I'm Jesse, and I am here to confess to you that I am a smart screwup. Once there did not seem that there was any mountain I could not climb. I wore the mantle of Martin Luther King. Black and white, people listened to me, because of my eloquence, the way I stood tall for justice, because I was a man who could close the door on a bad yesterday and open the door to a great tomorrow. I had the power to command the hour. Every word I spoke, and I loved to speak a lot of words, was golden. And then I spoke one word too many. One word. *Hymietown!* One dumb word. Why did I do it?"[19]

Several men and women rise. Taking turns, they proclaim, "We're the product management group at NYNEX. The damn customers weren't using their credit cards because they forgot their secret PIN numbers. So what could be more logical than to tell each one of them his or her PIN number in a mass mailing? Sure, if somebody gets your number he can charge calls to your account. But you can't make an omelet without breaking eggs. We had a bottom line to beef up."[20]

Now a compact figure takes the floor. The glasses and the hair parted in the middle are familiar artifacts of past celebrity. He says coolly, "My name is Bob and I am here because the logic of the situation dictates that I am a smart screwup. Today it is virtually impossible to defend our policy in Vietnam, or, for that matter, to even define the parameters of that strategy. Nevertheless it was then clear, to myself and my colleagues, that our optimum strategy was to stay the course, increase the pressure on Hanoi, and continue to increase our commitment of troops on the ground. The ultimate disaster does not alter the fact that the logic of the situation at the time indicated to rational analysis that we should ignore the pain and the destruction and the deaths and forge ahead."[21]

Another man rises. "My name is John. One day I was running one of the great corporations of the world, having my picture taken next to the first lady, getting mentioned for all kinds of high offices. The next day I was taking over a company that hardly anybody ever heard of. I had the job, I quit the job, I sued them, they sued me—what a mess!"[22]

Other eminent persons wait to tell their sad stories. As flies on the wall we're sort of enjoying it. It's human nature; when a man in a high hat and tailcoat slips on a banana peel, we smile. And when the Best and Brightest Blow It, we smile.

But when we put our instinct to laugh aside, we notice some significant things about the SSA meeting.

It takes *really smart people* to make mistakes as big as this.

Being smart is evidently no protection against doing dumb things.

If you're intelligent and accomplished, you are qualified for membership in SSA. If you've already done something self-destructively dumb—or know someone who has—you're aware of this.

If you haven't yet made your megamistake, *you will*, and it will hurt. It may smash your closest relationship, blotch your reputation, devastate your career.

That is, *unless you neutralize the virus.*

Notes

1. Political consultant Ed Rollins.
2. Margaret Thatcher.
3. Grocery entrepreneur Stew Leonard.
4. A Pennsylvania schoolteacher.
5. Senator Robert Packwood.
6. Leona Helmsley.
7. A former fast-tracker.
8. Hillary Rodham Clinton.
9. TV executive Stephen Chao.
10. An indigent divorcée.
11. Former New York chief judge Sol Wachtler.
12. Dr. Jules Masserman.
13. A grounded highflier.
14. Admiral Bobby Ray Inman.
15. Gary Hart.
16. Wall Street wonder Joseph Jett.
17. Cablevision chairman Charles Dolan.
18. City University of New York chancellor W. Ann Reynolds.
19. Jesse Jackson.
20. Sundry NYNEX executives.
21. Onetime secretary of defense Robert McNamara.
22. Former Apple CEO John Sculley.

Chapter 2.

SEEKING THE VIRUS OF SELF-DESTRUCTIVE INTELLIGENCE

Here's how this book came about.

For a long time we have worked together, a psychologist and a communicator, teamed up to study and solve problems affecting human beings on the job. We were dealing with the best and the brightest, intelligent individuals who used intelligence to get them where they wanted to be.

All too often we saw these gifted persons commit monumental blunders, damaging—and sometimes destroying—their careers, their reputations, their peace of mind, their relationships, and their lives.

Some of these episodes could be attributed to addictions of various sorts, to poor health, to mental illness. That's understandable; if you get really sick you're no longer smart.

But after eliminating such factors we still confronted the phenomenon of strange collapses of intelligence among persons with superior intellects. We started to ask ourselves a question: *Why do very smart people do very dumb things?*

We focused on those who not only have high intellects but who have the gift of using their brain power to achieve their goals in life. They think fast and deep, and they think *with impact*. We distinguish people with this kind of *dynamic intelligence* from those who score high on tests but whose intelligence is passive or diffused. For quick reference we've devised a term for the "impact thinker" who ascends to leadership in today's world: Superior Cognitive Intelligence Possessing Individual; SCIPI for short, pronounced "Skippy." (Some of us remember when smart kids skipped a grade in school.)

SCIPIs are able to make quantum leaps—in perception, in insight,

Seeking the Virus of Self-Destructive Intelligence

in creative accomplishment, in career advancement. The people who surge ahead to the forefront of business and society today may be Yuppies or Guppies or even Hippies or none of the above; but they are likely to be SCIPIs.

Those of ordinary intelligence make major mistakes because they lack the cognitive resources needed to handle the difficulties that confront them. They do the wrong thing because they're not smart enough to do the right thing. SCIPIs have the mental equipment. It is not just that they don't use it; it is that they seem to turn their intellectual firepower upon themselves.

When SCIPIs commit stupidities they are likely to be superstupidities. To do things as dumb as the things chronicled in this book, you have to be really smart.

Smart Stupidity Can Strike Anywhere

Eruptions of self-destructive intelligence run the gamut from embarrassment to debacle.

- A sharp, intuitive investor loses a fortune by taking a position, not because he really believed in the deal, but because he did not want to look like a wimp.
- A fast-rising brand manager blows a big promotion by insisting on a perk that she neither needs nor wants.
- Confronted with a choice among merger partners, an entrepreneur makes the worst possible choice, wrecking his beloved company and ending the jobs of hundreds of loyal employees.
- While speaking at a town meeting, a respected (and utterly unprejudiced) community leader blurts out a story that makes her sound like a racist, blemishing her reputation and ending her service to the community.
- A gentle and perceptive man, though genuinely in love with his

wife, humiliates and abases her before an embarrassed gathering of friends.

• Given an assignment that will make or break her career, a financial analyst, picking her team, skips over the talented people who can really help her, choosing instead a weak group that practically assures failure.

All of these people have one thing in common. They are too smart to have done the stupid things that did them so much harm. Nevertheless they did them. Just like Richard Nixon, Margaret Thatcher, John Sculley, and a parade of accomplished individuals who, in critical situations, have abandoned all sense and acted like imbeciles, inflicting great damage on themselves.

And we all ask, *How could he/she have been so dumb?*

Well, it happens. So often that it has come to be taken for granted. One day we decided to stop taking it for granted. We undertook an exploration that took us down many weird paths, brought us face to face with many episodes of strange behavior. We sifted, discussed, analyzed. We talked to professionals, businesspeople, therapists, academicians.

Gradually, a theory began to evolve. We call it the "Feinberg Factor": *Strong intelligence tends to subvert itself.*

We do not suggest that this formulation rivals the discovery by Watson and Crick of the double helix of the DNA molecule—but, after all, we do *soft* science.

Think of something you've done that's dumb; *really* dumb. Maybe it struck like a bolt from the blue: suddenly you said or did something stupid, amazing yourself as much as everybody else.

Or you were sucked into folly against your will. The rational part of your mind kept saying "Don't do it!" but you did it anyway.

Or the left and right halves of your brain were in perfect sync, saying "Go for it!" Only when you stood surrounded by the wreckage did you realize that everyone else, including all the dummies, knew it was a rotten idea.

Your intellect has trapped you by spinning a web of rationalization. Your disastrous impulse has acquired enough power to override your logic function. Your imagination has written and staged a scenario that is realistic, persuasive—and wrong.

You're not in trouble because you lack intelligence. You're in trouble because your intelligence willfully *got* you into trouble.

It takes real brains to do something that dumb.

Somewhere in your psyche there is a destructive influence. Think of it as a *virus*.

Originally meaning poison, as in snake venom, "virus" was appropriated by the medical profession to describe microscopic or submicroscopic agents that infect living organisms and cause disease. The term has come into broader use to mean a harmful, invisible influence, as in "computer virus."

We all know about computer viruses, even if we don't understand how they work. The virus is a destructive element—like a gremlin—lurking in a computer. You can't tell it's there. It's hidden in the labyrinthine maze of megabytes.

And then one day—BLOOEY! The computer goes crazy. Programs that, a moment ago, were performing positive miracles of data processing, now, with equal force and precision, destroy themselves.

Something similar happens to SCIPIs.

When political consultant Ed Rollins immolates himself at his moment of triumph with a gratuitous confession (perhaps exaggerated and maybe even untrue!) of fraud, it's as if a virus suddenly erupted within his mind. When corporate whiz kid Stephen Chao hires a male stripper to shake it in the face of his boss and a group of distinguished and straitlaced guests, his customary logical function has been short-circuited by a psychic malignancy exploding from the depths to the surface.

Computer viruses are implanted by others—for profit, for revenge, or just for the fun of hacking around. But there is no outsider transmitting the virus that destroys logic override. This is a *self-developed* virus. Besides being self-developed, it has another interesting and sinister characteristic. It *uses the power of the mind to sabotage the mind.* The virus feeds on the strength of the intelligence that harbors it. The smarter the individual, the greater the subversive power of the destructive force.

There is yet one more characteristic we must mention. The logic virus is endemic among smart people. A high IQ is a warning that you carry the seeds within you.

SCIPIs are high achievers because they are first-rate in all areas of cognitive performance. They are brilliant, imaginative, insightful. At the same time they are keenly logical. Their logic function arrays and deploys their other mental gifts, keeps them in balance, and, most important, keeps them from making bad mistakes.

When that faculty malfunctions you get *logic override.*

Logic override is one of the most devastating effects of the *Self-Destructive Intelligence Syndrome* virus.

SDIS is not like other viruses. It is not transmitted from one organism to another. Smart people come with the virus already installed.

And that brings us to one of the central themes of this book. *Intelligent people run the risk of self-destruction caused by their own brilliance. That self-destruction is caused by a virus that flourishes within strong intellects. And there is no escape. If you possess above-average intelligence you already have the virus.* It comes with the high IQ territory.

You don't protect yourself against SDIS by ignoring it or by avoiding contact with transmitters of it. Your protection lies within yourself. And, luckily, SCIPIs are capable, potentially, of deploying their formidable intellectual gifts against the inner force that works in its sinuous and powerful way to destroy them.

The SDIS virus need not be fatal. It is controllable, if caught in time. Your high IQ does not doom you to make a devastating mistake in your career or personal life. This book is a guide to help you catch and cope with the virus in time.

You're smart enough to immunize yourself against SDIS. This book will show you the way.

Seeking the Virus of Self-Destructive Intelligence

A *word about method*—our laboratory is the entire range of human behavior. We will use exemplars from politics, business, the law, the movies, et cetera. We will frequently summon up accounts of dumb things done by smart people. We will use these cases to illustrate our points. As we illustrate, we will extrapolate. We will speculate on causation. Thus when we analyze, say, Gary Hart's foolhardy challenge to reporters to catch him if they can, or the self-destructive maneuverings of a world-famous corporate leader, we don't claim to know the precise workings of the mind that led to the particular behavior. The individuals themselves don't know why they did what they did. That is one of the paramount features of the Self-Destructive Intelligence Syndrome.

The Four Pillars of Stupidity

As we examine the range of outbreaks of SDIS, we see that the virus manifests itself in four principal ways:

- **Hubris**
- **Arrogance**
- **Narcissism**
- **Unconscious need to fail**

They overlap. A typical case of SDIS will be dominated by one of these factors, but will contain elements of at least one of the others.

Take, for instance, Ed Rollins. Rollins (whose case we'll look at in more detail) pulled off the greatest win of his career with New Jersey's gubernatorial candidate Christine Whitman in 1993. Then Rollins blew it by proclaiming that he did it through bribery and chicanery.

This is one form of SDIS—the *sudden spasm*. The victim abruptly does or says something shockingly dumb and self-destructive. There is *narcissism* here, along with *hubris*. And, lurking in the shadows is the mocking face of the *unconscious need to fail*.

Other eruptions of SDIS do not come in a sudden rush. Amazingly enough, they are carefully planned by the victim.

Ciao Chao. Media-biz whiz Stephen Chao, rocketing toward the top of Rupert Murdoch's Fox TV empire, was given a star spot as a speaker before a 1992 management conference involving Murdoch, conservative intellectual Irving Kristol, Defense secretary Dick Cheney, National Endowment for the Humanities chairwoman Lynne Cheney, and other VIPs. As Chao lectured, a young man appeared and began to remove his clothes. The young man, a male stripper hired by Chao, performed his act right beside Mrs. Cheney.

Within hours, Stephen Chao was gone.

He had "pushed the envelope"—but the envelope pushed back. That's the compulsive act of a *risk junkie.* We'll be meeting a lot of risk junkies—people who take long chances for the sake of taking chances, or to prove that they are gutsier than the other guys, or just because they are bored. They're smarter and quicker than the people around them. They have no challenges. So they create challenges for themselves.

Risk junkies are driven by the need to fail, yoked to arrogance and hubris. As you look at Stephen Chao's stunt, you say, "He acted like a child." That's right. As we will see, intellect sometimes works in a curious way to retard maturity. The good news is that there are ways to build up your maturity component to help you fight off SDIS.

Watergate? What's That?

Another persistent form of SDIS is *reality blindness,* in which intelligent people suffer extreme logic override. They act in defiance of realities that are obvious to persons of far lower cognitive capacity.

One striking case is Whitewater—the mish-mash of speculation, innuendo, and accusation swirling around Bill Clinton and Hillary Rodham Clinton, involving real estate partnerships, sweetheart deals, and commodity windfalls. The Clintons cut their teeth on Washington politics at the time when Richard Nixon was being toppled by Watergate. As any dummy knows, Nixon's problem with Watergate was not the original break-in but rather the cover-up. But when they got to Washington, the Clintons forgot that.

Blindness to reality is a function of *narcissism*, which builds up our self-absorption so high that we lose sight of the real world; or, even when we see clearly what happened to others, we say, "It can't happen to me." Narcissism comes with success. It is part of the package. When we make it to the top we don't think of ourselves as narcissistic; we conduct ourselves modestly, deal with others patiently, and so on. And yet narcissism—an almost inevitable concomitant of success—is working to subvert our brainpower. It is even more irresistible when it is fueled by *arrogance*.

The Psychiatrist's Harem. Dr. Jules Masserman had scaled the heights of his profession. In his seventies, with the vigor of his intellect unimpaired, Dr. Masserman was one of the leading lights of psychiatry, a past president of the American Psychiatric Association. Then it all came crashing down when, after being rendered unconscious by an injection of sodium pentathol, a patient awoke on the couch to find the unclothed Dr. Masserman raping her. Nor, as it turned out, was she the only one. Evidently he felt *entitled* to treat his female patients as his harem.

Extreme feelings of entitlement stem from *intellectual arrogance*. The word *arrogance* comes from the Latin *arrogare*, meaning "to claim." Strong intellects tend to make sweeping claims (although, thank goodness, not many of them are as sweeping as those of Dr. Masserman).

A more typical form of arrogation is exemplified by the case of Stew Leonard.

The Great Milkman Skims the Cream. Stew Leonard had built his family's dairy farm in Norwalk, Connecticut, into the biggest and most renowned store of its kind in the world, a stupendous shopping theme park, with a petting zoo, life-size robot animals that sing and dance, dozens of pictures of the founder with his friends in high places, including Paul Newman and Ronald Reagan. Stew Leonard's was a shrine for entrepreneurs; they came from all over the world to see it. Tom Peters celebrated Stew Leonard as a paradigm of business excellence, a paragon of ethics and enterprise.

Then somebody at JFK airport noticed that Stew Leonard, on a trip to his place in Saint Martin, was carrying what seemed an excessive amount of pocket cash—$75,000. When the feds raided they found, in a hollowed-out book, the illicit computer program (called "Equity") that Leonard had been using for a decade to cheat the government of taxes.

This is the form of arrogance—bred by intelligence and success—that drives the individual to keep claiming more and more until the claims are all-encompassing. The lust to get everything that's coming to you combines with a need to fail. The result is explosively self-destructive.

Now, we'll take a whirlwind tour of the not-so-wonderful-world of SDIS.

Chapter 3.

MAKING THE ROUNDS
THROUGH THE SDIS
WARD

Let's take a closer look at the SDIS phenomenon in its varied aspects. We'll scan the cases of some notable high achievers whose brains have betrayed them.

Think about the cases. Analyze them in terms of the elements of SDIS:

- **Hubris**
- **Arrogance**
- **Narcissism**
- **Unconscious need to fail**

Note the ways in which these elements mix and work with one another to produce calamity.

From Champ to Chump— John Sculley's Wild Ride

Early in 1993 John Sculley was riding high. As the chairman of Apple he headed a company that epitomized the new world of technology. Sure, there were mutterings that Apple was not doing as well as it might. But Apple and its products were household words. Anything Apple did was big news. The man who sat at the top of this technological powerhouse was one of the most important executives in the United States. Since business is now essentially international—especially the computer business—that made John Sculley one of the most important persons in the world.

Why Smart People Do Dumb Things

John Sculley lived up to his role superbly. Personable and articulate, he shone on television, the epitome of business statesmanship. His opinions on profound questions of global importance were worth listening to; the media heeded them, and people listened.

There seemed good reason to think that Sculley might soon be moving to another stage. Millions of TV viewers saw him sitting at the elbow of Hillary Rodham Clinton, listening to the president. There was persistent talk that Sculley's talents would be put to work in the government, in a cabinet position or in some other high-level post. This was eminently logical: John Sculley's combination of vision, leadership, and charisma made him a logical mainstay of an administration geared to the new world.

But maybe the corporate world would hang onto this man, one of its brightest stars. There were, of course, only a few jobs that would be big enough, but every time such a job came open, Sculley was mentioned as being under consideration.

When IBM began to look for a new leader early in 1993, John Sculley's name came up, although Sculley still had a job to do at Apple. In fact, even before the IBM job opened up, there was a rumor floating around that Sculley might take over the troubled computer giant. Speculation continued; it was said that IBM had approached Sculley. John Sculley took himself out of the running in March, 1993. By this time, however, other names—including that of Louis Gerstner, the ultimate choice—had become more prominent than Sculley's on the speculative grapevine.

Then came the news that John Sculley was resigning from Apple. The resignation was portrayed as voluntary. One former Apple director said Sculley had been forced out.

Where would John Sculley go next? Avid speculation swirled around this corporate star. Many felt it would be government. How many top business jobs were big enough for a man of Sculley's stature?

Then, the bombshell. John Sculley would become chairman and chief executive at Spectrum Information Technologies, an obscure

Long Island firm. One of the marquee names of corporate America was joining a "tiny wireless-technology company that had no profits, no profile and a checkered past. . . ."[1]

Suddenly Spectrum was a hot item, the focus of competitors, investors, and industry observers. On the day that Spectrum announced the advent of Sculley, the company's stock soared $3.50 to $11.125, a gain of more than 45 percent. The company was automatically a player in the big new technological arena. People still shook their heads and asked how John Sculley could go from the top jobs at PepsiCo and Apple to an unknown company. But, more and more, they said that Sculley must know something. He was exemplifying the spirit of entrepreneurism by taking on this new challenge.

And then the saga of high-level entrepreneurism turned into tabloid low-jinks. Sculley suddenly quit the job after just four months. The stock crashed to $2.25. People gaped. Their jaws dropped even farther when Sculley sued Spectrum's president, Peter G. Caserta, for fraud. In response, Spectrum sued Sculley for breach of contract. The public was treated to stories of Caserta's long black limousine pulling into the driveway of Sculley's Greenwich, Connecticut, home . . . the unsuspecting John Sculley being seduced by slick operators who just wanted to capitalize on his name . . . Sculley's abashed admission that he had not really checked out his new company. . . .

As John Sculley insisted that he had been duped, Spectrum counterattacked by releasing documents purportedly demonstrating that Sculley knew all about Spectrum's troubles, which included a probe by the SEC.

A month later both Sculley and Spectrum agreed to drop their lawsuits.

Neither party was in good shape as a result of the imbroglio. Spectrum was no longer obscure, but it was hardly an industry bright spot. John Sculley, dogged by such headlines as *Newsweek*'s "From Champ to Chump," had become a laughingstock. Instead of people asking, "What will he do next?" they were asking, "How could he have screwed up so badly?"

John Sculley, perhaps disappointed by his failure to catch fire as a major national political figure or as CEO of IBM, and his parting of the ways with Apple, seemingly reacted impulsively when offered the Spectrum job. Who needs due diligence? He would show everybody!

Remote psychoanalysis of John Sculley became a popular sport. Writing in the *Wall Street Journal* (February 28, 1994), James E. Schrager made the provocative observation that there is a big difference between corporate executives and entrepreneurs. The big corporation provides a safety net; entrepreneurs work without a net. Schrager observed, "It must be particularly hard to be powerless after you've held the reins of a large corporation. This is not to say it can't be done—just that it takes an unusual individual to be willing to work without a net after having one for so many years."

And as for Sculley's actions following his parting of the ways with Spectrum, Schrager commented, "Real entrepreneurs don't start lawsuits." They don't have the time or the money. They think there is a better way to spend their energy than in legal proceedings. For the big corporation, the resort to law is a reflex.

It's likely that nobody, including John Sculley, knows all the motives underlying this melancholy tale. But it does qualify as a notable example of smart people doing dumb things.

The Injudicious Judge

In the fall of 1992, the FBI was trying to find out who was sending threatening letters and making obscene phone calls to Joy Silverman. Ms. Silverman was wealthy and well connected in the Republican party. She had been a potent fund-raiser for George Bush. She had talked with FBI director William Sessions about the letters.

So the case was an important one for the agents.

The letters and phone calls were bizarre. One contained a condom sent to Ms. Silverman's fourteen-year-old daughter. There were threats to kidnap the teenager. While the terror campaign carried some demands for money, it appeared to stem from motives far more twisted and weird than extortion. The letter writer seemed to know a great deal about Ms. Silverman's life. Some of the phone calls went to the number of Silverman's male friend, David Samson.

One theme of the campaign was that a private investigator named David Purdy was spying on Silverman and Samson. One day a man dressed like a Texas cowboy stopped at Samson's building and, according to a detailed account in *The New Yorker*, "left a message that David Purdy had stopped by; a few weeks later, a similarly dressed man gave Silverman's doorman a letter warning that he would be back by autumn."[2]

The FBI set up a wiretap in Silverman's apartment. Early in October Silverman's phone rang. The caller hung up quickly, but not quickly enough. Old movies and TV shows show, in innumerable scenes, that tracing a phone call takes a considerable amount of time ("Try to keep him talking!"). The fact is that today, with the right equipment, a call can be traced instantaneously.

This one was. It turned out to be a number that was only too familiar to Joy Silverman. Now the agents had their suspect; but they were dumbfounded when they learned the identity of the suspect. The number was that of the car phone of Sol Wachtler, chief judge of the State of New York. Judge Wachtler, sixty-two, had known Joy Silverman for many years. He was trustee of the estate she had inherited from her stepfather. And he had, until fairly recently, been Silverman's lover.

Sol Wachtler was one of the leading lights of New York politics. At one time he had been widely mentioned as a strong candidate for governor. He had a reputation as a brilliant jurist and politician.

Another call came through. In a disguised voice, the caller said that David Purdy would soon be in touch. Silverman would have to pay him $20,000 for tapes and photographs of her and Samson in compromising circumstances. This call had been placed at a pay phone a few miles from Wachtler's home in Manhasset, Long Island.

The agents went to the federal authorities with the hot potato. The federal prosecutor was naturally cautious. For example, it was possible that some member of Wachtler's staff had used Wachtler's phone.

Another phone call, contained nasty threats against Silverman's daughter. This call was made in Reno, Nevada—where, it turned out, Judge Wachtler was attending a conference. While it was still possible that some associate of Wachtler's had gone to Reno with the judge and made the call, the feds had to acknowledge that Sol Wachtler was probably the culprit.

So they set out to catch him red-handed.

The chance came when the extortionist specified that the ransom be left at a particular New York location at a designated time. The FBI covered the drop point. They were also protecting the Silvermans. And they were tailing Wachtler. Wachtler made a phone call. Shortly afterward, the receptionist at the hair salon near the drop point came out and got the package that had been left there.

The agent tailing Wachtler followed as the judge parked and put on a cowboy hat and a string tie. Then he hailed a cab, talked to the driver, handed the driver some money and an envelope, and sent the cab on its way without getting in. The driver delivered the envelope to Joy Silverman's building. Wachtler threw some envelopes in the trash: unused extortion notes.

By now the Feds had seen enough. They arrested Sol Wachtler, finding, in his car, a device for disguising the voice.

The case hit the headlines. Wachtler tried defaming Joy Silverman. Then he pleaded that he was just a victim of scorned love. He twisted and turned, but at last had to resign his judgeship, relinquish his trusteeship, and go to federal prison. Not long after Wachtler arrived in prison there was a story that he had been stabbed by another inmate. The authorities concluded that he had inflicted the wound, a superficial one, himself.

Brains Go over the Side on the Love Boat

Dante reserved a special place in his Inferno for those who had incurred damnation by an excess of passion. The poet was compassionate, but stern; these people, he felt, should have known better. Sol Wachtler was smart enough to have known better.

So was Kenneth Littman, a veteran assistant district attorney in Nassau County (on Long Island, New York). Littman, forty-four and married, was forced to resign after it emerged that he had offered a seventeen-year-old high-school girl $150 to kiss her feet while she wore high-heeled pumps. The offer was made inside the Nassau County Courthouse.[3] "He wanted to be my sex slave," said the girl.

Chuck Jones was smart enough to build a reputation as a top-flight PR practitioner and to land Marla Maples as a client. But Jones came a cropper when he could not overcome his obsession with Maples's shoes.

Pathology is beyond our province here. Human beings, smart or dumb, are prone to emotional sickness. The relevant question for us to ask is "Why don't intelligent people get help for their self-destructive obsessions before it is too late?" The fact is that supersmart persons are often the last to get help, because they use their brains to rationalize their *not* seeking help.

When passions remained private they were less dangerous to reputations, careers, and lives. Ask Austrian president Thomas Klestil. Early in 1994 the Austrian newspapers, which once steered clear of such stories, assailed Klestil with such headlines as "Girlfriend or Presidency" and "Divorce or Resign!" The occasion was the revelation that President Klestil's wife, Edith, to whom he had been married for thirty-seven years, had left him because he was having an affair with one of his closest aides.[4]

The Tutorial Trap

Smart and accomplished people achieve stewardship over other people. They are bosses, mentors, teachers. Over and over we see examples of brilliant persons lurching to destruction through disastrous involvement with those who come under their sway.

Why Smart People Do Dumb Things

Peter Abélard, the twelfth-century philosopher and theologian, has become a byword for what we might call the teacher's fallacy, or, in the case of male teachers, phallacy. Abélard was a great scholar. However, he is famous in song and story because of his affair with his teenage student Héloise. Abélard married Héloise secretly. The girl's uncle—who was the canon of the Paris cathedral—sent a band of thugs to emasculate the scholar. Abélard went into a monastery, Héloise became a nun. He composed a book of hymns and, with Héloise, compiled a book of their correspondence. These days that book would be on the bestseller list, and the lovers would be on Geraldo.

The prevalence of the tutelary temptation may be the reason that at no less a bastion of scholarship than Oxford University there were, in October 1993, 247 harassment advisers.[5]

The great British statesman William Ewart Gladstone was driven by strange impulses that he feared but did not understand. But at least Gladstone, in his own way, tried to do something about them. Today perhaps he would join a support group. In the nineteenth century Gladstone coped with his obsessions in ways that were dangerous—ways that would never withstand the media scrutiny beamed at politicians today—but which he got away with.

Gladstone walked the mean streets of London at night in search of prostitutes. He looked for, says a historian, "only the most disturbingly attractive young women—in order to accompany them to their rooms and lecture them on their shame, giving them money and often a Bible, then returning home to flagellate himself. During 1851 and 1852 he waited tremblingly for the same woman, Elizabeth Collins, twenty-five times, finding her on twenty occasions and then scourging himself. . . . In his diary he wondered whether what he was doing was 'unlawful' and whether his agonized 'rescue' missions were unpure temptation, but he lived on a razor's edge of emotional composure until each next streetwalking expedition."[6]

All of us cope with temptation. What's different about SCIPIs is that

- They achieve positions where they encounter many temptations and enjoy the power to indulge their urges.
- They are clever enough to talk others into acceding to their wishes.
- They can construct masterful rationalizations to persuade others—and themselves—that what they are doing is okay.

Short-weighting Uncle Sam

Everything about Stew Leonard's dream was big. His store ("World's Largest Dairy Store") in Norwalk was one of Connecticut's leading tourist attractions. Visitors—tourists, students, businesspeople—flocked to Stew Leonard's from all over the world. Outside the giant complex of store buildings, children and grown-ups lined the fence of the mini-zoo, which featured goats and lambs and ducks. A huge stadium-type scoreboard lit up to proclaim the specials of the day. A character in cow costume greeted you as you entered. You wheeled your cart along a winding track that took you past all the store's offerings and also enabled you to enjoy each of the establishment's famous troupes of performing automatons. A bovine band blared forth a ballad in praise of Dole canned food. Dogs strummed banjos. Chickens cavorted. Fantastic animation creatures—brought to big three-dimensional life as lovable robots—did vaudeville turns while urging you to buy. The walls were lined with photographs, typically a large picture of Stew Leonard with his friend and neighbor Paul Newman, whose Newman's Own products were featured in the store.

The Leonard family had run a small dairy in Norwalk, starting in the 1920s. Stew Leonard took over the dairy in 1951. The business was trying to adapt to changing times—for example, by placing a pioneering milk-dispensing machine on a strategic corner in Westport. Stew Leonard, a graduate of the University of Connecticut, saw the future. Fewer and fewer people wanted to have fresh milk delivered to their doorsteps.

So the Stew Leonard store was born. It succeeded, grew, and grew. The fame of the store, and its founder, spread worldwide. Tom Peters celebrated Stew Leonard in his book A *Passion for Excellence*. Television documentaries spotlighted the success story. The *Guinness Book of World Records* placed its seal on the store's leadership. President Ronald Reagan gave Mr. Leonard a Presidential Award for Entrepreneurial Achievement. When Stew Leonard started his own management school, the biggest corporations and government departments sent people to attend.

The Leonard legend flourished. Then, one June day in 1991, Stew Leonard was getting ready to board a plane to Saint Martin, where the Leonard family enjoyed a second home. Travelers headed for the Caribbean bring along enough pocket money to take care of their needs, but the customs agents felt that what Leonard was bringing along was a little excessive—$75,000 in cash. When you take that much money out of the country you're required to fill out a form, and this, the government said, Stew Leonard had not done.

On August 9, 1991, federal agents raided Stew Leonard's offices and the home of a company executive. What they found was astonishing. Stew Leonard, like a sovereign nation, was, beneath the surface, running a covert operation. The agents seized cash, records, and the computer program that had been used to execute the fraud, which had started as far back as 1981. The computer program was called "Equity." The disk containing the program was kept hidden in a hollowed-out book. The book was *The Business Directory of New England*.

Stew Leonard and three executives of the firm pleaded guilty to charges of diverting more than $17 million to evade taxes. Leonard was ordered to repay the stolen tax money; he was fined $850,000; he was ordered to pay nearly $100,000 for the costs of his imprisonment and release period. And the sixty-three-year-old entrepreneur was sentenced to fifty-two months in federal prison.

The IQ Scam

Cyril Ludowic Burt was the leading educational psychologist of his generation. After his graduation from Oxford in 1907, Burt plunged into the relatively new field of intelligence measurement. In 1932 he was appointed to the influential position of professor of psychology at University College.[7]

During these years, the discipline of psychology was embattled over a question that has erupted anew with the *Bell Curve* controversy: the relative importance of heredity as against upbringing in determining intelligence. Cyril Burt made decisive contributions to the controversy on the side of nature with his pioneering studies of identical twins who had been separated in early childhood and raised in disparate environments.

Burt's research showed that the twins who were his subjects had astonishingly similar IQs, even though their circumstances of life were radically different.[8] These findings helped to support the controversial theories of the psychologist Arthur Jensen, who advocates the proposition that intelligence is determined to a significant degree by race. (Jensen is cited by those who proclaim the superiority of the white race over the black race.)

With such a commanding figure as Cyril Burt weighing in on the side of heredity, those who argued for environmental circumstances were at a disadvantage. Not that the opponents did not try. They mustered arguments against Burt's persuasive studies of twins. But every time the opponents came up with new arguments, Burt seemed to come up with new twins. Initially he had reported on fewer than twenty pairs of twins. Over the years his sample grew to more than fifty pairs. The astonishing correlation between the IQs of Burt's differently raised twins remained the bulwark of the champions of inheritance.

Burt's published findings made the names of Margaret Howard and J. Conway, his research assistants, well known in the field. Most of the findings were statistical; however, one widely noted article, published by J. Conway in the *British Journal of Statistical Psychology*, told the story of "George" and "Llewellyn," sons of an Oxford don who died just before their birth. Llewellyn was adopted by a couple in North Wales, received little formal education, and became a farmer. George had a spectacular academic career. George's tested IQ was 136; Llewellyn's was 137.

It was fascinating material like this that made Cyril Burt world renowned, earning published tributes from such peers as the French psychologist J. Lafitte.

Burt towered above his field. Though specialists argued over interpretation, his findings were gospel.

Then, finally, somebody took a look at the work. Leon Kamin, a Princeton psychologist, studied the body of Burt's life work and did some arithmetic. Kamin discovered that, while the number of twins studied just about tripled, the average correlation between their IQs remained unchanged to the third decimal place. This was, practically speaking, a statistical impossibility.

Now more researchers tiptoed hesitantly toward the task of taking a cold hard look at the life work of Cyril Ludowic Burt.

And they found what Dorothy found when she looked behind the curtain: *the wizard was a fake.*

Or at least the latter part of the wizard's life was largely a fake. The twins did not exist. Burt's collaborators, Margaret Howard and J. Conway, did not exist—at least not as associates of Burt in conducting research. The improbably named French psychologist J. Lafitte, who had praised the work so highly, was a fictional person.

Cyril Burt's early work was valid and valuable. He made brilliant contributions to his field. But instead of defending his findings in the legitimate give-and-take of scientific debate, he bludgeoned his opposition into submission by fabricating results that supported his position. His brilliance turned into fraud.

Burt's reputation sustained the fraud for a while. And his reputation might have remained unblemished for a lot longer if he had not made puerile mistakes in carrying out his fraud. After all, Cyril Burt was intelligent enough to build a little more variation into the IQ scores that he was making up. And, while it might have been shrewd to make up a French professional supporter, it was reckless to give the creation the name "J. Lafitte"—recalling the swashbuckling pirate Jean Lafitte.

Who knows what drove Cyril Burt? Raymond Fancher[9] notes that Burt was "led by parental pressure to crave competitive academic success." Fancher cites Burt's own words: "As . . . examinations drew near, my mother regularly related how my father had once won so many prizes at . . . school that a cab was necessary to cart them home, and I felt I should be disgraced if I did not bring back at least one prize. To make quite sure, I generally aimed at the Scripture prize, which nobody else seemed to covet."[10]

Covering Up the Breast Cancer Fakery

Another case of falsification of scientific data hit the headlines in the early part of 1994. The National Cancer Institute found irregularities in research relating to a life-or-death question—the relative advantages of lumpectomy and mastectomy.

Attention focused on Dr. Bernard Fisher, a distinguished surgeon who had served on the University of Pittsburgh faculty since 1947 and had headed up the group conducting the studies. Dr. Fisher "was pivotal in changing the way breast cancer is treated by pioneering large-scale research and therapy studies of the disease and by overcoming the natural independence of surgeons."[11]

It came to light that some of the data that had gone into the landmark 1985 study—data originating in a Montreal hospital—had been falsified. There was no implication that Dr. Fisher had anything to do with faking the data. The furor that swirled around him was touched off by the revelation that he had found out about the irregularities and had not reported them to the National Cancer Institute. Women who had, with their physicians, made the agonizing choices about breast cancer, were confronted with the shattering news that they might have been relying on bad information.

Dr. Fisher said the results of the study came out the same when the tainted data were removed. This did not abate the controversy. Dr. Bernard Fisher was abruptly ousted from his position.

The New York Times said of Dr. Fisher that "the same forceful personality that allowed him to accomplish so much has contributed to his downfall.... Colleagues describe him as self-confident with a manner that is often perceived as arrogant and abrasive." Dr. Samuel Hellman, a radiation and cancer expert at the University of Chicago, called Dr. Fisher "outspoken, very clear, strong in his views and clearly not to be pushed around by the vicissitudes of smaller issues, a guy with a great deal of character and forcefulness of being right."

Dr. Fisher used to tell his students to avoid "politics, process and publicity." But here he was clearly involved in a process that was redolent of politics and susceptible to a high degree of publicity. His responsibilities as head of the study included a responsibility to the public in general and to those who had undergone lumpectomies or mastectomies in particular. Dr. Fisher overlooked that responsibility, and his omission was certainly not a function of lack of intelligence or character.

Being right all the time can have a terrible price.

Monkeying Around with Fate

Some episodes have it all: hubris, arrogance, narcissism, and the need to fail.

On May 19, 1987, a newspaper editor phoned his PR man to say that the paper had some interesting photos of some folks having fun on vacation. These photos would run in the next issue. The publication wanted maximum publicity.

The publication happened to be the *National Inquirer*. The folks on vacation happened to be Gary Hart, at that time the leading contender for the Democratic nomination for president, and a friend, Donna Rice. The two were frolicking aboard a yacht. One snapshot showed Ms. Rice sitting on Mr. Hart's lap. The presidential candidate wore a T-shirt bearing the vessel's name: *Monkey Business.*

Hyped to the hilt, the story led the evening TV news, made page one in the mainstream press, and rocketed the *Enquirer's* circulation to a new record.

The accompanying story announced that Gary Hart was planning to divorce his wife after being elected president, whereupon he would marry Donna Rice and bring her to the White House as his new first lady. Ms. Rice confided that she was getting abundant show business offers. Later Ms. Rice would say that no amount of success as an actress would compensate her "for the heartbreak of losing Gary Hart and the chance to live in the White House."

Despite these touching sentiments, some cynics said that Hart had been set up and exploited by Donna Rice. This perception was not diminished by the fact that the photos were taken (with Ms. Rice's camera) by a friend of the would-be first lady, also along on the cruise.

All of this came in the wake of Gary Hart's challenge to the press, which had been following up rumors about the candidate's extramarital activities. "Catch me if you can!" he said in effect.

Everything about the story, right down to the name of the yacht, came together to make Gary Hart the favorite target for every joke-smith in the world. Four years later, Bill Clinton would ride out a similar squall. But while Clinton might have looked like a guy who played around a lot, he did not look like a prize boob, who had dared the fates and who then allowed himself to be played for a sap.

The American public has demonstrated, in elections at least as far back as Grover Cleveland's, that it will accept a presidential womanizer—but not a presidential boob.

Fleeing from Success

Allard Lowenstein was an unlikely hero and an even more unlikely winner. In many ways a virtual caricature of a New York Jewish intellectual and social idealist, Lowenstein became a political power; a prime force in the undoing of President Lyndon Johnson; an activist for liberal causes who won the respect and regard of conservative foes, including William Buckley; a firebrand in the fight against apartheid in South Africa that has culminated in the tumultuous events of today; and a fearless leader in the civil rights struggle that changed the face of America forever.

Lowenstein achieved what few of his colleagues achieved. He upheld and espoused his principles eloquently; he was admired as a thinker of coruscating brilliance; and at the same time he scored astonishing triumphs in the rough-and-tumble world of power politics.

And yet, says the author of a searching biography,[12] Allard Lowenstein was driven by a need to fail, because he disliked himself—for, among other things, his homosexuality—and could not permit himself to win.

Lowenstein took on impossible challenges in his personal as well as in his public life. His biographer concludes that Lowenstein seemed to seek out questions that had no answer, to put himself in positions where he would not only come out a loser but a humiliated loser. He alienated idealistic supporters by failing to keep his distance from the CIA, which, in those days, was eager to provide clandestine support to organizations and leaders on the left.

The pure-burning flame of Lowenstein's idealism drew many adherents. He became friendly with many young followers, particularly young men, and then tended to move on to other relationships. One of his young followers was Dennis Sweeney, a dedicated but emotionally disturbed young man, whom Lowenstein realized to be dangerous. Lowenstein thought he could "handle" Sweeney. Sweeney became increasingly disturbed, hearing voices that he received through his teeth. Sweeney fixed on his former mentor as the cause of these voices and, on March 14, 1981, the crazed young man murdered Allard Lowenstein.

Penetrating Deeper into the SDIS Molecule

In the following chapter we will examine separately the elements of SDIS.

We begin with *hubris*.

Notes

1. *Wall Street Journal*, February 8, 1994, "Ups and Downs," by John I. Keller.
2. *The New Yorker*, December 21, 1992, "To Catch a Judge; How the F.B.I. Tracked Sol Wachtler," by Lucinda Franks.
3. *New York Newsday*, November 5, 1993, "DA Booted," by Susan Forrest.
4. *New York Times*, January 26, 1994, "The Talk of Vienna: President's Affair," by Stephen Kinzer.
5. London *Times*, October 26, 1993, "Sex Advisers Give Oxford Freshers the Third Degree," by Walter Ellis.
6. Stanley Weintraub, *Disraeli* (New York: Dutton, 1993), p. 324.
7. Raymond E. Fancher, *The Intelligence Men* (New York: W. W. Norton, 1985), pp. 169–175.
8. Stephen Jay Gould, *The Mismeasure of Man* (New York: W. W. Norton, 1981), pp. 234–238; 273–278.
9. Fancher, op. cit. p. 180.
10. Cyril Burt, *Autobiography*, in E. G. Boring and H. S. Langfeld, eds., A *History of Psychology in Autobiography*, vol. 4 (Worcester, Mass.: Clark University Press, 1951), pp. 53–73.
11. *New York Times*, April 4, 1994, "Fall of a Man Pivotal in Breast Cancer Research," by Lawrence K. Altman.·
12. William H. Chafe, *Never Stop Running: Allard Lowenstein and the Struggle to Save American Liberalism* (New York: Basic Books/HarperCollins, 1993), pp. 56; 392–393; 473.

Chapter 4.

THE GREEKS HAD A WORD FOR IT:
Ηυβριϲ

The ancient Greeks teach us about our world. Classic mythology gives us metaphors that help us understand our strengths and weaknesses, our lusts, rages and fears, the urges that drive us, the traps we make for ourselves. Athena, Hercules, Venus, Midas, Cassandra, Narcissus, Cupid, Achilles—the legends who loved, fought, and had adventures on and around Mount Olympus live today.

Classic mythology abounds with stories of brilliantly gifted creatures who commit acts of supernal stupidity. The usually clear-thinking Odysseus, bewitched by the nymph Calypso. The wise and noble Priam, king of Troy, ignoring Cassandra's warning that the wooden horse was full of Greek soldiers. Pandora (whose name means "the gift of all") opening the box. King Midas, given by Bacchus the privilege of having his wish come true, asking that everything he touched be turned into gold. (Since that included food and drink, Midas nearly starved to death before begging the delighted god to take back the gift.)

But for the most spectacular example of self-destructive intelligence in ancient Greece we turn not to a mythical creature, but to a real person: the Athenian leader Alcibiades, who was born around 450 B.C. Alcibiades is the ultimate SCIPI. We can see in him the traits that ruin the careers and lives of gifted people today.

Alcibiades, born of a rich and influential family, was related to the great Pericles. He studied with Socrates.

Deciding to go into politics while still in his twenties, Alcibiades put his magnetism, his brilliance, and his oratorical gifts to work, hoping to be elected general. He was shocked when he was edged out by an honorable and capable Athenian named Nicias. However, through trickery, Alcibiades discredited Nicias. Alcibiades was elected general—at the cost of intensifying and prolonging the war between Athens and Sparta.

As general, says Plutarch, he "possessed the people with great hopes, and he himself entertained yet greater."[1] Sweeping young Athenians along through his oratory and his charisma, Alcibiades unveiled the plan that would make him the greatest of the great, an immortal. He would lead the Athenians to the conquest of Sicily.

On the eve of the sailing of the armada came the Feast of Adonis. The next morning Athenians were horrified to find that, all over the city, statues of Hermes (Mercury) had been disfigured, noses and genitals smashed. Soon the story began to come out: Alcibiades and some of his companions, after a rowdy party at which they mocked the sacred mysteries, went out into the city and assailed the revered statues.

At the moment of his greatest honor and challenge, Alcibiades was disgraced.

> Pride that dines on vanity sups on contempt.
> Benjamin Franklin, *The Way to Wealth*

The general was recalled from Sicily to stand trial. Instead of going back, he fled to Sparta, turned his coat, and joined the enemies of Athens. (Another quality with which certain present-day SCIPIs are not overburdened is an oppressive sense of loyalty.)

Agis, king of the Spartans, befriended the renegade Athenian, heaped honors on him, and welcomed him to the royal palace. Alcibiades' thanks was to seduce the wife of Agis, impregnate her, and then boast that the fruit of his loins would one day rule over the Spartans. The king sent assassins to kill Alcibiades, but the intended victim, always fast on his feet, escaped.

Why Smart People Do Dumb Things

There is but a step between a proud man's glory and his disgrace.
Publilius Syrus, *Moral Sayings*

Always resourceful, Alcibiades defected to an enemy of both Sparta and Athens—Persia. There he found an admirer: Tisaphernes, the Persian satrap, was a connoisseur of guile and wickedness, and he welcomed Alcibiades.

But, following his lifelong pattern, Alcibiades changed sides again, becoming the front man for the anti-democratic Athenians.

As soon as these dissidents got the government of Athens into their hands, they turned their backs on Alcibiades.

But, in yet one more turn of the wheel of fate, Alcibiades would have another chance to use his greatness in a great cause and make himself immortal. The desperate Athenians, who were losing the war, agreed to make him the leader of their forces in the field once again.

Against the odds, Alcibiades' army and navy won a great victory. His fleet routed the enemy ships, driving them to destruction on the rocky shores of the Hellespont. Athens was prepared to welcome him back. Alcibiades was ready.

But first he had to make a little side trip. Let Plutarch tell it: "After the gaining of so glorious a victory, his vanity made him eager to show himself to Tisaphernes, and, having furnished himself with gifts and presents, and an equipage suitable to his dignity, he set out to visit him."

When the Athenian arrived in stately pomp at Tisaphernes' court, the Persian, instead of being impressed as he was intended to be, had the triumphant visitor seized and thrown into prison.

The end of Alcibiades? No. This brilliant, charming, and absolutely unprincipled man had a few more cards to play. He contrived to escape, and once again took the lead of the Athenian forces in the endless and confusing wars that swirled through the Aegean and into what we now call the Black Sea.

Alcibiades, who still harbored ambitions to divinity, determined to lead Athens in one last climactic fight, against his old enemy King Agis of the Spartans. This time, says Plutarch, "Alcibiades would engage in a holy war, in the cause of the gods, and in defense of the most sacred and solemn ceremonies." Thus the contemptuous cynic who had once profaned the holy rituals and statues of the gods would now lead the gods themselves to glory.

At first the holy war went without a hitch. Then Alcibiades' forces started to lose. The Athenians dumped him.

Alcibiades offered profuse advice to his successor, who ignored him. The deposed general, embittered, became a loud second-guesser. There was plenty to second-guess; the war was now going badly for Athens. And, finally, the Spartans broke through, occupied Athens, and ended the war.

The victorious Spartans did not capture Alcibiades. Knowing the hatred his old enemies bore him, he fled to Thrace, and then to Phrygia. One night a stealthy band of men surrounded the house where he was living, set it on fire, and, when Alcibiades emerged, killed him with arrows. Some said the assassins were sent by the leader of the Spartans. Some said that Alcibiades had debauched the daughter of a noble family, and that her brothers had murdered Alcibiades to avenge the dishonor.

"Certainly," says Plutarch, "if ever a man was ruined by his own glory, it was Alcibiades."

Analyzing Alcibiades

If we can identify the elements that make up the SDIS virus we can begin to look for a cure. Let's analyze the career of Alcibiades, distilling out the principal factors that made this fabulous highflier and foul-up do the things he did.

Start with *vanity.* Alcibiades loved himself to a degree that he never seems to have had room for an unselfish thought about anyone else. He is narcissistic.

A second thing that strikes you about Alcibiades is his tendency to go too far. He was capable of many things, but not of everything. He was smart enough to realize this. Nevertheless he acted as if nothing were beyond his capacity to achieve. Here, then, is a second factor in the makeup of people of self-destructive intelligence: *omnipotence fantasies*, growing from *arrogance*.

And yet, at the same time he is acting as if he were all-powerful, Alcibiades keeps doing things that lead inevitably to failure. A paramount example is his defacement of the holy images on the eve of the expedition to Sicily. We shall be talking more about the *unconscious need to fail*.

There is yet one more factor in the mix that leads to the catastrophe of self-destructive intelligence—a factor evident at every stage of Alcibiades' life. The Greeks—and we—call it *hubris*.

Hubris is a concept of paramount importance in exploring the self-destructive stupidity of intelligent people. Sometimes the word is used interchangeably with the useful Yiddish word *chutzpah*, meaning "shameless impudence." To many, hubris means arrogance, or excessive conceit, or self-centeredness.

Hubris includes all of these things. But it is something more, something deeper and grander and darker. Homer calls it "insolence against the gods." Aristotle calls it the *hamartia*, a tragic flaw, that strabismus that distorts the vision of the inner eye and brings even the wisest of mortals to ruin. An eminent classics scholar calls hubris *overweening pride*, which makes the individual oblivious to "shame or decency or the restraining force of public opinion."[2]

Hubris abounds in our society. It is one of the prime operative agents of SDIS. We see examples of it everywhere.

We see it even among scientists, who are usually taken to be models of calm rationality. Science has become so dominant in our lives that the most creative and successful scientists may occasionally assume, in their own minds, godlike status.

Steven Levy refers to this phenomenon in a *New Yorker* article about the biochemist Gerald Maurice Edelman, who shared the Nobel Prize for physiology and medicine in 1972. Dr. Edelman has, in recent years, developed some striking theories about the brain, which he advocates with an "in-your-face" approach. Levy writes, "The psychiatrist and writer Israel Rosenfield, who was an early supporter of Edelman's theory, now thinks that Edelman is an example of how the star system of science, and particularly the Nobel, can result in a sort of destructive hubris on the part of an ambitious scientist. In Rosenfield's view, Edelman's ambition 'raises all kinds of questions in science,' and he adds, 'Edelman to me is an example of the way one can go off the deep end.' "[3]

Hubris has destructive effects for others, but it invariably destroys the individual who possesses it. Alcibiades' life is one long display of hubris. His overweening pride rivals that of his counterparts among the mythical beings.

The Dark Star of High Intelligence

Astronomers have discovered that Sirius, the brightest star in the sky, has a dark companion: a lightless, infinitely heavy presence turning endlessly in space in a tight orbit with the blazing star. Hubris is the dark companion of personal brilliance. People of modest gifts have many troubles, but they are not hubristic. Hubris is ultra-individualistic. When people have little to be proud of, comments Richard S. Lazarus, a leading figure in the development of stress and emotion theory, they tend to "identify with a famous group, whether religious, sporting, political, ethnic, or national."[5] This kind of pride can be carried to extremes; it is not enough to glory in one's own group, one must make the group more important by excluding others, or denigrating others, or—when group pride is carried to pathological extremes—harming others.

Hubristic pride requires no identification with a group. Just the opposite; the hubrist scorns connection with groups. He or she (using chameleon-like qualities) may adopt the plumage of a favored group or class, but inside, the hubrist, feeling an overwhelming sense of personal superiority to everyone else, stands aloof.

Hubris is a powerful engine, driving the individual to extraordinary feats. Where would we be if Prometheus had not dared the gods and stolen the fire? But the hubristic engine revs so fast and generates such internal heat that it runs on the edge of destruction. Hubrists cannot live without danger. Their pride and insolence lead them constantly to sneer at the "gods"—meaning the contemporary counterparts of the Greek and Roman gods, the folkways, mores, and power structure of the society.

Hubris Among the Lawyers

Hubris abounds in every area of endeavor—business, politics, science, medicine, teaching, and so on.

We can find some interesting examples of hubris among lawyers. A good number of these modern-day tribunes of the people are worthy of wearing the mantle of Alcibiades. Success in the legal profession gives them great power. As advocates and judges they come close to playing god. It may be the god-playing role that generates so many cases of self-destructive hubrism among attorneys.

Milton S. Gould has made a study of hubris among lawyers. Gould, along with his partner William A. Shea, built the great New York–based law firm Shea & Gould. For thirty years Shea & Gould was a legal powerhouse. The firm's expertise in litigation and corporate restructuring was matched by its political influence on both sides of the aisle. William Shea was the muscular political arm of the firm, demonstrating immense sway over the life of the city. (Shea Stadium is named after him.) Milton Gould, described by the *New York Times* as a "legendary litigator," was the legal dynamo, building a winning team of attorneys and amassing a client list including Donald Trump, Aldo Gucci, William J. Casey, Aristotle Onassis, Leona Helmsley, and Jack Kent Cooke.

The Greeks Had a Word For It: Ηυβριο

Shea & Gould broke up early in 1994. The eighty-four-year-old Milton Gould saw the firm's dissolution as caused by the greed and folly of the lawyers he had chosen and nurtured: "We turned our clients over to these kids! We made them big shots! But they got drunk on their own liquor: they looked in the mirror and thought they saw Shea & Gould. And they were deluding themselves."[6]

The firm could have survived, Milton Gould felt. But that would have taken loyalty and commitment to the tradition of Shea & Gould. Gould said, "I was raised to believe that a law firm is a family. You stay together, love each other, protect each other. But now law firms are like ball clubs, and lawyers are free agents—when the season ends, you go looking for more money."[7]

In January 1994, seventy-eight of the eighty partners voted to dissolve Shea & Gould. Milton Gould said, "I have suffered a betrayal by people who owed a lot to me: they didn't discuss it with me, and they used bad judgment to further objectives that were selfish and unjust."

As Milton Gould expressed it to us as we talked to him about the topic of this book, the death of Shea & Gould was an example—the example closest to his heart—of hubris among lawyers and its malignant effects. It will be useful to venture more deeply into this tangled world, with Milton Gould as our guide.

No Limits

More than anything else, he was a person who refused to acknowledge limits. It was this quality, in large part, that made him at once so magnetic and so flawed . . . feeling exempt from legal, ethical and moral standards, he abrogated them at will. To violate all these standards, and never to be publicly caught at it—more, to be perceived by thousands as the very exemplar of some of these standards—now that, for someone like Ross, was winning.

Connie Bruck, *Master of the Game: Steve Ross and the Creation of Time Warner* (New York: Simon & Schuster, 1994)

Lawyers are our laboratory animals for this part of our exploration of why smart people do dumb things. They are undeniably smart, and sometimes they do spectacularly dumb things.

And their besetting sin is hubris.

Milton Gould wrote,[8] "Foley Square (location of the federal courthouse in New York City) is the peculiar habitat of hubris, not only because its courtrooms have furnished the proscenium against which so many of the victims [of hubris] have been annihilated, but because so many of the victims have come from our own ranks."

You would think that, seeing what they see, lawyers would be especially insulated from overweening pride. Every day they see the lofty brought low: tycoons, business leaders, community leaders, respected clerics, eminent academicians, hot media stars. Lawyers not only see this, they are part of the process by which nemesis overtakes the high and mighty. Gould observes, "The vagaries of our profession often force lawyers to become actors in the ruin of men who have enjoyed wealth, power, the high esteem of their fellows, and the other ingredients of a happy and fruitful life. As prosecutors, as defenders, as judges, even as witnesses, we become close observers of these men who, through the working of some tragic flaw in character or judgment, are hurled down from the heights to disgrace, to penury, and even to death."

When we see someone of high stature, who seems to have it all, stoop to follies that destroy him or her, we ask, "Why?" Why do they do it? In particular, why do lawyers do it? The law is an exacting discipline, requiring keen intellect, quick thinking, and practical and impactful application of brains to the solution of problems. Lawyers—who are pragmatic to the point of cynicism—should labor under no illusions about the consequences of quixotic stupidity.

Nevertheless, Milton Gould observes wryly, "When dinner-table conversation turns to the most recent of our reprobates, I am forced to explain that we lawyers are no more proof against the canker of hubris than are the soldiers or the statesmen, the sailors, the surgeons or the salesmen."

The Greeks Had a Word For It: Hυβρισ

As proof of Gould's opinion, it is sad but instructive to examine the case of a lawyer who had everything going for him, and threw it all away through an abysmal act of stupidity.

The Self-Induced Downfall of James M. Landis

James McCauley Landis was the golden boy of the legal world in the decades 1930–1960. An outstanding graduate of Harvard Law School, Landis found, in the early 1930s, a powerful patron—Joseph P. Kennedy, entrepreneur, speculator, millionaire, movie producer, political power, and father of John F. and Robert Kennedy. In the early days of Franklin D. Roosevelt's New Deal, Landis—with a powerful assist from Joe Kennedy—began to carve out a career that would make him federal trade commissioner, chairman of the Securities and Exchange Commission, dean of Harvard Law School, chairman of the Civil Aeronautics Authority, director of the Office of Civil Defense in World War II, the protégé of Felix Frankfurter, successful lawyer in private practice, and adviser to three presidents.

On a hot summer night in 1964, some boys climbed over the fence of a country estate in Harrison, New York. It was their practice to sneak into the grounds of stately homes to take a cooling, if unauthorized, dip in the pool. This night they had chosen the home of James Landis. They found Landis's body floating, face down, in the pool. It was never determined whether Landis suffered a sudden heart seizure or had killed himself.

There was reason to suspect suicide. Several days earlier, Landis had been suspended from the practice of law in New York and Washington following his conviction in Federal Court, Foley Square, for failing to file income tax returns for the years 1956–60.

James Landis benefited a great deal from his association with the Kennedy family, but he also performed distinguished and valuable services for the clan. When John F. Kennedy was first running in Massachusetts for the Senate, his campaign was endangered by charges of McCarthyism and anti-Semitism. James M. Landis put his impeccable reputation for liberal integrity on the line to support the young Kennedy. As a lawyer Landis was a key figure in the business dealings of the Kennedys. For example, notes Gould, "It was Landis who found a legal loophole in the tax laws to save the Kennedys vast sums in taxes on their acquisition of the Chicago Merchandise Mart."

When John F. Kennedy was elected president in 1960, Landis went to the White House as special assistant to the president. He had every reason to feel that, before long, his career would be crowned by the consummation that is just about every American lawyer's dream: appointment to the Supreme Court.

In the summer of 1961 a small cloud appeared on the horizon of this idyllic picture. Somebody in the IRS noticed that Landis had not filed tax returns for the past five years. Joseph Kennedy was alerted; he alerted his son Robert Kennedy, the attorney general. The brainpower and leverage of the Kennedy White House went to work to pull Landis out of the hole and avoid an embarrassment for the administration. Landis was dispatched to the office of the commissioner of Internal Revenue to "work things out."

The commissioner of the IRS, Mortimer Caplin, urged that the returns be filed at once. A *voluntary* disclosure of delinquent taxes would cost the taxpayer money, but there would be no criminal case. By June 1962 Landis had filed his returns and paid about $50,000 on account toward settling the affair. Evidently Joseph Kennedy loaned Landis some of this money.

Connoisseurs of stupidity among smart people have to ask two questions at this point:

- **Why didn't Kennedy lend Landis *all* the money he needed to pay off the IRS?**

- Certainly Joseph Kennedy had the money, and the whole idea was to settle the matter quietly.
- Why had Landis omitted to file returns for five years? This was an incomprehensible blunder for someone of Landis's position and sophistication.

To the first question there has never been a satisfactory answer. The only available answer to the second question involves the following story, told by Landis. It seems that in the 1950s Landis had sold some stock he had inherited from his mother thirty years before. The price was $3,000. Landis had a little trouble figuring out what the stock was worth on the date of acquisition. So he asked for an extension. That ran out and he asked for another extension. Then he stopped asking for extensions and also stopped filing returns for the next five or six years. Why? The tax form asks if you have filed a return in the previous year. Landis claimed he was embarrassed to answer no, so he just didn't make out a return. He talked vaguely about putting money aside to pay what he owed at some unspecified date.

Milton Gould comments that this explanation would sound lame coming from "the proprietor of a corner pushcart; from the former Dean of the Harvard Law School, the former chairman of the Securities and Exchange Commission and the chief tax expert for the Kennedy family, it is preposterous."

The massive damage control operation mounted by the Kennedys might have achieved its purpose except for the inconvenient fact that Landis had also failed to file his New York State income tax returns. The governor of New York was Nelson Rockefeller, a Republican who intended to run for president in 1964. The Kennedy administration was determined to keep Landis's troubles from becoming an issue for Rockefeller.

The key word now was "voluntary"—had Landis filed the overdue returns before or after the IRS started to investigate the matter?

There was no clear answer. Landis and/or his legal counsel could certainly get the benefit of the doubt. Case closed, right?

Wrong. In a breathtaking display of folly, James Landis went before an IRS hearing—without a lawyer—and, says Gould, "surrendered to that perverse impulse toward self-destruction that we recognize as the prime symptom of hubris: he conceded that his filing was *not* spontaneous, that it came from the tip-off by Joe Kennedy that he was under investigation."

Now it became a criminal matter.

In August 1963 Landis appeared in Federal Court in New York and pleaded guilty. Nicholas Katzenbach, the federal prosecutor, chose a sentencing date just before Labor Day, when media coverage would be minimal and when the presiding judge would be Wilfred Feinberg, a recent Kennedy appointee who, it was assumed, would be willing to go along with government recommendation that Landis *not* be sentenced to prison.

But Judge Feinberg knew Landis, was a friend of Landis's lawyer, and had ties to the Kennedy administration. He declined to handle Landis's sentencing. The task fell to Sylvester Ryan, a tough, plain-spoken judge with a reputation for ability and courage. Ryan refused to discuss the matter with prosecutors or defense counsel. He asked for the probation report. Astonishingly, it showed that Landis had *still* not paid his back taxes!

The Kennedy establishment had hoped for a small fine and a suspended sentence, with minimum publicity. Instead, Judge Ryan sent Landis to jail for thirty days on each of three counts, with two six-month sentences suspended. Ninety days might not be much for a career stickup man, but for Landis it was an eternity. The defendant threw up his hands in disbelief. The judge denied requests for a delay. James M. Landis was hustled away in handcuffs, says Gould, "to be fingerprinted and photographed and catalogued along with the common herd of drug peddlers and check forgers."

Landis served his time. On July 10, 1964, he was barred from the practice of law for one year. Twenty days later he was found dead in his swimming pool.

Just a Few Little Numbers on a Business Card

J. Vincent Keogh's downfall, says Milton Gould, "is one of the most harrowing examples of hubris among lawyers, because he was a man who radiated friendliness, who inspired love and confidence, and had an army of friends and admirers."

In 1961 Vincent Keogh was judge of the New York State Supreme Court in Brooklyn. Keogh was fifty-six. He had worked his way through college, attended Fordham Law School at night, achieved a distinguished record in World War II, and served as United States attorney for the Eastern District of New York. His brother Eugene was a powerful congressman (one of the creators of the Keogh Plan, which has provided retirement income for so many freelancers and small business proprietors). The Keogh brothers ranked high in Democratic politics, national, state, and city. Vincent Keogh was spoken of as a possible mayor of New York.

Early in 1961 a Federal Grand Jury in Brooklyn indicted three juke box operators for unlawfully diverting about one hundred juke boxes and slot machines from the Trustee in Bankruptcy of Gibraltar Amusements Ltd. The three pleaded guilty. According to later testimony, the juke box robbers enlisted influential friends to reach the sentencing judge.

Among those involved in the conspiracy was Dr. Robert M. Erdman, an orthopedic surgeon with an office on Manhattan's fashionable East Side and residences in Riverdale and Kings Point, where he lived with his wife and two children. Dr. Erdman numbered among his patients one Antonio Corallo, known as "Tony Ducks," a veteran hoodlum.

Dr. Erdman spent a lot of time testifying as a professional witness in personal injury cases. A federal agent would say that the doctor had "a penchant for fixing cases for kicks." Dr. Erdman had other somewhat unconventional interests. He was an investor in a slot machine business in Baltimore.

Erdman met Judge Keogh when he appeared as an expert witness in the judge's court. The orthopedist, declares Gould, "nurtured the Keogh relationship with the richest manure: flattery, gifts and lavish hospitality." Moreover, Dr. Erdman provided Judge Keogh and his family with free medical care.

So it may not be surprising that Keogh, along with Erdman and others, wound up in the toils of the law, accused of trying to fix the case of the juke box bandits so that they evaded jail time. Keogh admitted a lot of things. He admitted that the doctor had given him a new Dodge automobile, storm windows, and free medical care. Keogh admitted that Erdman had talked to him about the case, and that he—Keogh—had made a lunch date with the judge who would be doing the sentencing.

Nevertheless, Keogh denied that he had discussed with Dr. Erdman the possibility of rigging the sentence or that there was any question of taking a bribe from the doctor.

This was the key point; and it was here that the prosecution was able to produce two little pieces of cardboard with writing on them. Keogh admitted that these were his business cards. On one he had written an estimate of the cost of renovating his summer home. On the other he had written a request for a loan. But, testified Judge Keogh, these things had nothing to do with the juke box case; they were innocent indications of his financial situation.

What a heartwarming picture! Two old friends, chatting about this and that. One old friend says, "How're you doing?" The other, in reply, jots down the sums of which he is most in need.

Arguments like this did not convince the jury, which convicted J. Vincent Keogh.

Forget about all the other aspects of J. Vincent Keogh's story. Let's just focus on the little business cards. *Why would you put such things in writing?*

Hubris leads its victims farther and farther down the path toward the illusion of omnipotence. If you are a judge, and you believe you are all-powerful, and that nothing can harm you, then you don't worry about accepting cars and storm windows and free medical care. And you don't worry about writing potentially devastating notes.

Before we leave this tale, which focuses on the follies of lawyers, it is worthwhile to comment briefly on Dr. Robert Erdman, a SCIPI in good standing. Dr. Erdman, highly respected, successful and able to earn big money at his profession, liked to live dangerously. Whereas more conventional investors would have been in mutual funds or even government bonds, Dr. Erdman was in slot machines. He seems to have enjoyed the company of some shady characters. He enjoyed the feeling of being able to manipulate justice.

The Hubris of Douglas MacArthur

No discussion of hubris would be complete without discussion of one of the towering hubrists of the twentieth century, General Douglas MacArthur.

MacArthur, the son of a general who had served in the Civil War and the Spanish-American War, was marked for greatness from birth. He starred at West Point. As commander of the 42nd (Rainbow) division in France in World War I, MacArthur was called the "Boy Genius." He was the youngest chief of staff in U.S. history. His eagle profile, his elegant uniforms, and his titanic self-confidence made him a fabled leader in his lifetime.

All this was prelude to MacArthur's role as supreme commander against the Japanese in World War II. One of the indelible images emerging from the war's finale is that of the imperious MacArthur brusquely instructing the tiny Japanese delegates to sign the articles of surrender on the deck of the battleship *Missouri*.

As supreme commander of occupied Japan, MacArthur held the status of a demigod. When he had held high position in the Philippines before World War II, his position had been more like that of an Oriental satrap than that of a professional army officer.

In 1950 President Harry Truman committed the United States to war against North Korea, which had invaded South Korea. MacArthur was the obvious choice to command the U.S. forces. In a daring, brilliant maneuver, MacArthur defied conventional wisdom and landed troops behind the North Korean front lines at Inchon, reversing the course of the war, which had been going badly for the United States and its allies.

Buoyed by this success, MacArthur vowed to sweep the invaders back to the very northern borders of their country, the border with Red China.

Truman's advisers warned that the allied forces must not go north of the 38th parallel; this would run the risk of bringing the Chinese into the war. MacArthur scorned that risk. He hurled his troops north to the parallel.

The president arranged to meet with the general on Wake Island. Harry Truman had never met MacArthur. He looked forward to the meeting. To him, MacArthur was a great hero.

Truman was in many ways the antithesis of MacArthur. He was short in stature, unprepossessing in appearance. During World War I Truman had been a captain in the artillery in France. After the war he failed in a haberdashery business, got into politics, was backed for increasingly important offices by the Kansas City machine because he was loyal and dependable. FDR picked him to run for vice president in 1944 because he was a safe, inoffensive choice.

When Roosevelt died in 1945 the country was stunned. Roosevelt had led the country since 1933. His charismatic figure *was* the presidency. People were bewildered and despairing at the notion of a nonentity like Harry Truman trying to replace this strong leader. In

1948 the experts predicted that Truman would be swamped by the Republican Thomas E. Dewey. In the most staggering upset of U.S. presidential politics, Truman won.

And now this man from Missouri was coming face to face with Douglas MacArthur, a figure to match the noblest of the noble Romans.

At Wake Island observers noticed that MacArthur did not salute Truman. He was abrupt and imperious. Truman told MacArthur that the troops should stay clear of the Chinese border. MacArthur waved the caution away; the Chinese would *not* come in, he said.

Truman returned to Washington, troubled. MacArthur continued to penetrate past the 38th parallel.

On November 25, 1950, Chinese troops smashed across the Korean border to attack the Americans. Korean-War veterans remember those waves of infantrymen, wearing padded blue jackets, urged on by incessant bugle-blowing. MacArthur had been wrong about the intentions of the Chinese. He also underestimated their ability to fight. The Americans, pulverized, reeled back in retreat.

MacArthur had an answer: "Bomb Manchuria! Carry the war into China!" At this time China and the USSR were allied. There was good reason to think that expanding the war to China would bring in the Soviet Union. Truman told MacArthur that the war would have to be won or lost on the Korean peninsula.

MacArthur, used to running things like a warlord, bitterly resented this. He began to make pronouncements that were contemptuous of the president and his policy. Truman knew this could not be allowed to go on. The traditional relationship between the civil and the military authority was at stake. He told MacArthur that all statements would have to be cleared with Washington.

But General MacArthur, without authorization, issued an ultimatum to Red China: Surrender or I will attack you. He had defied a direct order of his commander in chief; he was challenging the president directly. MacArthur thought the country would back him. Many Americans did back him; but public disapproval did not keep

Truman from doing what he thought was right for the United States. He removed MacArthur from command.

The general thought his prestige was so great that Truman might be forced to back down. MacArthur returned to the United States, to tremendous acclaim. But Truman stuck to his guns. MacArthur's military career was over. Some toyed with the notion of MacArthur as a presidential candidate, and MacArthur seemed amenable. But the balloon never got off the ground.

Today Harry Truman is regarded as one of the country's great presidents. MacArthur is remembered as a great leader of troops in wartime. But the consensus is that Truman was right.

Douglas MacArthur's hubris drove him to tempt the fates once too often.

The Mother Motif—MacArthur's life contains a theme that we come upon in stories of great hubris: the maternal motif. Dr. Barry Perlman, chief of psychiatry at St. Joseph's Medical Center, Yonkers, New York, suggests that people with towering intellectual arrogance may have this characteristic fostered by a specially close relationship with a domineering and protective mother. Franklin D. Roosevelt had such a relationship.

Douglas MacArthur, too, was very close to his mother. Here is an example. While at West Point MacArthur refused to reveal the names of some upperclassmen involved in a hazing incident. His budding military career was threatened. MacArthur writes[9]

My mother, who was at West Point at the time, sensed the struggle raging in my soul and sent me this message during a recess of the court:

> Do you know that your soul is of my soul such a part
> That you seem to be fiber and core of my heart?
> None other can pain me as you, son, can do;
> None other can please me or praise me as you.
> Remember the world will be quick with its blame
> If shadow or shame ever darken your name.

Like mother, like son, is saying so true
The world will judge largely of mother by you.
Be this then your task, if task it shall be
To force this proud world to do homage to me.
Be sure it will say, when its verdict you've won
She reaps as she sowed: "This man is her son!"

When Overconfidence Can Mean Death

Hubris can make you a risk junkie.

When intelligence agencies place spies in target countries, the spies must at all costs retain their cover identities. This often means that they have to appear to lead the humdrum lives of ordinary citizens. This takes brains as well as training. Good intelligence operatives are intelligent.

There are many dangers. Author Feinberg's good friend and former student, General Meir Amit, former head of Mossad, the renowned Israeli intelligence agency, says, "I can mention one important reason for mistakes made by smart and able people: *overconfidence.*"

Many agents, after they penetrate into their new environments and settle down, become overconfident; they are less careful, and as a matter of fact "they cut *the branch on which they are sitting.*" General Amit cites particularly two cases, in which Mossad agents in Damascus and Cairo settled in so well that they became careless and were caught: "They became victims of their own success."

Arrogance as a Career Minus

Hubris, leading to excessive arrogance, can drive an individual into an act of destructive folly.

The *perception* of arrogance—even if it has not yet given rise to a virulent case of SDIS—can be a career-breaker. Robert Hogan and

Why Smart People Do Dumb Things

Joyce Hogan of the Department of Psychology, University of Tulsa; and Gordon J. Curphy, Personnel Decisions, Inc., Minneapolis, tell us that "many managers who are bright, hard-working, ambitious, and technically competent fail (or are in danger of failing) because they are perceived as arrogant, vindictive, untrustworthy, selfish, emotional, compulsive, overcontrolling, insensitive, abrasive, aloof, too ambitious or unable to delegate or make decisions. . . ."[10]

So even if the hubrist avoids sudden disaster, he or she may be accumulating gradual disaster by acquiring a reputation for arrogance.

Keeping Pride in Proportion

You are justifiably proud of what you accomplish. But pride tends toward hubris; and hubris rockets you far beyond pride, to the outer reaches of dangerous fantasy.

Now we'll examine another, closely related, element of SDIS: *narcissism*.

Notes

1. Plutarch, *Lives of the Noble Greeks*, ed. by Edmund Fuller (New York: Dell, 1959), p. 201.
2. Michael Grant, *Myths of the Greeks and Romans* (New York: Mentor Books, 1962), pp. 59–60.
3. *The New Yorker*, May 2, 1994, "Dr. Edelman's Brain," by Steven Levy.
4. Proverbs 16:18.
5. Richard S. Lazarus, *Emotion and Adaptation* (New York: Oxford University Press, 1991), pp. 273–274.
6. The *New York Times*, February 7, 1994, "An End to a Law Firm That Defined a Type," by Jan Hoffman.
7. *New York* magazine, February 21, 1994, "The Firm," by Eric Pooley.
8. *New York Law Journal*, December 7, 1981, "A Homily on Cause & Effect of 'Hubris' in Foley Square," by Milton Gould.
9. Douglas MacArthur, *Duty, Honor, Country*, (New York: McGraw Hill, 1965), pp. 4–5.
10. *American Psychologist*, June 1994, "What We Know About Leadership," by Robert Hogan, Gordon J. Curphy, and Joyce Hogan.

Chapter 5.

NARCISSISM AND THE DISCONNECT EFFECT

Richard Nixon's career provides abundant material for students of SDIS. He demonstrated all the elements: hubris, arrogance, narcissism, and the unconscious need to fail.

Let's glance at one small incident. As the Watergate scandal began to engulf his regime, Nixon looked around for a new lawyer to defend him against the determined threat posed by special prosecutor Leon Jaworski. Alexander Haig, Nixon's chief of staff, and aide Charles Colson recommended a Boston trial lawyer, James D. St. Clair.

St. Clair, a graduate of Harvard Law School, enjoyed impeccable credentials. His courtroom skills were held in extremely high regard by a roster of prestigious clients. Nixon was pleased to get such a high-class attorney.

Bob Woodward and Carl Bernstein describe an evening in May 1974, shortly after St. Clair joined the team. Nixon took his new advocate for a cruise on the presidential yacht *Sequoia*.[1]. The limousine took them to the Navy Yard. They climbed to the *Sequoia*'s upper deck. The president told the stewards to bring drinks. The yacht steamed down the Potomac toward Mount Vernon, the home and burial place of George Washington. It was dusk. The president and his men sat in the mild spring breezes, sipping their drinks.

The *Sequoia* arrived at Mount Vernon. Here it was the custom to carry out a brief ceremony. Nixon and St. Clair stood near the bow, with a couple of Nixon's close aides a few steps behind. Woodward and Bernstein write, "The boat's bells tolled eight times at five-second intervals. Taps was played. A recording of the national anthem was broadcast.

"The President turned to St. Clair and said, 'They pay you nickels and dimes, but this is what makes it worth it.'"

Nixon's aides cringed. Crew members looked away in embarrassed silence.

Here is Richard Nixon, a man of great intelligence, president of the United States, leader of the free world, explaining his willingness to work for peanuts. Why? Part of it is the sense of entitlement that, as we will see, can become all-consuming. The sense of entitlement affects most politicians; the higher the office, the greater the effect. (Once an escort said to Lyndon Johnson, "Sir, this is your helicopter." Johnson responded, "Son, they are *all* my helicopters.")

There's another driving factor: *narcissism*.

The Narcissistic Intelligence

The psychiatrist Aaron Stern told a gathering of business executives in Berlin, "The single most malignant force in the human mind is narcissism."

Narcissists are deficient in connection with the world outside themselves. They interact with other people, of course, but their relationships are faux relationships, because they are one way. The world and the people in it exist only to provide gratification to the narcissist.

The original Narcissus is a self-centered youth who scorns the love of the nymph Echo. His cruelty and indifference to others finally draws the dread attention of the goddess Nemesis, who pronounces the words, "May he who loves not others love himself." We all know the payoff for poor Narcissus, who bends over a clear pool, falls in love with his own reflection, and remains there, pining away, until he dies. As Charon's ferry conveys Narcissus' shade across the river that encircles the underworld realm of the dead, the youth leans over the gunwale to catch a last glimpse of his reflection.[2]

Narcissism and the Disconnect Effect

Nowadays narcissists of both genders find far more active ways of self-destructing. (If they just sat around the pool they would do less harm to others.) Their inner-direction becomes hard-wired. Love turns to trinketry; their companions are ornaments. Every bit of praise they receive, no matter how fulsome or self-serving, is deserved. Perks, large and small, are no longer functions of title or status but are personal tributes. Every shred of recognition that goes to someone else is an injustice, often perpetrated by envious enemies.

The Narcissist on the Fast Track

Narcissists often get ahead with breathtaking swiftness—at least for a while. We find a good description of the career advantages of narcissism by the clinical psychologist Norman Tallent, written more than a quarter of a century ago:

> The narcissist in his competitiveness uses several typical approaches, both fair and foul. He may inflate his self-image through achievement that calls the attention of others to his prowess. He will "hit you over the head" with his qualities. Thus even the drive for genuine deeds is in the service of exhibitionism; what is done in private and is not available to draw the admiration of others is of little consequence.
>
> The exhibitionism of the narcissist is seen in as many areas as he can effectively manage. It may be conspicuous in speech, in dress, in carriage, and in gait. . . . The impression the narcissist seeks to give is of strength, competence, confidence, superiority. . . . The narcissist is extremely threatened at the prospect that he does not have these, or that he will not be able to exhibit them.[3]

"Strength, competence, confidence, superiority"—these characteristics of narcissism sound like the qualities a multitude of job interviewers are looking for. No wonder narcissists get ahead!

Why Smart People Do Dumb Things

The Climate of Narcissism

Success always conduces to narcissism. 'Twas ever thus. That's human nature. When we win we preen ourselves; we strut a little, even if we don't show it.

Luckily for us—at least until recently—life has offered most of us sufficient doses of antidotes. For one thing, the average person responds to setbacks as well as to triumphs. Our self-esteem is boosted by a win, but it is diminished by a loss. The give-and-take of life keeps us in a state of reasonable equilibrium.

Most societies maintain tacit limits on narcissism. Parents caution us not to get too big for our britches. Childhood companions bring us back to earth when we get too conceited. As grown-ups we used to be reminded constantly that we accomplish nothing entirely on our own, that we are not flying solo through life, that we exist in a network of other-connectedness.

> No man is an *Island*, entire of it self; every man is a piece of the *Continent*, a part of the *main*; if a *clod* be washed away by the *sea*, *Europe* is the less, as well as if a *promontory* were, as well as if a *manor* of thy friends or of *thine own* were; any man's *death* diminishes *me*, because I am involved in *Mankind*; And therefore never send to know for whom the *bell* tolls; It tolls for *thee*.
>
> John Donne

Donne's measured cadences still resound magnificently, but in an increasingly broader sector of today's society they are quaint; passé; something of a joke. At upper levels of achievement, we *live in a culture of narcissism.* Self-absorption, once deplored, is celebrated. The world gives us perks (which Stern calls "narcissistic variables") to feed our inwardness; to *hook us.*

Narcissism and the Disconnect Effect

One of the most fascinating effects of narcissism is that it makes its victims so self-absorbed that they lose touch with reality. We call it the *Disconnect Effect*.

Narcissistic Disconnection in Washington

There is no better place to study narcissism and the Disconnect Effect than Washington, D.C.

Visitors to the National Archives building in Washington who have listened to the Watergate tapes (which led to the resignation of President Nixon) may note the impersonality with which Nixon, Haldeman, Erlichmann disconnect themselves from the immediacy and reality of what is happening to them. They discuss themselves as if they were characters in a movie that was unfolding on a screen. President Nixon is frequently heard talking about "The President"—the President could say this, the President could take this position, what if the President were to issue a statement, this must not touch the President, et cetera.

It's Happening to Those Guys, Not to Me

Nixon and his key advisers are calm and analytical when they speak in the third person of themselves. You feel as you listen that you're a fly on the wall in a Hollywood studio where movie-makers are talking about a forthcoming production, "How We Saved the Presidency." Nixon offers line readings as if he were directing a play: "Here's what the President can say: *Since not one shred of credible evidence has been brought forward to support these allegations, we can only conclude that the entire episode is a politically motivated attack on this President and this Presidency. . . ."*

This goes beyond role-playing; it is detachment carried to an extreme degree. You might call it *creative denial*—an adroit use of brainpower to insulate the consciousness from unpleasant reality.

Ordinary mortals engage in denial. They try to shut out unwelcome truth. But they do not carry it out with such ingenuity. It takes superior minds to reach the fullest measure of the Disconnect Effect.

The true Disconnect Effect, which we see in Nixon's presidency and in other presidencies, does not help the individual to do the job better. It is a manifestation of SDIS—a self-destructive use of intelligence that impels us to step out of our own skins and look at ourselves and our lives as if we were looking at fictional events on a screen.

Here we must make a distinction. A certain amount of detachment from oneself is very useful. From time to time we all need to be able to step back and look at ourselves with some degree of objectivity. Industrial-strength narcissists lack this capacity.

The Disconnect Effect does not foster healthy self-examination. It's an escape mechanism. And it is a twisted form of narcissism.

> Many people today don't want honest answers insofar as honest means unpleasant or disturbing. They want a soft answer that turneth away anxiety.
>
> Louis Kronenberger, *The Cart and the Horse*, 1964

The feeling of omnipotence, spiced up by the narcissism that is almost essential to any successful political career, assails powerful people in certain ways. For one thing, it causes them to add the fateful three letters *ALL* before the word *powerful*. If you are a privileged presidential adviser or the chairman of a pivotal congressional committee or, indeed, the president, to consider yourself powerful is just realistic. However, to consider yourself *all*-powerful is suicidal.

The sense of invulnerability is as old as the legendary Achilles, who, when he was a baby, was dipped by his mother, Thetis, in the River Styx to make him impervious to injury. As we know, Thetis was careless or in a hurry; she held the infant by his foot, and did not immerse all of the tiny foot in the magic waters. In the Trojan War Achilles threw himself into harm's way, always in the forefront of the battle. And indeed for a long time it seemed that nothing could harm him. And then one fateful day Achilles drove the Trojans before him to the very walls of Troy, whence Paris shot an arrow at him. That was not bad in itself; plenty of arrows were shot at Achilles, without effect. But Achilles had done something else that SCIPIs do; he had offended a creature more powerful even than himself—namely, the god Apollo. Apollo guided the arrow, and it flew fatally to the one square inch of the warrior unprotected by the waters of the Styx: now called the Achilles' heel.

Government teems with the spiritual heirs of Achilles, who think they have been immersed in the Styx of invulnerability. It happens to the smartest of them. Take Michael K. Deaver. Deaver was a confidant of Ronald and Nancy Reagan, a key figure in the deliberations of the Reagan White House, a shrewd public relations operative who was widely credited with creating and maintaining the Reagan image by manipulating patriotic crowds and orchestrating flag-waving demonstrations.

Michael Deaver was like many image makers in coming to think that image was more important than substance. The last big act that he stage-managed was Ronald Reagan's notorious trip to Bitburg in 1985. Reagan was headed for an economic summit in Europe. Deaver saw the trip as yet another opportunity for him to work his wonders. He enjoyed his reputation; in his memoirs he writes, "The daily press and the weekly news magazines had hailed me as 'Magic Mike' and 'The Vicar of Visuals.' . . . If I qualified as an expert on anything, it was said to be the staging of a media event; blending the gifts of Ronald Reagan with the proper pageantry."[4]

Deaver discusses the president in the kinds of terms used by Hollywood directors in describing actors of limited talent: "He was not at ease with, nor eager to confront, scenes of unrelenting depression. He was at his best when he could touch the nostalgia, the longing of each of us for a more romantic time. You put him near a flag, around uniforms, or in sight of a parade, and he could lift anyone's spirit."[5]

Thus, when Deaver visited Germany in February 1985, as advance man for Reagan's trip, he seems to have thought of himself as far more than a public relations functionary preparing the way. He was the impresario of American power. His stage management of Reagan's trip would have a profound effect on the world.

Helmut Kohl, the chancellor of what was then West Germany, suggested to Deaver that, when Reagan came in May, the American president and the German leader might go together to the military cemetery at Bitburg to lay a wreath.

PR people get paid to pay attention to *image* and *context*. When their bosses decide on an action, the PR person's function is to look at the proposed action and ask some hard-boiled questions:

- **How will this look?**
- **On balance will it enhance our image?**
- **What can go wrong?**
- **Are there any boobytraps that might embarrass us?**
- **How will the story be handled on TV, radio, and in the press?**
- **What's the upside—the best thing that can happen?**
- **What's the downside—the worst that can happen?**

Kohl's idea sounded fine to Deaver. Deaver checked out the military cemetery. It was February, and most of the grave markers were covered by snow. However, Deaver could imagine how it would look in the spring. The trees beginning to bud, the shrubs beginning to bloom, two great leaders of the free world, their countries once locked in a great war, now side by side, bareheaded in tribute to bravery, pledging friendship and the continued quest for peace. A great spectacle, rivaling John F. Kennedy's spectacular visit to Berlin; and everyone who mattered would know that Michael K. Deaver stagemanaged the whole thing.

Planning for Reagan's trip proceeded. Then, in mid-April—three weeks before the visit—German newspapers carried the story that the Bitburg cemetery contained the graves not only of soldiers in the regular German army but also of forty-nine members of the Waffen SS, the notorious military and paramilitary arm of the Nazi party, Hitler's elite guard.

"Suddenly, the Bitburg visit was a battleground," Deaver writes. "In Europe, the United States, and the Soviet Union, the outcry was immediate and bitter. Wounds long unhealed but ignored surfaced again. Veterans marched and mailed back their medals. Jewish groups demonstrated and begged the president to back off. No newscast, no edition of any newspaper, was complete without an interview with a person who had lost someone, or everyone, in the Holocaust."

Reagan did not see why he should change his itinerary. He said, "Today, you have a German people who are our staunchest allies and friends, for thirty years an ally in NATO, forty years of peace."[6] At Reagan's right hand was Pat Buchanan, the White House communications director, a hard man but one who could find a warm spot in his heart for Nazi death-camp guards. Buchanan urged the president to do nothing to appease his opponents and to, in Deaver's words, issue what was "virtually an amnesty for the Third Reich."

Advice poured into the White House. Richard Nixon, that most reliable advocate of toughing everything out, warned Reagan not to retreat. Henry Kissinger declared that cancellation of the Bitburg visit would do enormous damage to American foreign policy. Helmut Kohl, who had his own political problems in Germany, implored Reagan not to back out.

And, perhaps worst of all for Michael K. Deaver, Nancy Reagan was convinced that the public relations master had ruined her husband's presidency, and maybe the rest of his life.

Reagan made the visit to Bitburg. He did not linger; eight minutes after it entered the cemetery the presidential motorcade was on its way back to the airport.

Michael Deaver Becomes His Own Best Customer

Not long after this, Deaver left the government. He stayed in Washington, though. Once people have enjoyed the power and perks of the capital, they become addicted to the place and all that it means.

Deaver set up a consulting firm in Washington, Michael K. Deaver and Associates. He enjoyed boasting to reporters of his "access" to Ronald Reagan. A PR man to the core, he went after the maximum amount of media exposure. When he started to make big money, he saw no reason not to let everybody know about it.

Deaver was certainly taking a different tack from most Washington "consultants," who prefer to keep a very low profile. Another factor that he blithely ignored was that there was now a law aimed at limiting the ability of high government officials to profit from their contacts immediately after leaving government service.

In February 1986 *Time* magazine ran on its cover a picture of Deaver in the backseat of a chauffeur-driven Lincoln Town Car, talking on a cellular phone. The cover copy read: "WHO'S THIS MAN CALLING? Influence Peddling in Washington." The fellow on the phone was identified as "Lobbyist Michael Deaver."

The storm broke. Deaver became a symbol of influence peddling and corruption. He says, "Actually, no one ever accused me of breaking a law. It was the *appearance* of wrongdoing that brought forth so much righteous indignation." Deaver, of all people, should have known that, in Washington, appearance can be much more important than reality.

Deaver was called to testify before a congressional committee. He was indicted for perjury. His friends and clients deserted him in droves. He was revealed as being an alcoholic. His business was ruined, and his life was pretty nearly ruined. He writes, "I kept wondering what had happened, where had the train left the rails? Had I really miscalculated this badly? Had I ridden the wind and, in seven months, blown a reputation for integrity that had been twenty years in the making? To borrow a famous Watergate phrase, had I lost my moral compass?"

Washington, D.C., is like the core of a nuclear reactor, pulsing with immense power, available to those who know how to manipulate the controls. Those who enjoy the vast power forget the dark side: the lethal radioactivity lying in wait to burn up unwary victims. Those who work around it for a long time come to take it for granted, just as anybody who remains involved with power comes to take it for granted. They develop the illusion of immunity from harm. They know exactly how to harness the power to damage others; they are shocked and helpless when the pitiless radiation is beamed at them.

Some of the most successful people we know do much the same thing. They trash their own accomplishments, the tributes that are paid to them, the rank to which they have been elevated. Typically, an advertising copywriter who has just won a Clio award shrugs it off, saying to her companions, "That bunch of jerks, what do they know."

Part of this is "downplaying"—the self-deprecating posture of people who are really very proud but who don't want to be thought conceited. We accept this kind of talk as symbolic rather than actual. The golfer who wins the Masters says, "I was lucky." We know he won because he played well; and we know he knows that. The actress accepts her Oscar with the words, "I owe it all to ——" (the blank is filled by the names of directors, producers, writers, agents, relatives, accountants, chauffeurs, cooks—you name it). We have seen her act; we know how talented she is. We don't believe for a moment that she really thinks her own skills had nothing to do with her triumph.

People who have reached elective office get to thinking that they achieved their positions entirely on merit; that they are doing their constituents a favor by serving; and that any political opposition to them is mean-spirited, unfair, unethical, and probably un-American.

This phenomenon—Officeholder's Afflatus—strikes politicians at all levels, local to the White House. They campaign as politicians. They rely on political managers to do what is necessary to get them elected. Most are ethical enough to avoid going to extremes of duplicity or mudslinging, but, in seeking the job, they give little thought to the merits. You don't hear many candidates on the stump saying, "My opponent has many pluses and minuses. So do I. In some ways he would be better at the job than I would. . . ."

No. You win elective office through political means, which often have little or nothing to do with performance in office. Presidential rivals vie to outflank each other on crime and education, areas in which the federal government has not all that much impact. Big Bill Thompson, mayor of Chicago in the 1930s, stirred voters with his repeated threats to punch King George of England in the nose. Candidates for first selectman in a small New England town attack each other over the issue of rap lyrics.

Anything goes during the campaign. But once the winners are in office, their outlook changes. "How can he/she run against me on the basis of rap lyrics? Rap music has nothing to do with municipal governance. Why can't I be judged on my solution of the storm drain problem out on Turkey Hill Road?"

The most intelligent and level-headed political officeholders suffer from the feeling. Far more than corporate executives, they develop the notion that they deserve the jobs, and that criticism is unfair and partisan. In a corporation, politicking plays a considerable part, but there is, by and large, more attention to actual ability in filling jobs than there is in the government. However, most private sector officeholders understand that someone else is always after their jobs; it's part of the game.

Board Games

Intellectually gifted and accomplished persons can be infinitely resourceful in persuading themselves that the rules of the game don't
apply to them. This may be why W. Ann Reynolds, chancellor of the
City University of New York, pursued her penchant for joining corporate boards in spite of the danger signals.

The position of chancellor carries immense prestige. It is also politically sensitive. Therefore, when the City University trustees learned
about Dr Reynolds's outside activities, they were a little upset. The
chancellor's job is a big one, involving supervision of the university's
twenty-one campuses. At the same time, Dr. Reynolds was serving on
the boards of five corporations and one nonprofit institution. Her
board memberships were reaping almost as much in compensation as
her main job. She seemed to be spending far more time on her board
work than she was entitled to.

Then it emerged that when Dr. Reynolds was chancellor of the
California State University system, the trustees there had ordered her
to resign from all but two outside boards. This fostered the impres-
sion that Dr. Reynolds liked playing board games more than she liked
doing her primary job.

With Me It Will Be Different

Watch two championship golfers—say, Davis Love III and Fred Couples—as each tries to score a birdie on a difficult hole. Both have
reached the green of a par-four hole in two. Love has an eighteen-foot
putt; Couples is four feet closer to the hole. The balls are close to
each other. Couples marks his ball; Love putts first. The putt breaks
slightly to the left just before reaching the hole, rims the cup, stays
out. Couples, who has watched carefully from behind Love, replaces
his ball and putts, allowing just a little more for the break to the left

that defeated Love's effort. Couples's putt goes in. He "went to school on" the other golfer's shot. Good players do it all the time.

You would think politicians—especially smart politicians—would do the same thing. After all, politicians have matchless opportunities to "go to school on" one another. They have seen, close up, how their predecessors handled situations just like the ones they are now called upon to handle. Very often, if the predecessor comes from the opposing party, the present incumbent has exploited the predecessor's mistakes for political gain.

Today just about everything a politician does is fair game for the media. Freedom of information legislation and sunshine laws have practically abolished secrecy. So aspiring officeholders have a great advantage on their counterparts in industry. When you're angling for a job with a corporation, you may know the person holding the job now is having trouble, but short of being a fly on the conference room wall you can't learn for sure what's going on. You need to do some guesswork. Politicians can usually learn much more about the mistakes of other politicians.

And they do. Over and over again you'll hear candidates chortling at the difficulties into which office-holding rivals get themselves. "One thing you can be sure of," they say, "you will never see me making a dumb mistake like that."

Hillary Rodham Clinton and Bill Clinton are among the smartest people ever to go to Washington. Their road to the White House was not an easy one. The opposition hit them with everything they had. The Clinton candidacy often seemed belly up. And yet Clinton won.

It was a new kind of presidency. One of its most interesting—and most important—features was the ascendancy of Hillary Rodham Clinton to power. During the campaign the Republicans had tried to win votes by belittling Mrs. Clinton as a dupe of her skirt-chasing husband. They had tried to depict her as a career-mad super-feminist who scorned all the good women who stayed home and baked cookies. They had derided her for speaking out too much and for keeping quiet and gazing soulfully at Bill Clinton while he spoke.

None of it worked very well. Then, in office, Bill Clinton made his wife a real player in national politics. This was the first time a first lady had been given such official responsibility. There continued to be grumbling that "Hillary" (opponents invariably use her first name, managing to hiss it, even though it is hard to hiss a word with no *s*'s in it) was not elected to anything. No matter. Her articulateness, her cool self-possession, her command of her subject (the vital health care issue), and her intellectual brilliance blew the minds of friends and foes alike.

Hillary Rodham Clinton, of all people, should have been a person who would not fall into the trap of making the same mistakes that brought down a predecessor. At least as intelligent as Bill Clinton, she enjoyed the further advantage of having been outside partisan politics while he had been embroiled in political strife. Her long suit was cool analysis of complicated situations, and the ability to focus on what is really important.

Hillary Rodham Clinton's first experience in Washington involved the Watergate imbroglio that destroyed the Nixon presidency. She worked for the select congressional committee that held the televised hearings before which the country sat riveted, watching a parade of high officials and low-down rogues trying to deny the truth.

The genesis of the brouhaha was a break-in at Democratic national headquarters in Washington's Watergate office building. The intruders had planted bugs in the Democratic headquarters. They had connections to CRP—pronounced "creep"—the Committee to Re-elect the President. The committee, leaving no stone unturned in its efforts to give Richard Nixon another four-year mandate in 1972, had been somewhat overzealous, particularly in view of the fact that Nixon's first term was viewed as successful and that there did not seem any way he could lose the election.

All this was bad enough. But not necessarily fatal, or even particularly damaging, to Nixon's presidency. After all, as someone once said, "Politics ain't beanbag." The populace of the United States knows that politicians play rough. Yes, the bugging of the other party's headquarters was a step over the line, but the episode would probably have blown over in due course without costing the Republicans enough votes to threaten their victory.

It was not the crime itself (derided by Republican stalwarts as a "third-rate burglary") but rather the cover-up that destroyed Nixon's presidency. Day after day the American public saw a procession of officials—higher and higher in rank—twisting in discomfort as they tried to deny that persons in the White House had tried to quash the investigation. And not just persons close to the president; it began to appear that even the president himself might know something about it.

It was the *cover-up*, not the break-in, that did in Richard Nixon. Everybody acknowledges this. It would certainly have been obvious to a young lawyer like Hillary Rodham Clinton, working for the Watergate committee at the time.

It's 1994. Bill Clinton is in the White House. The country begins to hear about something called Whitewater. Even the name is reminiscent of Watergate. Republicans, understandably, seize upon the potential scandal as a way of damaging Clinton.

Well, what *is* Whitewater? It has to do with events that took place sixteen years earlier, in Arkansas, when Clinton was governor. Through the Whitewater Development Company, the Clintons, with two partners, bought 230 acres of land in northern Arkansas. The partners were James B. McDougal and his wife, Susan. Years later the Clintons were to sell their remaining stake in Whitewater, claiming that they suffered a loss of more than $68,000.

Four years after the Whitewater investment, McDougal, the Clintons' partner, bought Madison Guaranty Savings and Loan. Madison failed, costing investors and, ultimately, taxpayers a lot of money. The Resolution Trust Corporation began looking into the failure of Madison, as it looks into the failure of other S&L's.

The Clintons did not borrow money from Madison; they were not investors or officers of the S&L. Hillary Rodham Clinton did serve as Madison's attorney for a while. This would not be altogether astonishing, since the Rose law firm, in which she was a partner, was one of the biggest in the state.

Narcissism and the Disconnect Effect

Déjà Vu All Over Again

When it first began to surface, and for a considerable time afterward, the affair made scarcely a dent on the public consciousness. Watergate involved a sitting president trying to cover up wrongdoing that took place while he was president. Whitewater and the failure of Madison Guaranty had happened years before, in Arkansas.

Without denigrating the state of Arkansas, it is fair to say that most people do not confuse politics there with Athens during the Golden Age of Pericles (and the Golden Age of Pericles was by no means free of influence peddling and scandal).

During the 1992 campaign for the presidency, the Clintons had withstood volleys of accusations involving all kinds of matters. The voters of the country knew that, in electing Bill Clinton, they were not convening as the College of Cardinals to beatify a saint.

What was the worst that could come out about Whitewater and Madison? Had the Clintons been given a sweetheart deal? Had they exaggerated their loss for tax purposes? Had the Rose law firm enjoyed a special advantage because one of its partners was the wife of the governor? Had a partner of the Clintons in the land development deal made political contributions, and had he benefited from his association with the Clintons?

Assume the answers to all of the above are yes. Then ask, "So what?" During the campaign Clinton had been hit with Sleazegate and Bimbogate, and had maintained his course to victory. Yes, if it came out that the Clintons had cut corners and pulled some fast ones back in Little Rock, it would be embarrassing. But it was unlikely that many voters would allow these things to outweigh their feelings about health care, crime, welfare reform, and so forth.

During the 1992 presidential campaign, the formidable political manager James Carville had a famous sign hung in Clinton headquarters in Little Rock: "It's the ECONOMY, Stupid!"

The crystal-clear meaning was that those working on the campaign should never be distracted down side paths involving foreign policy, term limits, abortion, prayer in the schools, and so on. They had to make a clear distinction between what was important and what was a sideshow.

As the Whitewater situation continued to play out, the White House could have used a similar sign: "It's the COVER-UP, Stupid!"

But the sign should not even have been necessary. Hillary Rodham Clinton, who had a close-up look at the self-destructive dumbness of the Nixon crew during Watergate, should certainly not have needed it. Nor should Bernard Nussbaum have needed it. Then it was the cover-up, not the matter being covered up, that brought down the house.

The same would be true of Whitewater. By covering up, the Clinton team took an affair that was old stuff and too complicated to bother about and made it immediate and easily grasped.

Success Breeds Success— But Not in a Different Context

Bernard W. Nussbaum was unable to cope with the job of White House counsel. Certainly he was smart enough. And he was accomplished enough—a SCIPI par excellence. He was an immensely successful lawyer, commanding large fees from big corporate clients during the takeover frenzy of the 1980s.

When Nussbaum joined the Clinton administration he "deployed his style as a New York corporate litigator with a vigorous take-no-prisoners defense of Mr. Clinton and his wife, Hillary. In the end, such behavior vastly increased suspicions about what the Clintons had done. . . . Mr. Nussbaum always seemed baffled that his style, which was so successful in the world of New York corporate litigation, often reaped scorn in Washington" (The *New York Times*, March 6, 1994, "Nussbaum's New York Tactics Falter in Washington," by Neil A. Lewis).

Tennis players have a saying, "Never change a winning game." But when you move from the tennis court to, say, the basketball court, you had better be ready to change, no matter how successful you have been, because you are now in a different game.

It's the *cover-up*, stupid! A stupid cover-up carried on by smart people.

Deadly Detachment

Hillary Rodham Clinton *detached* herself from experience and logic. Her firsthand experience showed her the lethal effects of the Watergate cover-up. Logic would dictate that the appearance of a cover-up of Whitewater would be equally damaging. A dumber person would have put the two together without questioning it, saying, "Bad as it might be to get the facts out now, the alternative is worse. So we'd better bite the bullet and do it."

Michael Deaver detached himself from experience and logic in the Bitburg affair and in opening his lobbying firm. Someone with less brilliance would have said, "This is a German military cemetery. Are there real Nazis buried here?" And, after leaving the government, that same person might have said, "Sure I have dynamite contacts in the White House, and that's why clients would pay me a lot of money. That's also why they passed the law about influence peddling. Since I would be a high-profile target, I guess I'll have to pass up the loot for now."

Richard Nixon detached himself from his own existence as president. He viewed "the president" as a puppet, with him and his associates pulling the strings. He spoke of the position of leader of the free world, the position for which he had schemed and fought, in terms that might be used by a hamburger flipper at McDonald's: "They pay you nickels and dimes. . . ."

People of low intelligence do illogical things because their logic systems are deficient. Deaver, Nixon, Hillary Clinton, John Sculley, Margaret Thatcher, et al.—these are smart people. So we have to seek another reason for their abandonment of logic. They possess logic; but sometimes they act illogically: *logic override*.

The Disconnect Effect is a prime cause of logic override. This is the kind of megadetachment that enables the mind to disconnect it-self from experience, perception, and common sense. The Discon-nect Effect does not happen casually. It requires real effort—albeit unconscious—by a strong and agile mind.

Politicians disconnect in spectacular ways. Margaret Thatcher dis-connected from her roots in the tough-minded but traditional Brit-ish middle class. Mrs. Thatcher was really hurt—though the damage did not appear on the surface—when she took to referring to her-self as "we." In Britain the imperial we is still the privilege of the monarch. Queen Victoria said, "We are not amused." The British public were not amused at the prime minister's usurpation of the royal pronoun.

Mrs. Thatcher's Conservative party soon demonstrated, as a group, an impressive and self-destructive affinity for the Disconnect Effect. The new prime minister, John Major, was of course at a disadvantage. He had a tough act to follow. Moreover, Great Britain was wallowing in economic woes that translated into political problems for the party in power. Unemployment remained high. Taxes were raised. Public morale and confidence waned. Hostility among ethnic groups and classes heated up. These ills were by no means confined to the United Kingdom. Germany, France, and Italy were undergoing their own tor-ments. In certain ways things were not as bad in Great Britain as in the rest of Europe. Across the globe, Japan was not in great shape ei-ther. And the United States, while on the whole better off, had its own troubles.

But voters in Britain—like voters everywhere—refuse to take the philosophical view. They don't care what's happening in other coun-tries; they want a better deal in their own country. The Tories were not delivering, so voters blamed John Major and his cabinet. Opinion polls showed the Labor party leading the Conservatives by around 47 percent to 28 percent.

So the Tories needed a new theme, something to capture the imag-ination of the masses. And, like a lot of parties in various corners of the world, the Tories were drawn to the magnetic concept of Morality. Not morality as a way of life, morality as a campaign idea.

The leading lights of the British Conservative party devised what they called the "Back to Basics" agenda, based on law and order and on public morality.

As we have noted, voters, by and large, do not expect elected officials to be saints. That has been true in Britain for a long time. The great Benjamin Disraeli's financial and sexual adventures were accepted by no less straitlaced a figure than Queen Victoria, who adored him.

Disraeli never set himself up as a model of rectitude. That is what makes all the difference. It is when politicians—and leaders in other areas—claim higher morality than other people that the public is ready to turn like a wolf pack on these leaders when they slip.

For a whole party to mount a morality program was a triumph of detachment from reality. The Conservative party, from the outset of Back to Basics, was beset by frequent (and gleeful) media revelations about the private lives of prominent party members.

A look at recent—indeed, current—events should have made the Tory leadership at least think twice. A look, for example, at the misadventures of Norman Lamont, who had been chancellor of the Exchequer under Thatcher and then under Major, and had been regarded by many as a potential prime minister. Lamont's transgression was not paying his credit card bills. Late in 1992 the chancellor of the Exchequer was revealed (in the *Sun*, one of Britain's more lurid tabloids) as buying liquor and cigarettes with credit cards, and exceeding the limit on his Access credit card by £470. Moreover the politician in charge of the country's treasury had, according to *The New Yorker*, "breached his limit twenty-two times in the previous eight years, and had received no fewer than five written warnings after failing to make the required monthly payments."[7]

Norman Lamont seems to have achieved a total disconnect, never having dreamed that sloppiness about his personal finances would be of interest to the public at large and would be seen as a reflection on his ability to run the country's finances. Poor Lamont. The storm broke. They dredged up all kinds of things about him, nor did they stop with him; their scrutiny extended to his tenants. The job of chancellor of the Exchequer gives the incumbent the use of two houses: 11 Downing Street and a forty-five-room mansion in Buckinghamshire. So Lamont was able to rent out his own place in the Notting Hill area of London. It turned out that the tenant in his basement, who, reported Julian Barnes in *The New Yorker*, "had described herself in her rental agreement as a 'therapist dealing with stress and nutritional management,' was, in the language of the *News of the World*, a 'busty hooker,' and that her therapy involved punishment and payment (ninety pounds per hour) of an all too predictable nature. . . ." Lamont had never met this professional; she was just his tenant. Nevertheless the burden of his tenant (named Sara Dale) was added to the lists of wines and spirits he had bought with overdrawn credit cards.

The pillorying of Norman Lamont should have been a warning for any government thinking about staking its future on a posture of superior rectitude. Another warning bell might have been heard in the downfall of David Mellor, Major's secretary of state for National Heritage, who made a phone call to his actress girlfriend in which, says the *New Yorker* article, "he maintained that their previous sexual encounter had been so exquisite and so prolonged that he did not have the energy to write his next ministerial speech." Now, Mr. Mellor was probably using a little poetic license. He was probably perfectly capable of writing a speech up to his usual standard, but he was indulging in a gallant tribute to the lady.

Such lovers' talk no doubt takes place all the time. It was Mellor's misfortune that the phone he was talking into was bugged. Maybe the phone tap was illegal, but that didn't help Mellor when the content of his tribute was aired. He had to go.

Despite the lessons of experience, the Conservative party proceeded with its Back to Basics slogan. The presentation of the Tories as superior in morality and reverence for law started to unravel quickly. In December 1993 Tim Yeo, a junior environmental minister, had fathered a child in an extramarital affair. He fought to keep his job, but he was forced to resign. Then another Tory MP disclosed that he had "shared a bed with a man in a French hotel, though he insisted that they were merely friends and that no sexual act took place."[8]

Just a few days later, the wife of another Tory minister, the Earl of Caithness, killed herself because she was distraught about her husband's relationship with another woman.

Early in February 1994 yet another Tory member of Parliament, Stephen Milligan—widely regarded as one of the most talented young members of the party—was found dead with a length of electric cord wound around his neck and a plastic bag over his head. Milligan's body was clad only in a pair of woman's stockings.

The Perils of Superdisconnection

A thread runs through these stories—the thread of *disconnection from context.*

O.J. Simpson Disconnects

In June, 1994, when O.J. Simpson set off on his bizarre freeway ride before surrendering, he left a letter, which a friend read at a news conference. The letter wound up with a classic expression of disconnection: "Don't feel sorry for me. I've had a great life, great friends. Please think of the real O.J. and not this lost person."

(Quoted from text of letter in The *New York Times*, June 18, 1994.)

Here are all these intelligent people who have used their intelligence to achieve high position—the ultimate SCIPIs—compromising their reputations, losing their jobs, and making themselves into the butt of jokes. They have done these things to themselves by acting as if they were totally unaware of the realities of existence around them—the *context* within which they live, work, and are perceived by others.

Nothing happens without context. There is an old French saying that, translated, goes, "There was a tree of Provence that said, I will be tree and naught else. Not sunlight, not rain, not earth—shield me from the air!"

The people in these episodes, acting alone or in concert, are not so ignorant or insensitive that context does not register on them. Nor are they sick. Psychosis disconnects its victims from context. They fantasize states of inner reality, within which they dwell. The comic crazy man wearing a cocked hat and proclaiming himself Napoleon really *is* Napoleon in the only world that is real to him. That world is furnished with the same details as our real world. He speaks and acts in a perfectly proper manner, a manner befitting his context. Of course he is so at variance with what we know to be real that we laugh or grimace in pity, but we certainly say, "He's nuts!"

Our Disconnect Effect falls far short of pathology. Nevertheless, it has similarities. The mind reconstructs context. It obliterates unwelcome implications, like the implication that certain behavior will lead to criticism, or embarrassment, or failure, or, in some cases, jail.

Intelligent people outthink those who are less intelligent for a number of reasons. One reason is their superior ability to apprehend and interpret context. The SDIS virus redirects that cognitive superiority to the task of renovating reality. It's a hard job; lesser minds cannot accomplish it. It takes a really vigorous intelligence to create a context within which black is white.

Once created, though, that context has a rock-solid texture. We trust it implicitly. It's wrong; it's delusional; but by turning our capable minds to it we make it right. And in the process we venture to the edge of the precipice. By cutting ourselves off from contextual reality we dramatically heighten the chances of catastrophic error.

"Keep in Touch"

Politicians especially need to "keep in touch." They acknowledge this; they are always talking about going back home and getting in touch with their constituents. Politicians become adept in *looking like* they are talking with, and listening to, ordinary people. They speak in "I'm just folks" tones; they wear "I'm just folks" clothes; they are coached in how to walk and gesture in ways that say, "I'm just like you, folks."

Actually, of course, they are isolated by privilege and power, and they become more isolated the longer they hold power. In a newspaper story on goofs made by politicians,[9] Frank Mankiewicz, a veteran public relations counselor to Democratic politicians, observes, "Isolation and hubris account for most of it. You get someone who's been in the Senate for twenty-four years, probably never paid for a haircut, never made a dinner reservation or parked a car. So they're likely to make dumb mistakes."

You Don't Have to Be a Politician to Disconnect

We've examined the Disconnect Effect through the lens of politics. But the men and women we vote into office have no monopoly on isolation from reality. In practically every line of endeavor, the higher you go, the more you are in danger of disconnecting to a really dangerous degree. The splendid isolation of bossdom puts you in an ivory tower. Insulated from the concerns that beset lesser mortals, your natural immunity to Self-Destructive Intelligence Syndrome seeps away.

People at the top say they hate their isolation. The CEO declares, "My door is always open." Nobody ever crosses his threshold with any problems. The CEO is experienced and sophisticated—and smart—enough to know there really are problems out there. But he/she doesn't go out into the corridors, rounding up people and demanding, "Tell me what's wrong!"

We know about the addictive aspects of being at the top—the privileges and perks, the big money. but there is less recognition of another habit-forming element of high office—the seductive charms of always having people tell you what they think you want to hear. Brendan Sexton, vice president of the Rockefeller Group and, for many years, a top-ranking aide of Mayor Edward Koch of New York, says, "You get hooked on good news."

Corporate executives get hooked on good news, as do scientists, publishers, physicians, performers. It keeps them in a state of bliss. At the same time it destabilizes their inner compasses, and heightens their vulnerability to the big dumb mistake.

Keeping in touch is acutely necessary to stability and success today. When we disconnect we lose touch with key elements of reality. Intellectual isolation goes hand in hand with high intelligence. Unfortunately, that handclasp is sometimes used to drag the intelligence to its destruction.

Narcissism and Corporate Failure

Harry Levinson, leading psychologist and student of organizational behavior, finds narcissism at the root of the difficulties besetting some of the world's leading companies. All organizations, says Levinson, "recapitulate the family structure and the behavioral practices of the culture in which they are embedded."[10] He studies the current problems of a number of large corporations and pinpoints certain causes for their inability to adapt to changing world conditions. Among them are these:

1. **General Motors and IBM and most of the other prominent troubled companies have been significantly "family organizations."**
2. **All promoted exclusively or disproportionately from within.**
3. **All became significantly narcissistic.**

Levinson observes that many large companies, though they now hire and promote female executives, retain a significantly male orientation and patriarchal culture. He says, "The combination of collective, masculine, competitive striving, attachment to aggressive self-images and established corporate structures, and efforts to avoid failure and indictment reinforce organizational narcissism."

Levinson comments further that narcissism, while essential for self-confidence, becomes potentially self-destructive when it "becomes inflated or less subject to social controls...." Narcissistic inflation "becomes overconfidence and a sense of entitlement. That, in turn, leads to denial of those realities that threaten the inflated self-image and to contempt for other individuals and organizations. It also leads to less tolerance for deviations from the already successful model."

Narcissism is useful in limited doses. Overindulged, it is intoxicating and ultimately fatal.

Notes

1. Bob Woodward and Carl Bernstein, *The Final Days* (New York: Simon & Schuster, 1976), pp. 180–181.
2. Edith Hamilton, *Mythology* (Boston: Little, Brown, 1940), pp. 87–88.
3. Norman Tallent, *Psychological Perspectives on the Person* (Princeton, N.J.: D. Van Nostrand, 1967), pp. 197–198.

4. Michael K. Deaver, with Mickey Herskowitz, *Behind the Scenes* (New York: William Morrow, 1987), pp. 179–188; 215–223.
5. Deaver, op. cit., p. 180.
6. Deaver, op. cit., p. 182.
7. *The New Yorker*, December 28, 1992/January 4, 1993, "Over the Limit," by Julian Barnes.
8. *Wall Street Journal*, February 9, 1994, "As Scandals Mount, 'Morality' Program Backfires for Tories," by Nicholas Bray.
9. *New York Times*, April 4, 1994, "In Political Bloopers, Practice Is Everything," by Richard L. Berke.
10. *American Psychologist*, May 1994, "Why the Behemoths Fell," by Harry Levinson.

Chapter 6.

INMANIA: THE DANGER OF INSULATION FROM CRITICISM

The world is full of sharp edges and rough corners. We bump and scrape as we make our way through it; and it hurts.

Some "lucky" people seem immune. Nobody criticizes them. Nobody questions them. Great, huh? Well, actually, not so great. Ask Bobby Ray Inman.

It is unlikely that any Washington figure has ever been called "brilliant" so frequently as Bobby Ray Inman. Throughout Admiral Inman's naval service and his stints in the National Security and Central Intelligence agencies, he floated past pitfalls that had consumed lesser mortals, bathed in a spotlight of admiration for his superlative mental capacity.

Not only did Bobby Ray Inman possess a great brain, he knew how to use it to achieve practical results and, at the same time, to burnish his reputation and speed his career. Washington runs on inside information, authentic and spurious. Officials, lobbyists, and journalists seize upon any shred of knowledge that seems to float across the lunch table, over the transom of the conference room, along the bar at the cocktail party, even in the intimacy of the boudoir. Bobby Ray Inman—particularly when he became the deputy director of the Central Intelligence Agency in President Reagan's administration—held the keys to the Fort Knox of inside information. He could tell you things that could build your bank account and boost your career.

Inman, by all accounts, used his position with transcendental shrewdness. He "became the intelligence community's liaison with both Congress and the Washington media."[1] What an opportunity!

Unfortunately, experience tells us that it is the kind of opportunity that contains a multitude of hidden dangers, that winds up destroying the "lucky" individual who received it.

Bobby Ray Inman played it superbly. He built bridges to people at all points along the spectrum from liberal to conservative. At the same time he imparted information he collected information. One of his strengths lay in his trustworthiness. John F. Lehman, Jr., secretary of the Navy under Reagan, said (as quoted in the *Wall Street Journal*), "He was totally honest, so people confided in him. It enabled him to put together fuller pictures than anybody else, whether it was Washington intrigues or Kremlin intrigues. When I was in government I talked to him a lot, mainly to get advice."

Bobby Ray Inman did not confine his inquiring mind and useful advice to matters of defense and intelligence. And here, perhaps, he was venturing a little way into dangerous waters. Lehman says, "He was constantly buzzing around like a honeybee piecing together pieces of what was going on. The reason Inman had so much staying power with so many different people is that people over time found he generally came up with the right answers and he was not loath to share it."

Washington is a sieve of information. Part of Inman's job was to plug leaks, or at least narrow them. So he got very close to many of the capital's top reporters, like Bob Woodward of the *Washington Post*. When you are trying to persuade a reporter to refrain from publishing leaked information, you must bring something to the table in return. Inevitably, Bobby Ray Inman was dispensing secrets from his golden treasury in order to accomplish what he needed to accomplish. And, inevitably, there would be those who, though they might not go public in criticizing the widely admired admiral, would suspect that Inman was also cultivating journalists to achieve his own ends.

> It is folly to censure him whom all the world adores.
> Publilius Syrus, *Moral Sayings*

One of those who held back from membership in the Bobby Ray Inman fan club was William Safire, a one-time public relations man who had become a speechwriter for Richard Nixon, a supporter of generally conservative causes, a noted semanticist, and, finally, a columnist for the powerful *New York Times*.

Safire was very close to William Casey, the director of the CIA and Inman's boss. Bill Casey came, increasingly, to be regarded as something of a rogue operator who played fast and loose with Congress and who could not be trusted in his sensitive position. Safire, probably reflecting Casey's feelings, concluded that Bobby Ray Inman had used calculated leaks to the press to undermine Bill Casey.

When Inman left government and went home to Texas to go into the private sector, his reputation was still extraordinarily high. Those who expected his brilliance to be as effective in business as it was in government (and this probably includes Inman himself) would be disappointed; his ventures did not fare very well.

But Washington still remembered the brilliance. And so, when President Bill Clinton needed a secretary of Defense, his choice of Bobby Ray Inman was greeted with hosannas. From both sides of the aisle came the assurances that Inman would be approved by acclamation. And indeed, at the press conference in which the president announced the appointment, the nominee projected the air of a crown prince on his way to a coronation. He stated, though he could easily have avoided it, that he had not voted for Clinton—at which the president winced slightly but continued to grin gamely. Inman, whose image had not previously been marked by perceptions of arrogance, talked about his need to be "comfortable" with President Clinton and his administration, making it sound like the ultimate accolade for the president that Inman had at last consented to be a member of the cabinet. This performance raised a few eyebrows, but there was no doubt of Bobby Ray Inman's brilliance, nor of the ease with which he would be confirmed.

Then William Safire wrote a column denouncing Inman as, among other things, duplicitous—a characterization that the Chicago columnist Mike Royko said sounded like a job description for membership in the administration of Richard Nixon, for whom Safire continued to express abundant admiration.

Well, so what? The media, and especially the newspaper/TV opinion mongers, have become increasingly self-confident, vocal, and ferocious. The wonder was not that a journalist attacked Inman; the wonder was that there were not many other attackers. The feeding frenzy is now normal behavior in the Washington pool. Surely a man as smart and experienced as Bobby Ray Inman would laugh this off.

> Censure is the tax a man pays to the public for being eminent.
> Jonathan Swift, *Thoughts on Various Subjects*

Laugh it off? Just the opposite! In a stunning development, Admiral Inman went on television for a rambling news conference in which he excoriated the media, especially Safire; accused Safire of making an unholy deal with Senator Bob Dole to destroy both Inman and Clinton; described himself as the victim of McCarthyism, which would produce even more dirt to be thrown at him; and referring vaguely but knowingly to Safire's "involvement"in a plagiarism suit many years ago. As a result of all this, Inman withdrew his name from nomination.

Supporters were dumbfounded and embarrassed—at the withdrawal itself, and even more so at the weird way in which this cool, brilliant operator had made it. William Safire was able to point out that the "plagiarism" implication did not concern anything Safire himself had written, but rather a case in which Safire's old public relations firm was involved.

Bobby Ray Inman went on the *Nightline* show, where Ted Koppel commented that it was somewhat odd that a man who called himself a martyr to McCarthyism would use such a patented McCarthyite tactic: smearing a critic with insubstantial and inaccurate allegations. In the face of this, Bobby Ray Inman—the icy paragon of applied intelligence—practically collapsed into a virtual admission that, yes, it was a little weird.

Once again Admiral Inman went back to Texas—but this time with his reputation in tatters, with pundits speculating on his sanity, with comedians targeting him as a figure of fun to rival the politically defunct Ross Perot.

Bobby Ray Inman's intelligence had been his weapon, but it had also been his armor. He had flourished within the polished, brilliant protection of his mind; but, free of the bumps and bruises that most ordinary mortals encounter, he seems never to have built up any inner toughness. The first touch of criticism seemed to totally short-circuit his logic function.

How to Avoid Inmania

Bobby Ray Inman was cosmically thin-skinned. Very few people would act as he acted in his situation. But the example underscores one factor that causes smart people to do self-destructive things.

The brain is an extremely sensitive physical organ, and the psyche is equally sensitive. Megaminds build up complex defense mechanisms to avoid hurt. One such mechanism is *selective listening*.

Selective listeners hear only what they want to hear. And what they want to hear is praise. People of all calibers of mental attainment prefer boosts to knocks, or course, and we would all like to hear only pleasant things. Most of us cannot avoid hearing the negatives.

So we hear the bad things, absorb them into our consciousness, and then try to deal with the discomfort, often by forgetting the negatives as quickly as possible. Another way of coping is to twist the negatives into positives. That is one of the big problems in performance reviews. The reviewer tends to take the sharp edge off criticism, perhaps through the "sandwich technique," which cushions negative commentary between slabs of positivism. The person being reviewed hears the criticism, but chooses to place equal or greater value on the positive comments.

There are other ways in which the mind eases the sting of unpleasant input. The point, however, is that the unpleasant input *is* received.

Certain brilliant minds use their brilliance to create *screening mechanisms* that fend off criticism altogether, so that the subject truly does not hear it. It's an invisible shield, much like that which protects the Starship Enterprise from the killer blasts of the Klingons. Nothing that is not benign gets through.

> The greatest of faults, I should say, is to be conscious of none.
> Thomas Carlyle, *On Heroes, Hero-worship, and the Heroic in History*

It takes a certain kind of complex and supple intelligence to build and maintain such a screen. For one thing, the individual must be motivated by a high level of narcissism, so high that no negatives at all can be tolerated. Then, the mental equipment must be sophisticated and powerful enough to intercept bad messages before they penetrate the sphere of consciousness.

We do not believe that nobody ever criticized Bobby Ray Inman before Safire got on his case. Inman's charmed life is part of the myth. Washington loves instant myths. It became the journalistic fashion to heap praise upon the admiral, and thus it was easy to infer from the fact that Inman got a lot of praise the assumption that he never got any criticism. From this point, it is an easy step for the media to ignore any criticism they may hear, because it conflicts with the convenient myth.

And Bobby Ray Inman gave the no-criticism assumption life because he *really did not hear any negatives*. Most of us are able to bear with a few blemishes on our self-image (because we cannot avoid it), but Inman's self-image had to remain spotless. Luckily (or, as it turned out, unluckily) for him, he possessed the extraordinary qualities of mind that enabled him to screen out all the bad stuff.

Everybody has critics. We don't have to go very far to hear them; often we need only tune in to our spouses, companions, family, and friends. Indeed, sometimes it seems that negativism is the main commodity provided by one's nearest and dearest. Let's face it; it is very human to point out the faults of others, even those we like. When the penchant for criticism collides with the ego, especially the well-developed ego, it can be like the meeting of matter and anti-matter.

> Next to the joy of the egotist is the joy of the detractor.
> Agnes Repplier, "Writing an Autobiography," *Under Dispute*

So we all work out ways to shield ourselves from the full, blistering beams of criticism, just as we use sun screen at the beach. But at the beach we are letting *some* of the rays through. We are *being selective*.

The Inmanian Mix

Bobby Ray Inman does not appear excessively hubristic, at least not by Washington standards. He was brilliant, capable, and conscientious. But he was not immune to the narcissism that creeps through the psyche of any successful person. You can hardly blame him. When so many people keep telling you what a genius you are, who are you to deny it?

There is one more factor of the SDIS virus here. Given the circumstances under which this melancholy farce played out, we might well think that, at some level of his being, Bobby Ray Inman did not really want this job, did not really think he could do this job. Result—an unconscious ordering of events to bring about failure.

Notes

1. *Wall Street Journal*, January 21, 1994, "Herd Instinct: How Inman Could Go from Star to 'Bizarre' in Such a Short Time," by Thomas E. Ricks and Michael K. Frisby.

Chapter 7.

THE UNCONSCIOUS
NEED TO FAIL

As we watch all these smart people charge, lemminglike, over the cliff, we ask, "What's the matter with these guys? Do they *want* to screw themselves up?"

You've got it. That's exactly what they want—or, at least, that's what the inner gremlin of the SDIS virus wants them to do. The need to fail is the dark underside of the hubris of intellect and achievement.

Business, the arts, sports—every walk of life abounds with examples of senseless self-destruction that seems to have only one purpose, to avoid success. At the very moment that you stand on the brink of a great success, your rebellious intelligence can be working to make sure you fail.

Ask the boxing fans who still remember one of the most startling heavyweight fights of the twentieth century.

Nobody Can Beat Joe Louis

Was there *anybody* who had a chance against Joe Louis? In 1941 fight promoters, sportswriters, and boxing fans scoured the bushes of the fight game for credible heavyweight contenders.

Billy Conn, a stylish Irish boxer from Pittsburgh, had risen through the middleweight and light heavyweight ranks through speed and cleverness. Conn was not a terrific puncher. Of his fifty-eight wins (he had lost eight times), just twelve were knockouts. Conn made up for his lack of power with his footwork, his canniness, and his strategic command of the ring. He was hailed as one of the smartest boxers who had ever stepped between the ropes.

But, most agreed, being smart was not enough. There was no way to outthink Louis's left hook. Louis outweighed Conn by twenty-five pounds. Billy Conn had his rooters, but the consensus was that he did not have a chance.

The fighters met at the Polo Grounds in New York on June 18, 1941. As a crowd of 55,000 sat dumbfounded, Conn—improbably—took command. He had studied Joe Louis's style. He had formulated a plan: keep moving, jab-jab-jab, constantly circle the ring, keeping away from Louis's lethal weapons, stay off the ropes, *never* trade punches with the heavier, more powerful man.

Radio listeners (there was no TV then) goggled as the fight went on, round after round, long beyond the point at which the experts said Billy Conn would be flat on the canvas. Even more bizarre was the assertion of the announcer that, incredible as it might seem, Conn was winning the bout. The peerless Joe Louis appeared befuddled by his opponent's elusive, dancing footwork and crisp jabs, which, though they lacked power, scored points. Conn was beginning to laugh as he taunted the champion.

As the thirteenth round started, even the most skeptical observers at last had to acknowledge the truth; they were witnessing the biggest upset in boxing history.

And then the fight changed. Conn's blows got harder. Instead of circling, he set himself, smashing through the surprised Louis's defenses. Conn's punches were landing; the fans could see that they were registering with dead aim on target.

Billy Conn was trying to knock Joe Louis out!

Conn stalked the champion now, slamming in hard punches. Louis tried to cover up. His shoulders were hunched; his eyes followed Conn like the eyes of a wounded bull following the matador.

And then, a blur of motion. Conn waded in with lefts and rights. He left a momentary opening. Louis suddenly connected with a right to the jaw. Conn, moving confidently a moment ago, was back on his heels, a quizzical look on his handsome face. Louis, expressionless, plodded toward him, letting loose a volley of punches. A right to the head spun Conn around. He fell, struggled to get up, but was counted out with just two seconds to go in the thirteenth round.

Afterward Conn said that he was beating Joe Louis so badly that he decided to knock Louis out. In other words, his strategy was working so well that he abandoned it to adopt the only tactics that gave Louis a chance—a chance the champion did not miss.

In one sense Billy Conn was doing what other smart athletes—and smart people in other walks of life—do on occasion. Not content to win by sticking to the game plan, they say, in effect, "Now I'll show you I can beat you at your own game!" A few years ago Boris Becker— an eminently intelligent tennis player—astounded the crowd at the U.S. Open by abandoning his successful net-rushing style and trying to show that he could outslug the backcourt player Andre Agassi from the baseline. Marveling at his good fortune, Agassi won.

Choosing to Lose

Good players in sports, business, or life are occasionally overwhelmed by the temptation to see if they can successfully adopt somebody else's game. The French painter Camille Pissarro, captivated by Georges Seurat's Pointillism, went over to Seurat's painstaking placement of multitudes of tiny dots on the canvas. Some of Pissarro's friends, along with other artists, critics, and dealers, lamented that a great Impressionist had transformed himself into an indifferent Pointillist.[1] Pissarro was undeterred; he experimented with the new approach until he was satisfied, then moved on.

This is intellectual curiosity; the vibrant mind resists ruts and restlessly seeks new fields.

But when someone on the verge of a great triumph does something that brings about, instead, a complete debacle, there is something else at work: the *unconscious need to fail.* Sometimes we need to lose because we are afraid to win.

The psychiatrist Leon Tec defines the fear of success as "an unconscious fear of what one consciously considers important and desirable."[2] *Winning* is the sine qua non of desirability in our culture. But winning can be a burden. For one thing, winners have to *keep on winning.*

Take as an example a marathon like the one held annually in New York. At the start, more than 26,000 people in running shorts jam together on the Staten Island side of the Verrazano Bridge. On television, the aerial shot shows a heaving undifferentiated mass, one huge organism. Only two individuals from that mass—a man and a woman—will be crowned as official winners.

But of course there will be a multitude of winners. Hundreds of runners will chalk up personal bests. Others will win simply by finishing the race. Still others will come out ahead in competition, friendly or otherwise, with running companions. A special group of competitors will roll their wheelchairs along the 26-mile, 385-yard course winding through the five boroughs of the city. And just about everyone is a winner by sharing the exhilaration of participation in the big event.

So who are the losers? Curiously enough, the losers are the best runners, all of the outstanding marathoners who started at the head of the pack. Sure, they got "appearance money" for showing up, but if they did not come in first, they lost. When TV reporters stick microphones in the faces of those who finished second or third, they don't ask, "Will you tell us how you were able to achieve this marvelous result, finishing ahead of all but one of the 26,000 runners who started?" No. The question is "How do you explain your failure to win the race?"

When others perceive you as superior, they expect you to win all the time. When *you* perceive yourself as superior, you demand superior performance from yourself. That's fine; but it isn't so fine when you demand of yourself that you *win every race*. Any time you come in second, you have failed.

In their valuable book *When Smart People Fail*, Carole Hyatt and Linda Gottlieb say, "It is important to understand what failure is . . . and what it isn't. Success and failure are not polar opposites, they are parts of a continuum. One can lead to the other with great ease. Neither is likely to be permanent; the irony is we believe both will last forever."[3]

Hyatt and Gottlieb write about the ways in which we can survive and profit from setbacks. Here, we are concerned with exploring the reasons for certain egregious setbacks suffered by people who appear to have all the equipment to succeed and, indeed, who seem to have already succeeded when—unaccountably—they throw it all away.

The Thirteenth Round

The danger zone starts when the contest is not officially over but the winner is clear. This was the point at which the great jockey Willie Shoemaker threw away a Kentucky Derby win by standing up in the irons before his leading horse reached the wire, only to be passed by an opponent. The danger zone continues past the finish line, through the moments of relaxation, congratulation, and celebration.

Our Secret Goal: Failure

All management books, films, videos, training programs, and so on, assume that the individual on the receiving end has a high—practically unlimited—level of aspiration. If you don't "want it all," what are you doing in business?

Highly gifted people—SCIPIs—are assumed to have aspirations consonant with their gifts. If you're really smart, you are labeled as sinful or sick if you don't perform up to your potential. So you accept as a matter of course that you are driven by an overwhelming urge to "be everything you can be."

But—*suppose something deep inside you does NOT want success*, or at least the kind of success that you've defined for yourself and that others expect of you?

If that's the case, the Anti-Genius Gremlin goes to work, termite-like, eating away the foundations of the triumphal arch that you are building higher and higher. Then one day, with success in your grasp, you blow it.

Sigmund Freud was among the first to recognize that many people have a secret passion for failure. Sooner or later, they turn their triumphs into disasters. Consciously, they revel in their success. But unconsciously, they reject success. They consider themselves unworthy; they don't believe they can handle it; in the core of their being they just don't want it.

Not Sick Enough to Succeed?

Lady Macbeth predicted that her husband would make it to the top— but that he lacked the necessary sickness to keep him there:

> Glamis thou art, and Cawdor; and shalt be
> What thou art promis'd. Yet I do fear thy nature;
> It is too full o' the milk of human kindness
> To catch the nearest way; thou wouldst be great,
> Art not without ambition; but without
> The illness should attend it;
> *Macbeth*, act 1, scene 5

Some people need to fail because they are "nice guys"—too nice to triumph in their particular arena. If you're lucky enough to find this out about yourself before it's too late, find another arena.

The Fatal Flaw

The unconscious need to fail runs like a toxic stream through many of the cases of smart dumbness we examine in these pages.

One CEO told us that he had made it in the consumer products game by developing a working knowledge of all aspects of the business: R&D, research, advertising, sales and merchandising, cost control, and so forth. He was a master at keeping all these elements working in harmony. Then he reached the pinnacle—and suddenly seemed to forget everything he knew. He looked at some preliminary scores on a new product, liked what he saw, and said, "Let's go with it!"

"Needs more testing," said key subordinates.

"The hell with that! Competition will beat us to the punch!"

The Toscanini-like orchestrator of all the elements of package goods success was now a hunch player, winging it. His performance dropped off and so did his support on the board.

Here's how it works. Imagine that you're watching the Dallas Cowboys. Quarterback Troy Aikman is picking the San Francisco defense apart with his passes. Now and then he varies the attack by giving the ball to Emmitt Smith for a run. Dallas builds a comfortable lead.

But now look! Aikman starts acting as if the Cowboys are alone on the field. He ignores the defensive alignment, sends running plays into masses of tacklers, passes into clusters of defensive backs. Result? Interceptions. Turnovers. Enemy touchdowns. And, ultimately, defeat. People do the equivalent every day.

I've Got It Made, So Who Needs Friends?

Some self-destructive people, on reaching the top, decide they no longer need anybody else. They dump colleagues, partners, spouses.

They insult and alienate those with whom they were friendly. This may be a naturally vicious personality, held in check for years, emerging at last. But, at least to a degree, it may be the need to fail.

One method of ensuring failure, used by a lot of successful people we know, is to organize the opposition. The logic seems to be, once you defeat an opponent, make sure he remains an opponent. On a megascale, the winners of World War I, notably France, ground Germany into the dust with the Versailles Treaty, making it possible for Hitler to rise to power and diverting the course of history down a bloody and tragic path. A fast-track manager, promoted to head a division, treats her unsuccessful rivals with uniform disdain, impelling them to paper over their differences and band together against her.

> I never let the four guys who hate me get together with the five who are undecided.
>
> Leo Durocher (former major league manager)

Compulsive Womanizing in the White House

John F. Kennedy's astounding predilection for copulation anywhere and at any time is now part of American lore. Kennedy's escapades—including entertaining the mistress of a Mafia chieftain in the White House—would seem to lead us deep into the labyrinths of pathology Dr. Harvey Feinberg, a psychiatrist at Mt. Sinai Hospital in New York, observes that compulsive sex is, in certain cases, a release from depression.

We'll never know why he did it. But it is perhaps permissible to mention the topic of the unconscious need to fail. Every fresh episode put Kennedy more firmly into the hands of his hated enemy J. Edgar Hoover, as well as other even more sinister figures. Maybe there was a deliciousness about the risk, as well as the feeling of conquest and whatever else went into the experience. But, as with all highly intelligent risk junkies, we have to assume he knew the long-term downside was not worth the short-term upside—but he went ahead anyway.

The Unsuffering of Fools

The word *politic* means tactful and adroit in dealing with people. Of all the professions, why would you go into politics if you openly scorned people who were not as smart as you?

Actually, some people of consummate ability have gotten very far in politics even though they made little or no effort to please those whom they deemed their inferiors. But, by and large, politicians who make enemies get ahead in spite of that characteristic, not because of it.

Everyone agrees that Stephen J. Solarz is brilliant. Elected to the U.S. House of Representatives in 1974 from a Brooklyn district, Solarz built a reputation for brilliance, especially in the area of foreign policy. The *New York Times* observed, "In his climb to prominence, Mr. Solarz never suffered fools gladly, often condescended to less brainy colleagues and irritated scores of Foreign Service officers in posts around the world."[4]

In 1992 it was revealed that Solarz and his wife had written 743 overdrafts at the House of Representatives Bank (more than any other member). Some members of Congress received considerable support from colleagues in riding out this scandal. Not Solarz. Then his seat was further jeopardized by redistricting. If the redistricters had been kinder to Solarz he might have fared better, but instead they put him in an impossible bind. His congressional career was over.

But Solarz had been a strong supporter of Bill Clinton. It looked as if he were in line to be ambassador to India. But his appointment ran into various problems, not the least of them caused by foreign service officers making anonymous calls to reporters. The appointment was shelved.

A politician who consistently makes enemies among those who may decide his fate seems to harbor a career death wish.

Lyndon Johnson: The Art of Suffering Fools Gladly

Lyndon Johnson did not court failure by alienating people. (Johnson's Vietnam disaster was fueled by a complex of factors, but not, it would seem, by the unconscious need to fail.) If Johnson lost to an adversary, he sought reconciliation, and at least acted as if he harbored no grudges. That's why, after losing out to John F. Kennedy in 1960, Johnson was able to take second place on the ticket and thus become president.

> I'd rather have him inside the tent pissing out, than outside pissing in. [Said of a potential adversary.]
>
> Lyndon Johnson

Notes

1. Ralph E. Shikes and Paula Harper, *Pissarro: His Life and Work* (New York: Horizon Press, 1980), pp. 212–214; 247.
2. Leon Tec, M.D., *The Fear of Success* (New York: Reader's Digest Press, 1976), p. 4.
3. Carole Hyatt and Linda Gottlieb, *When Smart People Fail* (New York: Simon & Schuster, 1987), p. 37.
4. *New York Times*, March 20, 1994, "Solarz, Who Made Enemies, Pays the Price in a Lost Job," by Todd S. Purdum.

Chapter 8.

THE ARROGANCE OF ENTITLEMENT

Arrogance is another element of SDIS.

We don't mean arrogance in the sense of bragging or pushiness. The word comes from the Latin *arrogare*, meaning "to claim for oneself." An individual can be soft-spoken and cordial, and still be arrogant, because he/she makes sweeping claims for admiration, money, perks—and most of all, power, especially power over others.

Many brilliant people are motivated more by power than by achievement. As children, these bright ones found themselves relatively powerless in an arena that is cruel to the smart kids. As adults they can use intellect to achieve power.

The arrogation of power manifests itself in a strong sense of entitlement.

The feeling of entitlement encroaches insidiously. The powerful mind, wanting more, constructs elaborate and plausible rationalizations for getting more. Unchecked, the feeling of entitlement leads on to folly that would appall the rational mind. But the rational mind has been elbowed aside by the willful urge to enjoy what one is "entitled" to enjoy. Parts of the psyche urge caution, fairness, and decency. But the urge snarls, "Because I'm entitled, that's why!"

With the urge out of control, the results can be horrendous.

Jules Masserman was a titan of the psychiatric community, a former president of the American Psychiatric Association, in practice for more than forty years. He brought to his practice a mastery of his discipline and a command of the various methods of treatment that might be used to heal psychic wounds.

One of his techniques was the sodium amytal interview, which Dr.

Masserman reserved for selected patients. The patient would stretch out on the couch in Dr. Masserman's Chicago office. Dr. Masserman would then administer the drug intravenously, rendering the patient unconscious. The doctor was still using this approach in 1984, at a time when such treatment was no longer widely used. Since amytal is highly addictive, there is the danger that patients may become dependent on the drug and on the doctor who supplies them with the drug.

This, however, was not a major concern to Dr. Masserman. This became evident to Barbara Noël—a patient for eighteen years—on a September day in 1984. Noël later described[1] how she awoke on the couch as the seventy-nine-year-old psychiatrist, naked, was raping her.

Barbara Noël was warned that it would be futile for her to go to court. The doctor was too important. There was no chance of getting other psychiatrists to testify against him as expert witnesses. It was her word against his; he could dismiss her as "just one crazy female patient suffering from some delusion."

But Noël persevered. Other patients came forward to make similar charges against the eminent psychiatrist. Four malpractice claims were settled out of court, while others remained pending. Dr. Masserman was suspended from the American Psychiatric Association, which he once headed. While maintaining his innocence, he surrendered his medical license and retired from practice.

The Entitlements of Superiority. Alas, the story of Dr. Jules Masserman is not unique. People of intelligence and accomplishment—physicians, teachers, political leaders, executives—all too often act as if slavery were by no means dead, especially sexual slavery. In the bad old days of feudalism there was the practice called *droit du seigneur,* purportedly entitling the lord of the manor to spend the wedding night with any bride in his domain.

That's gone out of style. Feudalism still exists, but in far fewer places than it did then. The landed aristocracy is gone, but that doesn't mean the concept of aristocracy is gone. Today we have various aristocracies, of money, fame, and achievement. A common thread runs through these aristocracies: *followership*. Aristocrats of the mind, those who achieve leadership, have followers, people who look up to them, people who are placed under their tutelage.

Certain members of the elite find it increasingly hard to distinguish followership from sexual slavery. The modern equivalent of *droit du seigneur* becomes a perk. The brainy achiever (traditionally, though not exclusively, male) takes care of the physical side of things by using his position to arrogate to himself the privileges of the harem. Senator Robert Packwood is one of our recent examples, besieged by women who claim that he kissed, fondled, or otherwise sexually harassed them.

> Men who possess all the advantages of life are in a state where there are many accidents to disorder and discompose, but few to please them.
> Jonathan Swift, *Thoughts on Various Subjects*

"Because God Entitles Me!"

Today we are besieged by stories about bad things done by people whose profession is supposed to be goodness. Pedophile priests. Corrupt evangelists. Megalomaniac cult leaders. Their transgressions are often sexual. They take carnal advantage of those with whose souls they are entrusted.

Nor do all the stories make the headlines. In a not untypical example, a Methodist minister in an eastern-state town listened to a distraught congregant. The congregant told the minister about her friend, a Jewish woman, who was being sexually abused by the rabbi. The minister, after some thought, spoke to the president of the rabbi's congregation. Asked about the story, the rabbi went into denial. How could he do such a thing? He was a rabbi! But he had indeed done such things.

The theme of the lustful religious person runs through literature at least from the time of Chaucer. Molière's Tartuffe was a titanic religious hypocrite, bent on stealing the wife and the money of his credulous victim. Somerset Maugham's 1921 short story *Miss Thompson* (later dramatized as *Rain*) tells how the ultra-righteous Reverend Davidson self-destructs in his obsession with the prostitute Sadie Thompson. Sinclair Lewis's *Elmer Gantry* (1927) foretold the doings of holy men like Jim Bakker and Jimmy Swaggart.

Religious stewardship can be particularly dangerous to those who are vulnerable to the lure of entitlement. Their followers implicitly believe them to be surrogates of God. They are in a position to indulge their impulses.

Most, of course, do not. But a depressing number succumb to the temptation.

King David's Lethal Sense of Entitlement

The Bible sets off its great spiritual message with stories of events that, if they took place today, would steam up the tabloid TV screen with depravity and scandal. The highest and the lowest are subject to the urges of base human nature.

David—slayer of Goliath, author of the Psalms, great king of Israel—is one of the Old Testament's most brilliant figures. He was a wise and brave leader. But on one notable occasion his sense of entitlement impelled him into one ignoble act that forever besmirches his name.

It begins as King David sees "a woman washing herself; and the woman was very beautiful to look upon."[2] The beautiful woman turns out to be Bathsheba, the wife of Uriah the Hittite, a captain in the army of Israel.

"David sent messengers and took her; and she came in unto him, and he lay with her. . . . And the woman conceived, and sent and told David, and said, I am with child."

At this time Israel was at war with the Ammonites. David sent a letter to Joab, his general, saying, "Set ye Uriah in the forefront of the hottest battle, and retire ye from him, that he may be smitten, and die." It is a macabre touch that King David sent this death sentence, sealed, by the hand of Uriah.

In the climactic battle with the Ammonites, Joab assigned Uriah to the hottest, most exposed position—and then hung the captain out to dry. Uriah was killed. Bathsheba mourned her husband; then, "when the mourning was past, David sent and fetched her to his house, and she became his wife, and bare him a son."

A brutal and murderous use of power by a great and gifted man. But, after all, David wanted Bathsheba and he was entitled to her.

The Bathsheba Effect

We see recurring examples of the Bathsheba Effect among leaders who allow their sense of entitlement to flood out the impulses of fairness, decency, and, often, common sense.[3]

No less a figure than Mao Ze-dong was depicted (in a BBC documentary) as a leader with an insatiable appetite for young women. Mao's personal physician, Dr. Li Zhisui, says, "Women felt honored to have sex with Mao. It was a glorious and natural thing to do, because Mao was God and the Supreme Ruler." Relations between China and Great Britain, already strained by the dispute over Hong Kong, were further frayed by the documentary.[3]

David McCullough, author of a distinguished biography of Harry Truman, commented that the kind of arrogance epitomized by Senators Packwood and Gary Hart, among others, is epidemic among people who skate on thin ice and think it will never break, because they are the ones doing the skating. We might comment in passing that

McCullough's subject, President Truman, was a paragon among leaders, because he kept his intelligence linked to his common sense. However, even Truman encountered occasional logic override, as when he offered to wreak havoc (by way of trauma in the genital area) on a music critic who dared to comment adversely on the singing of the president's daughter, Margaret.

The human resources manager of a large communications company passes along an example of dumb things perpetrated by smart people:

The CEO of a $350 M company meets a young woman, falls completely in love, marries quickly. The young woman, a former beauty queen, decides to enter the lists again, as a competitor for the "Mrs. Georgia" crown. The CEO arranges for the company to sponsor her. As a show of support, he decrees that a national sales meeting be held at the site of the pageant.

Everybody on the sales staff is offended.

The Trap of Entitlement. The infatuated antics of the CEO are more pathetic than vicious. However, they resemble the haremizing of some of the other luminaries of this chapter in one important respect: *the authority figure uses power to satisfy personal appetites.*

These are smart people. They wouldn't be world-famous psychiatrists, or high elected officials, or leaders of enormous countries, if they were not smart. How do they persuade themselves that what they are doing is right?

They rationalize their actions by means of two words: "I'M ENTITLED."

Our organization conducted a study of attitudes about sex and sexual harassment in the workplace. The theme of entitlement cropped up again and again. Some rather straitlaced executives were frank to acknowledge that, on learning of a peer's affair with an attractive employee, they felt resentment: "Why with [him or her] and not me?"

The feeling of entitlement goes with the territory in the higher regions of accomplishment. It seems as if the superior brain gets tired of operating in the realm of pure thought and decides to get down and dirty, go out for a blast, get laid. Well, you don't have to be a genius to lust, but the distinctive feature of the phenomena we are discussing is the ingenious use of strong intelligence to justify the most outrageous behavior.

> Man errs not that he dreams
> His welfare his true aim,
> He errs because he dreams
> The world does but exist that welfare to bestow
> Matthew Arnold, *Empedocles on Etna*

Entitlement and Narcissism

The overwhelming feeling of *entitlement* is a characteristic of the *narcissistic leader*. Recently the role of narcissism in leadership has come under increasing scrutiny. Dr. David W. Krueger, clinical professor of psychiatry at Baylor College of Medicine, writes in *Bottom Line* (November 15, 1992):

Narcissists are drawn to leadership positions by a deep need for power and prestige. They are often highly talented, hard-working and charismatic. But feelings of inferiority lead to self-aggrandizement and the need for constant, unconditional affirmation and positive feedback from others.

The psychologists Robert Hogan, Robert Raskin, and Dan Fazzini, in their insightful paper, *The Dark Side of Charisma* write:

In the modern literature of personality disorders narcissism is defined as a constellation of attitudes that includes exhibitionism, *feelings of enti-*

tlement, the expectation of special privileges and exemptions from social demands, feelings of omnipotence in controlling others, intolerance of criticism, and a tendency to focus on one's own mental products and to see others as extensions of oneself.[4]

One effective test for measuring narcissism is the *Narcissistic Personality Inventory* (NPI; Raskin & Hall, 1979, 1981). Persons who score high on the NPI are described by others in terms like this: highly energetic, extroverted, self-confident, competitive, achievement oriented, aggressive, exhibitionist, egotistical, manipulative, and self-seeking.

The most pathological aspects of narcissism, according to the authors, are exploitiveness and entitlement. The entitlement factor is exemplified by statements like *"I will never be satisfied until I get all that I deserve."*

A charismatic figure finds himself surrounded by all kinds of supporters, volunteers and staffers. He singles out those whose looks he likes. If they're on his payroll, he leans on them. If they are acolytes, he uses his charisma. In extreme circumstances he uses knockout doses of sodium amytal.

The chief executive of a company, treated like a pasha everywhere he goes, finds it fitting to adopt the customs of the real pashas of old Turkey. The young women working around the place are his property.

Is it love? Or affection? Not bloody likely. It probably doesn't have all that much to do with sex. The "entitlements" seem to be designed to assuage what Dr. Krueger calls the "feelings of inferiority."

What? Captains of industry with feelings of inferiority? Senators, presidential candidates, outstanding professionals? *Mao Ze-dong?*

Yes. The kind of narcissism that leads to extreme feelings of entitlement reflects weakness rather than strength. The powerful mind finds all kinds of ways to layer healing tissue over the weak spot. Elsewhere we discuss what might be called the identical twin of "I'm entitled"— the feeling that can be summed up as "I don't really deserve this."

"Life Is Passing Me By!"

Judge David B. Saxe of the New York State Supreme Court makes an insightful point about the sudden self-destructive brainstorms that attack intelligent and successful people in public life.

"They are grabbing the 'last ride,'" said Judge Saxe in an interview. "Their lives have been devoid of passion. Forced to live up to a certain public image, they forego certain pleasures. Then, suddenly, they panic: 'I'm missing life!'" Desperate to live the unlived parts of their lives before it's too late, they rush into astounding folly.

All kinds of people confront the moment when they can view the downslope of life. For certain individuals who have lived in a fishbowl (as do public officials), the situation is worse because they feel they have had to forego pleasures enjoyed by others. "Some of these men [and we see it most in men] are highly developed in some areas of their personalities but undeveloped in others," says Judge Saxe. A successful career politician, superb on the platform, in the TV studio, and at pressing the flesh at political dinners, is socially infantile.

When we develop one part of the personality while another remains undeveloped, a static charge builds up. When the charge gets too big there is a lightning bolt release of tension. The individual, who has spent a lifetime pacing the straight and narrow path, bolts over the precipice.

Later in this book you'll find exercises designed to bring all salient areas of your personality into synch, to preclude self-immolating excess.

The Wonderful World of "I'm Entitled!"

We've been discussing what we might call *libidinal* entitlements. There are other kinds: *ceremonial* entitlements and *financial* entitlements. Whether the rewards involve money, or a corner office, or sexual advances, they all stem from the same root cause: the brain has concluded that the perk is deserved, and thus any excess is justified.

Ceremonial and financial entitlements often overlap, blending into the imperial style. When a small elite group shares in its conviction of entitlement—in spite of evidence to the contrary—the entire enterprise is threatened.

WQED, Pittsburgh, is the first community-sponsored education television station in America. Readers of the *Wall Street Journal* were treated, early in 1994, to the story of entitlement intoxication at the station.[5]

WQED was in big financial trouble. Nothing unique about that. Public television has been tossed by turbulent seas for some time. For one thing, cable—with offerings like the Discovery Channel—now gives viewers a choice of the kinds of programming once available only on public TV. Another factor is the increasing resistance of businesses to sponsorship of public TV programming. A show like the "MacNeil/Lehrer NewsHour" has national sponsorship from large corporations, foundations, and institutions. For the show to be aired in a particular locality requires additional sponsorship from local funders. Businesses must justify such expenditures. Increasingly it is difficult for some businesses to justify support of such programs against other forms of advertising or promotion.

In addition, state and local governments are not willing to give public TV the amount of funding they used to provide. No wonder public television stations around the country are stepping up the intensity and stridency of their appeal periods, which seem to recur so frequently as to be almost continual. And no wonder they have cut back staffs, abandoned ambitious production plans, and reduced salaries.

Certainly there was good reason to think that WQED in Pittsburgh was not immune, and that the station would have to take some of the same measures being taken by other stations. But at WQED the watchword seemed to be that of the immortal Alfred E. Neuman: "What? Me worry?"

The Arrogance of Entitlement

The *Wall Street Journal* declared that the station's "greatest problem has been insouciance." The station's executives continued to spend lavishly. As high-powered telethons urged viewers to send in money, WQED's top executives enjoyed big salaries and benefit packages, which they maintained staunchly in spite of the gathering clouds.

The station's top brass did not have to worry about carping from the board of directors. A former board member commented, "I'm not sure how much any board member—even the officers—was aware of the nuts and bolts of what was going on over there. It was a big operation with a big board, and authority gets a little bit fragmented."

What fragmented was the financial base of the station. WQED lost Gulf Oil, its principal sponsor, and National Geographic, its main co-producer. Nevertheless, the gravy train rolled on. In the fiscal year ending June 30, 1992, the station's top four executives enjoyed packages of up to $325,995. The *Journal* notes, "The packages included annual car allowances ranging from $15,000 to $22,000, and the executives were able to cash in insurance policies for amounts ranging from $34,000 to $68,191." The policies were apparently bought without the board's knowledge.

Now, these compensation packages are not up there in the stratosphere with, say, the arrangements secured by the CEOs of IBM and GM. But corporations don't go on television asking the public for contributions to enable them to keep going.

> Why do men seek honour? Surely, in order to confirm the favourable opinion they have formed of themselves.
> Aristotle, *Nicomachean Ethics*

Word of the plush arrangements in the executive suite of WQED leaked out. Loyal viewers and supporters felt betrayed. Community volunteers who had been slaving away to raise money for the station were outraged. Potential supporters and sponsors were alienated.

Why Smart People Do Dumb Things

THEY HAD EARNED IT—WQED had enjoyed a long period of success. Two top executives, Lloyd Kaiser and Thomas Skinner, came to Pittsburgh in 1970 from a public TV station in Hershey, Pennsylvania, and built WQED from a small station with $2 million in annual revenue to a $36 million complex comprising a classical music radio station and a monthly magazine.

The station launched the famed "Mister Rogers." With National Geographic it produced a string of programs, a dozen of which rank among the most-watched shows ever seen on public TV. The station won twenty-eight Emmys, putting it in the same class as the bigger stations in New York and Boston.

In the mid-1980s the atmosphere began to turn sour. But life was still sweet in the executive suite at WQED. The station went merrily on, spending as it had always spent.

What happened? A great many things, no doubt. But prominent among them is, we suspect, the *entitlement syndrome*.

The satisfaction of achievement is augmented by other rewards: money, status, promotion, recognition. The work is hard, but the pay-off is worth it. But when brilliance is linked with narcissism, the payoff always lags behind the accomplishment. We're paid big money—but we're worth even more to the firm than we are paid. We reach the highest possible levels of recognition, but that recognition is not universal, nor is it adulation. The head of a Washington think tank told us that one of George Bush's problems in his failed run for reelection in 1992 was his anger at the American people. Bush felt that he had won the Cold War, was a great commander in chief in the Gulf war, and was entitled to be reelected. When a substantial number of Americans did not seem to agree, Bush grew angry. When we are angry we don't pay attention to the needs of others, especially people whom we perceive as ungrateful.

And when they don't pay attention to the needs of others, smart people do dumb things.

One spectacular example is Leona Helmsley. The ads for her hotels proclaimed her attention to the needs of her guests. Her monumental inattention to the needs and feelings of her subordinates and colleagues won her the title, "Queen of Mean." Her contempt for paying taxes might have been covered up if some of her scorned lackeys had not been eager to strike back at her. She was smart in real estate and in certain other areas. Her dumbness in human relations was a decisive factor in putting her behind bars.

Macho Madness at Kidder, Peabody

When Kidder, Peabody & Company appointed Joseph Jett its chief of government trading in 1993, some people grumbled that Jett had no experience in government securities. Jett's track record was not awesome; he had been, reported the *Wall Street Journal*, "laid off by Morgan Stanley and dismissed by CS First Boston."[6]

At first Joseph Jett lost money. Then things turned around. Jett started to show phenomenal results. At the same time he took bigger and bigger positions. His portfolio swelled to around $18 billion. His marvelous trades earned him a $9 million bonus for his first year in the job.

Then, in April 1994, the horror burst over Kidder, Peabody. Joseph Jett was accused of faking $350 million in phantom trades to cover losses amounting to $100 million. Jett was stripped of his job and his directorship. The firm moved to recover the $9 million bonus. Jett's superiors found the swirling tides rising to engulf them. Some speculated that John F. Welch, Jr., chairman of GE, Kidder's parent company, would be so disgusted that he would dump the sinning subsidiary.

Pressure and Illusion. We don't list pressure-for-results as one of the prime causes of SDIS, because it is a catalyst that causes all kinds of people, smart and dumb, to make mistakes. Tell a dumb basketball player that he's got to put more points on the board and he'll start taking wild three-point shots. A smart player may do the same thing.

However, there are certain aspects of the Kidder episode that fit into our thesis.

- **The power of wishful thinking.** Jett's bosses wanted him to do well, so they persuaded themselves that he was doing well, despite unpromising auspices. A commonplace person might say, "This guy has been let go from two places before, and he's lost money at the start. We'd better watch him closely and keep a tight rein on him." Kidder did just the opposite. It takes a supple mind to rationalize such a translation of wish into the illusion of reality.
- **Bottom line fixation.** There is often a tacit agreement among talented, high-achieving people that it is unseemly to examine what they are doing. That's how the spy Kim Philby fooled British intelligence for so long, and how the CIA was able to overlook the clues that should have spurred scrutiny of Aldrich Ames. The effect is even more pronounced in corporations when the high achiever is thought to be making big money for the firm.
- **Where money meets macho.** Highly intelligent people (usually men) sometimes adopt a supermacho image. They talk tough. They brag about their ruthlessness. They use words of violence ("I'll cut his balls off!" was the constant cry of a renowned IBM executive).

To some extent this happens because, when they were children, the bigger (and dumber) kids humiliated the smart ones. On the big-money fast track, "trash talk" is as prevalent as in the National Basketball Association.

This may be harmless (although embarrassingly immature) up to a point. Then it becomes dangerous. After the bad news about Joseph Jett began to come out, co-workers talked about his intimidating demeanor. He would loom up in front of colleagues, piercing them with a challenging eye. He was fabled as a master of the martial arts. He was hard-boiled and confrontational, a kind of Darth Vader of Wall Street.

To ordinary mortals, tough talk and martial arts have no connection to trading government bonds. In the arena we are studying, the two go together.

Worse, the cerebral macho man buys his own act. He goes further and further in chest beating. What might have started as an act becomes essential personality.

As the Jett story unfolded, other Kidder stories surfaced. One concerned John Kliebert, a former Kidder bond salesman who, said the company, had been fired for inflating commissions. Kliebert, described as a "tall, stocky man with steely blue eyes," called himself "The Klieb."[7]

Kliebert, unhappy over his dismissal, began to "stalk" his ex-bosses, accosting one in front of Kidder's headquarters and telling him that his "shirt would look good with a red splotch in the chest area." Kliebert also made phone calls that were taken to be threatening. Kidder people complained to authorities, and Kliebert was arrested.

Terminal toughness is one manifestation of the SDIS virus. It is fed by arrogance and narcissism, and nurtured by an injured sense of entitlement. It is a childish pose that can, if unchecked, warp the workings of the superior mind.

Take Advantage of Your Position— Why Else Would You Have It?

Stanley Friedman, once one of the most powerful political leaders in New York City, went to federal prison in 1988, convicted of racketeering, conspiracy, and mail fraud for illegally using his influence to sell portable computers to New York's Parking Violations Bureau. (One of Friedman's partners in power, Queens borough president Donald Manes, killed himself when his illegal involvement with the Parking Violations Bureau began to come out.) Friedman said that "the longer you're in, you acquire a proprietary interest in the position. Because you justify you're doing a good job governmentally you rationalize that you're above the law," according to the *New York Times.* "You must take advantage of the position you have or why have it? You feel you own the job. It begets arrogance."[8]

The urge of entitlement can have strange manifestations. A large brokerage house used an executive search firm to lure a young, promising manager away from another company. The inducements included a high base salary, a liberal bonus, a hefty up-front payment, and perks including cars, country clubs, and health spa privileges. The new manager moved into an office furnished to his specifications. One morning another executive, who had an office nearby, found her computer terminal missing. The new man, it turned out, had appropriated it. Protests! Meetings! Mollification! The victim of the ripoff got her computer back, and the new hotshot was given an identical computer. Not long afterward it happened again. The new manager had spotted yet another computer that he liked (one, in fact, deemed inferior to the one he had) and, after hours, had simply appropriated it.

Top management now decided that the turmoil was not worth the brilliance. They fired the computer purloiner.

Another case of *I'm entitled!* linked with *I don't really deserve it.*

Your feeling of entitlement can lure you into acting dumb. At any given time, a large proportion of the population feels unappreciated—by spouses and companions, friends, communities, bosses, colleagues, the world at large. When intelligent and accomplished people are consumed by such feelings, they are capable of using their positions to satisfy their feelings of entitlement.

And, by the very use of their power, they proceed to destroy the base of that power.

The Delicate Art of Living a Lie

The lure of entitlements traps smart people into stupidities of a number of types. For those who depend on the support of others—politicians answering to voters, CEOs relying on their boards—the gap between projected image and actual behavior can be damaging, sometimes fatal, when it becomes known. And, these days, those things *do* become known.

Once politicians got a free ride from the media, which overlooked their "peccadilloes," on the theory that what the rulers did in private was none of the business of those who were ruled, as long as it did not impinge on performance. As we know, that notion has definitely gone out of fashion. Every nook and cranny of the lives of elected officials, candidates, and political appointees is ransacked for specks of dirt. "Entitlements" that could once be enjoyed with impunity now bring down governments and wreck careers.

In France, where the public is, perhaps, a little more relaxed about sex in the upper echelons, money has been the biggest engine of scandal, and in 1993 (counterbalancing the misadventures of the Tories across the Channel) the French Socialist party had a cataclysmic fall from power, helped over the brink by public disgust at a plethora of financial shenanigans charged to the leaders of the left. One Socialist ex–prime minister committed suicide.

Business bigwigs aren't faring any better. Time was when top corporate executives could enjoy a resplendent lifestyle, with the kinds of perks once reserved for royalty, the company footing the bill. Executives took for granted that they were entitled, and they could act out that entitlement itch without fear of rebuke. No more. The kill-joys at the IRS and SEC have whittled away many of the bejeweled baubles of bossdom. Aroused stockholders are even worse. If a big executive stumbles just a bit, the predators swarm, like ants covering a wounded caterpillar. Ross Johnson was a big moneymaker for his stockholders at RJR Nabisco for a long time, but when one misstep made him vulnerable, all his foibles and somewhat childish yens were held up to scorn and ridicule.

The vast majority of SCIPIs is not driven to the monstrous excesses of a Jules Masserman. The feeling of entitlement traps them in more subtle ways. They lust for perks. They eye the other guy's perks to make sure they have more. Bit by bit they regress toward nursery school grabbiness. They lose sight of what is important. They offend others. And they ultimately reach too far.

The Bottom Line

Feelings of entitlement are understandable. However, the use of power and position to obtain what is "entitled" impels the entitlee into a minefield of stupidities of increasing inanity and lethality. Finally the individual reaches too far for the wrong entitlement and self-destructs.

Notes

1. Barbara Noël with Kathryn Watterson, *You Must Be Dreaming* (New York: Poseidon Press, 1993), pp. 19–21; 124.
2. 2 Samuel ii, 2–5, 14–27.
3. *New York Times*, December 19, 1993, "China Protests Documentary About Mao," by John Darnton.
4. Hogan, R.; Raskin, R.; and Fazzini, D., "The Dark Side of Charisma," in K.E. Clark and M.B. Clark (Eds.), *Measures of Leadership* (Leadership Library of America, West Orange, N.J., 1990), pp. 348–350.
5. *Wall Street Journal*, January 17, 1994, "Missed Signal: Pittsburgh's WQED Failed to See Change in Public-TV Industry," by Valerie Reitman.
6. *Wall Street Journal*, May 2, 1994, "Kidder's No. 2 Man Comes Under Scrutiny in Trading Scandal," by Laurie P. Cohen, Alix M. Freedman, and William Power.
7. *Wall Street Journal*, April 29, 1994, "An Employee Fired by Peabody Casts a Pall of Fear," by Michael Siconolfi.
8. *New York Times*, November 23, 1992, "Stanley Friedman on the Lesson He Learned Late, in Metro Matters," by Sam Roberts.

Chapter 9.

E PLURIBUS STUPIDITAS: COLLECTIVE DUMBNESS

So far our melancholy survey of dumbness among the brightest has focused, for the most part, on individuals. Now let's look at how groups of smart people, working together, can reach heights of almost unbelievable folly. The elements of SDIS—hubris, narcissism, arrogance, the need to fail—interact and spread until the whole organization is infected.

"**FLOPS**" is the bold headline on an article in *Business Week* (August 16, 1993). That stark word is followed by the grim reminder that "Too Many New Products Fail." The next few pages toll the dreary litany of disasters. La Choy frozen egg rolls and Fresh and Lite low-fat Chinese foods. Coca-Cola's tiny soda fountain for the office. Time Inc.'s *TV-Cable Week* magazine. Toyota's T100 pickup truck. Dell computer's notebook. The Osborne portable computer. And, of course, that paragon of folly, the notorious Edsel.

They all have one thing in common. They *looked like a good idea at the time*—to a lot of very smart people, acting together.

Most successful corporations are headed by a team of policy-making executives who may come from various backgrounds but who are undeniably smart. When they operate on their own, their brilliance is decisive. When they combine their intelligences, the cumulative product should be so overwhelming that no riddle would be too difficult.

At least that's what we might think—if we didn't know better. The failure rate of products and businesses attests to the proposition that strong intelligences can band together to take the enterprise in exactly the wrong direction. That might well be what happened in the case of the Triplecast fiasco.

In the summer of 1992 Cablevision and NBC got together to offer coverage of the Olympics on a pay-per-view basis. The public did not buy. As the date of the Olympics drew nearer, the public still did not buy. They kept cutting the price; still no sale. NBC and Cablevision sustained huge losses.

"Clearly we did not read the research well," said Charles "Chuck" Dolan, Cablevision's chairman. Amen to that.

As you might expect with an idea as new as this, with so much riding on it NBC and Cablevision would want to test it to the best extent that they could. They invested a lot of money in extensive sophisticated research to test the idea's viability.

The test results were overwhelming. The numbers showed that only one percent (or less) of the total potential market would "definitely" buy the Triplecast.

So, did the TV executives heave a big sigh of relief, exclaiming, "Wow! We dodged that bullet!" Did they thank heavens that they had had the foresight to test the idea so rigorously? Did they say, "Okay, it won't fly, so let's forget it"—and go on to explore more profitable areas?

No, they didn't do that.

Well, did they then revise the concept substantially, offering different packages, and then go back to test the new idea to see if it would be greeted any more favorably?

They didn't do that, either. They took a third course. They adjusted the test results by adding the "probables" to the "definites." This is like a doctor finding a patient to have a temperature of 106 degrees and then putting the thermometer on ice to get a more favorable reading.

Let's Put Our Heads Together to Reshape Reality

Confronted with the facts, most people accept them, like it or not. But powerful minds are capable of deploying powerful rationalization mechanisms that override reality. Individuals fall into this trap; so do groups. A group of powerful minds, working together, can accomplish marvels. But, as in the Triplecast fiasco, a constellation of brilliances can generate a kind of self-destructive power leading to a devastating implosion.

The Deadly Baby Nursers

Market research has been honed to a razor-keen edge. It is a powerful, and usually reliable, tool. But its value is negated when its message is misread or altered.

There can be other problems as well. A company felt it had developed a superior baby nurser. The product was thoroughly tested. The results were positive. The product went on the market.

And soon the company was facing the worst nightmare possible. The baby nurser was unsafe, to a possibly fatal extent. Complaints began to come in about the nipple pulling loose. Luckily, no infant had choked to death thus far. Horrified, the company pulled the product off the market.

While working to rectify the defect, management also wondered what had gone wrong with the research. The raw materials of the research findings were examined. It turned out that, in test, there *had* been a few instances in which the nipple pulled loose. However, they were not numerous—so the coding supervisor included them in the "All Other" category.

This is a management failure. The coding supervisor deals with numbers, not implications. Somebody should have said, "There are certain problems that are so potentially serious that even *one* instance must be red-flagged."

PIN Heads—NYNEX Overlooks the Obvious

In April 1994 customers of New York Telephone (NYNEX) were stunned when they received a mailing urging them to use their phone credit cards and qualify for a big sweepstakes promotion. It was not the promotion that boggled the minds of NYNEX's flock; it was the fact that the mailing—a folded card glued at two corners—contained each addressee's own PIN number. The PIN (Personal Identification Number) is the secret code needed by credit card users to validate phone calls and other transactions.

The whole point of the PIN is that it is Top Secret, Eyes Only, the bulwark against fraud. PINs are usually sent in sealed envelopes, separate from the cards. Users are instructed to memorize the number, never carrying it with them.

So PIN numbers are a prime target of criminals: "shoulder surfers," who watch callers at public booths and try to decipher the PIN, and "dumpster divers," who rummage through trash looking for exactly such information.

And here was NYNEX, sending out three million of these valuable personal codes in a fold-over card that, though mailed first class, was easily disposable as junk mail.

Pandemonium! NYNEX customers got a Western Union "Important Information" flash:

Dear NYNEX Customer:
   Recently we sent you a sweepstakes mailing as a reminder of the value of your NYNEX Calling Card. It also included your Personal Identification Number (PIN).

Some customers, however, have expressed concern over the security of this mailing. Please be assured that customer privacy is a major priority to us and we acted with only the best of intentions. . . .

NYNEX tells customers they can get new PINs, reassures them that they won't have to pay for unauthorized calls, and winds up:

I hope this hasn't caused you any inconvenience. And I want to encourage you to continue using your NYNEX Calling Card with confidence, as you always have.

The promotion was dreamed up by executives in NYNEX's product management group, working with a direct marketing firm. The head of the direct marketing firm said, "There are always ways to improve a program. We would definitely take additional precautions" in any subsequent promotion. A NYNEX spokesperson said, "In hindsight, maybe we should have done it differently. If we had it to do over again, we'd give it more thought."[1]

What D'You Mean, the Emperor Is Naked?

The NYNEX PIN debacle sounds a theme we can see recurring throughout this book. When a bunch of bright, intense, competitive SCIPIs get together, they are in danger of skipping right over the obvious.

In this case a group of high-achieving individuals—certifiably intelligent—joined to address a problem. Customers were not using their Calling Cards enough. It did not take extensive research to uncover the principal reason: the customers had received their PIN numbers but had hidden them away or destroyed them—and promptly forgotten them.

So why not remind people of their PINs while giving them the incentive of a sweepstakes promotion? It would be an expensive mailing, of course, but worth it.

Someone with a more mundane mind might say, "But hey! Isn't the whole idea of the PIN number that it is *confidential?* We can't send out the code alongside the name and address in a piece of junk mail!"

That would have been too obvious.

High-pressure intellects, reinforcing one another, can soar so high that they lose all contact with the basics.

He Can't Be a Mole, He's One of Us

Look at another example of group folly among the best and brightest. Early in 1994 the country watched in astonishment as a senior CIA official, Aldrich H. Ames, and his wife were handcuffed and bustled off to jail, accused of being Russian spies for many years, for selling out reams of our country's most closely guarded secrets, and, most horrifying, for selling out—and sending to their deaths—untold numbers of U.S. agents during the Cold War.

Aldrich Ames burrowed away as a mole, undetected, for years. Why wasn't he caught? It turns out that the Ameses lived in a mansion, drove expensive cars, altogether enjoyed a lifestyle that simply did not jibe with the way a CIA officer of Ames's rank was supposed to live. If Ames had worked for, say, Agriculture or Commerce, his lifestyle would have been, no doubt, his own business. For obvious reasons, CIA people—and their colleagues in other highly sensitive positions—court scrutiny when they seem to live beyond their incomes.

The explanation for the anomaly of Ames's lifestyle was, supposedly, attributed to the fact that Mrs. Ames came from a wealthy Colombian family. (Some murmured that certain members of that family were aligned with Colombian drug cartels, but that didn't bother the watchdogs at CIA. Indeed, such an association might even have been viewed as a plus.)

One observer, familiar with the CIA, says, "They would not look twice at Aldrich Ames because he fitted in so perfectly with the ruling elite. Here was a gentleman, a guy with a last name for a first name, a personal style that made him an ideal spook. This was still a game for the Ivy League gentleman, even though most of them had never been near the Ivy and were definitely no gentlemen."

In Ames's case—as in the cases of other CIA moles and in the cases of Philby, Burgess, and McLean, the celebrated British traitors—there was a general assumption that all of these people were above suspicion because they were "one of us." The assumption in every spy shop is that *everybody* on the other side—Kremlin, East Germany, wherever—is a potential double agent. This assumption is justified; our spooks are often able to turn their spooks.

You would think, then, that logical counterintelligence doctrine would turn that assumption around and apply it to our side as well. Look at every official and agent with the thought that he or she could be working for the other side.

No such thinking applied at Langley. The notion that Aldrich or anyone like Aldrich Ames could be working for the other side was totally unacceptable. The power of group folly at the CIA is demonstrated by the tale of the polygraphs.

CIA officers are routinely given lie detector tests. So, people asked, what happened with Ames? Did he somehow get out of taking the tests? Or was he such a cool customer that he somehow fooled the polygraph when he passed the tests? Neither was the case. It turned out that Ames *flunked* at least three lie detector tests after he began spying for the USSR in 1985. In each case (according to an op-ed piece in the New York Times, March 8, 1994, by Ronald Kessler, author of Inside the CIA) Ames was reported by the examiner as not telling the truth when he denied giving out classified information. Since Ames could not possibly be a spy, the polygraph results had to be adjusted. This was done.

Groupthink Dumbs Down
Intelligence

Group thinking has long been accepted as being superior to individual thinking in solving a wide range of problems. Moreover, there is a parallel assumption that a group of capable thinkers avoids the kind of sudden stupidity that strikes individuals. Typically, a basic psychological work on individual behavior within society[2]—one familiar to generations of psychologists—refers to the great advantage that groups have "in the solution of difficult problems when compared with individual workers." The authors go on to say, "The advantage of group work depends inevitably upon the relative importance assignable in any given case to fertility of association, rejection of inappropriate suggestions, possibility of modification of a suggestion to make it usable, and, in fact, upon a great number of attributes relating to the past experience and intelligence of the subjects . . . the superior value of group thinking over individual thinking, when demonstrated, is clearly due in part to (1) the larger number of ways of looking at the problem; (2) the larger number of suggestions for a solution; (3) the larger number of effective criticisms of each proposed plan; (4) the patent need to accept social criticism and not be 'bullheaded' (as subjects working alone frequently are)."

The advantages enjoyed by intelligent people thinking together (as summed up in the passage cited above) are that there are more ways of looking at the problem; more suggestions; and more good criticisms. There is the added advantage that recalcitrants are more easily persuaded not to hold out against the majority.

Ah; here, perhaps, we have a clue. Yes, no doubt there was a lot of great input from all the strong brains beaming their power together on the subject at hand. But, once a consensus started to form, individual holdouts, while articulate in their objections, would be opposed by an increasingly potent counterfire of brilliant argument.

And then we have the questions of which members of the group thought what. A lot of the theoretical and experimental work underlying the idea of the superiority of group thinking assumes a relatively homogeneous group. Orwell said (in *Animal Farm*), "All animals are equal but some animals are more equal than others." Here we assume a bunch of bright people discussing an important project. Early in the discussion, everybody feels comfortable about tossing out ideas and opinions. But then it begins to emerge that the CEO of the corporation favors the project. The path becomes increasingly steep and lonely for those who disagree. There is a persistent tendency in even the most "democratic" groups to observe the principle of *primus inter pares—*" first among equals."

Not that these bright and accomplished people are sitting there saying to themselves, "Aha! It looks as if Chuck is for this, so I better be for it too." CEOs of successful companies don't get that way by encouraging key people to be blatant yes-men. Or at least that used to be the case. As we discuss elsewhere, in recent years we have seen the rise of the "in-your-face" management style, in which the boss relishes his ability to scare underlings.

No. Smart, opinionated people don't usually turn into toadies when they find themselves in disagreement, even with the topmost bosses. They adjust in another way. Their subconscious minds do the job of rearranging reality.

The psychologist Leon Festinger has given us the valuable concept of "cognitive dissonance." Difficult decisions or conflicting challenges set up a dissonance in the mind. Below the conscious level the mind works to resolve the dissonance. One means of resolution involves changing perceptions to conform with wishes.

Cognitive dissonance pops up in various contexts throughout our study. It's a powerful factor in individual and group thinking. People who make decisions should be aware of it.

Smart groups make dumb mistakes when they stop using their minds to look for answers and start using their magnified mental power to justify what they want to do. Self-justification is by no means exclusively confined to high IQs. We all do it. But smart people do it adroitly and imaginatively; and smart groups of people can become like mighty mechanisms linked in series to perform astounding feats.

In the condition *folie à deux* two persons share the same delusional beliefs. *Folie aux beaucoup* sweeps many people, lemminglike, over the precipice of dumbness. When those people are particularly smart people, they use particularly effective ploys to urge one another on to catastrophe.

One such device is *punishment of the deviant individual.* When you disagree with a person of average or lower intelligence you may risk a punch in the jaw, but you need not fear rapier thrusts of mockery and laser beam attacks on your reasoning processes that make you look and feel like a dummy.

A shrewd observer postulates the six phases of a project:

1. Enthusiasm
2. Disillusionment
3. Panic
4. Search for the guilty
5. Punishment of the innocent
6. Praise and honor for the nonparticipants

Groups tend to require conformity. Elite groups—though they may give lip service to individual freedom and the right to dissent—can be especially effective in keeping people in line. Richard S. Lazarus, professor emeritus of psychology, University of California, Berkeley, writes, "The more confidence a subject has in the group (e.g., if it is believed to be highly expert or composed of high-status persons) the greater the pressure to conform."[3]

Lazarus calls attention to the ways in which "the group punishes deviant individuals, thereby demonstrating a motivational basis of conformity in us all." He cites particularly a classic study by S. Schachter[4] in which university groups responded to heretics, first by reasoning and arguing with them, then by ignoring them, and ultimately by giving them low ratings and refraining from giving them important appointments.

Lazarus also calls attention to studies that "show powerful and damaging conformity pressures on presidential advisers responsible for governmental policy blunders such as the Bay of Pigs invasion and the Vietnam war."

The Cult of Expertise

Organizations pay so much for expertise that they can be led astray by it. *The PA Perspective*—a March 1994 newsletter from Princeton Associates, a management consulting firm—draws our attention to "that insidious, mind-crippling disease that Herman Kahn referred to as Educated Incapacity: 'Experts so often turn out to be mistaken because they are experts: they know the past and present in such detail, and have formed such ironclad assumptions, that their knowledge prevents them from anticipating surprises.'

"It seems that the bigger the organization, the more it's affected and infected with this disease. Perhaps that's the reason the average life span of a Fortune 500 company is less than 40 years."

The Best and Brightest Lead Us into the Quagmire

The war in Vietnam remains a salient, bloody, and tragic example of how smart people can group think themselves and many others into calamitous idiocy.

The brain trust assembled by John F. Kennedy was called the "Best and Brightest"—a collection of some of the most powerful intellects in the public and private sector, people with tremendous academic credentials who had also won their spurs outside the scholastic areas. The Best and Brightest included Dean Rusk, McGeorge Bundy, and, notably, Robert McNamara, Kennedy's Secretary of Defense.

McNamara had been one of the brightest stars among the Ford "Whiz Kids," those scintillating thinkers who were able to generate theories and turn those theories into money-making solutions in one of the most brutally competitive of big industries.

After Kennedy's assassination in November 1963, McNamara and his associates put their abilities at the disposal of the new president, Lyndon Baines Johnson. The most important baggage they carried over from the previous administration was Vietnam.

The Best and Brightest were the intellectual mainspring of the United States war in Vietnam, a war that today is almost universally seen as a tragic blunder that killed 60,000 Americans and 1.3 million Vietnamese, blighted a large area of the world, and hacked gashes in the American psyche that have yet to heal.

Here is a key memorandum, signed by McNamara, Rusk, and Bundy, along with Generals Maxwell Taylor, William Westmoreland, and Earle Wheeler (as quoted in Doris Kearns's book about Johnson):[5]

The Viet Cong seem to believe that South Vietnam is on the run and near collapse. There are no signs of their settling for anything less than a complete takeover.

We must choose among three courses of action:

(a) Cut our losses and withdraw under the best of conditions that can be arranged—almost certainly conditions humiliating the United States and very damaging to our future effectiveness on the world scene.

(b) Continue at about the present level, with the U.S. forces limited to say 75,000, holding on and playing for breaks—a course of action which, because our position would grow weaker, almost certainly would confront us later with a choice between withdrawal and an emergency expansion of forces, perhaps too late to do any good.

(c) Expand promptly and substantially the U.S. military pressure against the Viet Cong in the South and maintain the military pressure against the North Vietnamese in the North while launching a vigorous effort on the political side to lay the groundwork for a favorable outcome by clarifying our objectives and establishing channels of communication. This alternative would stave off defeat in the short run and offer a good chance of producing a favorable settlement in the longer run; at the same time it would imply a commitment to see a fighting war clear through at considerable cost in casualties and matériel and would make any later decision to withdraw even more difficult and even more costly than would be the case today.

A brilliant document in its way, which is not surprising when you consider the brilliance of its authors. The memo purports to present three options, as if they were the only options available. But of course the way options (a) and (b) are presented, they are not viable options at all. Look at the language in which they are couched: "cut our losses . . . humiliating . . . damaging . . . playing for breaks . . . weaker . . . too late to do any good." When the choice is put this way, to the Texan Lyndon Johnson there is only one way to go—option (c). This was the path that Johnson took, and the result was ten more years of conflict and ultimate defeat.

What all the wise men promised has not happened, and what all the damned fools predicted has come to pass.
  Lord Melbourne (British prime minister, 1834, 1835–41)

This pivotal memorandum is of course most important because it exemplifies the thinking that pushed the country deeper and deeper into a hideous, brutal, and finally unwinnable war. Beyond that, it is useful to us as an example of collective stupidity perpetrated by highly intelligent people.

Here we see the grip that *idea infatuation* can get on intellectuals. Most people of average cognitive attainment don't become theoreticians to any great degree. We tend to be pragmatic. But to outstanding minds, theory is important, and it can become all-important. Einstein was something of an endearing figure of fun when he came out with his theory of relativity, which no one understood and which most people could not see as having any practical application. When Einstein's pronouncement that light could be bent by gravity turned out to be true, the world paid attention and acclaimed him as a genius, though the products of his extraordinary brain were not regarded as eminently practical. But when the equation $E=mc^2$ turned into the atom bomb that destroyed Hiroshima, the world knew once and for all that the formulations of intellectuals can have immense consequences. The world has been relearning that lesson ever since.

Neurotic Organizations

The president who relied on the expertise of the best and brightest was Lyndon B. Johnson. Johnson's presidency failed when he was unable to provide both guns and butter—to fight on to victory in Vietnam and, at the same time, give America the Great Society. Johnson, seeing the disgust of the country rising at the endless slaughter in Indochina, decided not to run for re-election in 1968.

Under Lyndon Johnson the United States government was an unfortunate paradigm of the organization that collapses because smart people do stupid things—and keep on doing them.

Johnson himself manifested some of the great flaws discussed in this book. His ego was vast. It required constant feeding. Doris Kearns writes:

The constant encouragement he demanded deadened the critical faculties of those still allowed access, creating a vacuum around himself and making him a prisoner of his own propaganda. Screening out options, facts and ideas, Lyndon Johnson's personality operated to distort the truth in much the same way as ideology works in a totalitarian society. . . .

Over time, Johnson tacitly developed an anticipatory system that discouraged views that the President would not receive favorably from being communicated to him.[6]

But the people around Lyndon Johnson were not wimps or lightweights. How could they have collaborated in folly for so long? Why did they permit themselves to be treated as vassals by Johnson?

Kearns explains:

To understand how the men in Johnson's White House, few of whom could be considered weak or submissive, eventually played a role in what might be called a *folie à plus*, it is important to understand the state of dependency imposed on a President's top advisers by the modern structure of the White House.

Kearns quotes Johnson's aide George Reedy, who said, "The life of the White House is the life of a court." The leader "is treated with all the reverence due a monarch."

Kearns and Reedy are describing a sick organization. Corporations, like governments, get sick. They become addictive; the addictions of the group are the sum total of the addictions of the individuals in the group. Elsewhere in this book we quote Brendan Sexton, an official in the New York mayoral administration of Edward Koch, on how executives become hooked on good news. Johnson got hooked on good news. So did his key people. So all they got from Vietnam was good news, while in reality the situation was very bad and getting worse.

Anne Wilson Schaef and Diane Fassel wrote an insightful book called *The Addictive Organization*. They comment:

The organization becomes the addictive substance for its employees when the employees become hooked on the promise of the mission and choose not to look at how the system is really operating. The organization becomes an addictive substance when its actions are excused because it has a lofty mission.[7]

Like individuals who abandon logic in the pursuit of a large goal or a worthy cause, groups of likeminded, intelligent people lobotomize themselves collectively when they are hypnotized by the mission they jointly pursue. And they support each other in folly; when one member gets an occasional glimmer of sanity, the others band together to bring the errant member back to a satisfactory condition of idiocy.

Here is an example of an addictive pattern followed by an individual that becomes a pattern for the group. John Safer, a banker and prominent sculptor, tells the story of an entrepreneur—let's call him Joe Wilbur—who went into the real estate business in the Washington, D.C. area in the 1950s. Wilbur got a few friends to invest some money with him. He bought some land, leveraged it via bank and insurance company loans, put up an apartment building. His timing was excellent. The value of the building went up while it was being built, and continued to go up after it was completed.

In less than two years, Joe Wilbur was worth nearly a million dollars. (John Safer remarks, "Remember, this was in the fifties, when you could still buy a Cadillac Fleetwood for three thousand dollars and a nice home in the Washington area for twenty thousand dollars, and in many parts of the country for half that.")

By the late 1960s, Wilbur was considered one of the wealthiest developers in the United States. He owned apartments, office buildings, a sports arena, a professional team.

Wilbur had developed a pattern. He would buy land for top dollar, outbidding all competition. The land was almost always in marginal neighborhoods, from which more conservative developers would shy away. Wilbur would personally sign notes to finance his purchases.

Wilbur now had an organization. He decided to undertake his most ambitious project yet, a huge office building. His team went along with him, leveraging everything to the hilt to get construction started. And then—disaster! There were unforeseen problems with the ground on which the building was to stand. The foundations began to sag. Construction stopped. So did the loan advances.

And Joe Wilbur lost everything.

He still had his old magnetism. He attracted new backing, started up his organization again, followed the same approach as before.

And disaster struck again!

Here was a pattern of addiction to a certain approach. It's a hair-raising approach. Some become hooked on it. It seems to have a special appeal to real estate operators. Someone once asked William Zeckendorf, Sr., the extreme risk-taking developer, why he operated the way he did. Zeckendorf replied, "I'd rather be alive at twenty-eight percent than dead at the prime rate."

A magnetic leader communicates the virus to his whole organization, even when that organization comprises bright, independent individuals who don't have to kiss the boss's boots to make a living. They go along with doomed policies, when they know them to be doomed. And, amazingly enough, they'll go along with the same policies a second and a third time!

Schaef and Fassel write, "*Loss of corporate memory, or forgetfulness, is an outstanding characteristic of the addictive organization. People have said of addicts that they cannot learn from their past behavior, because they have no memory. This is one of the aspects of the disease. Addictive organizations have the same problem.*"

The business consultants Lisa J. Marshall and Sandra Mobley—in a 1992 white paper called "Too Smart to Learn: Musings on an Organizational Paradox"—ask, "What causes an organization to succeed at one moment in time and fail at another? While each example [of corporate failure] has its own context, its own realities and constraints, the authors believe they all share one thing in common. They were built and staffed by brilliant people who became convinced that they had figured out 'THE WAY' to do their business. They were right, given the circumstances. Yet when these circumstances changed, these brilliant people failed to see it or believe that it mattered. In other words, they failed to learn."

It happens over and over. The leader has a pet idea. A young manager in a food company, like multitudes of young managers, used to think about his ideal product. He came up with one: Nut Yogurt.

The young manager reached the policy-making level. Unlike many of us, who discard the dreams of youth, he retained his dream. Nut Yogurt would be a winner! He plunged ahead, carrying his marketing staff with him. Huge supplies of the product were produced. Customers would not touch it with a ten-foot spoon. The executive was compelled, in effect, to eat all the Nut Yogurt.

Dr. Valentine Appel, the well-known market research consultant, says, "Strong leaders can become so dedicated to a particular idea or concept that they cannot see the flaws. And they are so good at defending their ideas that nobody can get through to them."

The Ostrich Outlook

There's an old story about the band of ostriches that hears something approaching. Being ostriches, they do what comes naturally. The newcomer is a fellow ostrich who looks at all the birds with their heads in the sand and exclaims, "Hey, where is everybody?"

Some organizations have an extraordinary inability to see outside their own perimeters, or to consider how certain activities, which seem perfectly all right within the ostrich circle, might seem from the outside. We see one example in a sidelight of the story of the decline and fall of Gitano Jeans.

Gitano had been in trouble for some time. The company hit the headlines in December 1991, when gun-waving U.S. Customs agents stormed Gitano's headquarters in New York, seizing cartons of financial records.

Following the raid, the company—along with the Dabah family, which had founded the jeans empire—was engulfed in scandal. Charges of ineptitude and corruption jostled with charges of abysmal financial controls and illegal internal deals.

The clouds had been gathering over Gitano for quite a while before the storm broke. But the Dabahs—although they were smart and successful entrepreneurs—acted as if they did not have a care in the world. "These guys thought they were bulletproof," said one observer.

For some people close to the scene, the last straw came a few months before the raid. Haim Dabah, the son of Gitano's founder, hosted one thousand guests at his son's bar mitzvah in the Grand Ballroom of the Waldorf Astoria. The *Wall Street Journal* reported, "There was Lester Lanin's forty-piece orchestra, a cake baked in the shape of the Wailing Wall and a troupe of lambada dancers that the family flew in from Brazil. But the flourish that brought gasps was a glass-enclosed wind tunnel filled with one-dollar bills. Each child at the party was briefly escorted into the chamber to grab as many fistfuls of dollars as he or she could."[8]

People in the clothing business know appearances are important. The Dabahs knew they were under scrutiny. The unrestrained festivities would surely inflame the feelings of creditors and regulators. But the show had to go on.

"Let's Put Our Heads Together and Screw Up"

We see collective dumbness by smart people at all levels, in government, in community work, in industry. An August 16, 1993 *Business Week* story on product failure gives some telling examples. In the 1980s, General Motors saw younger buyers being lured away from

Cadillac by BMW and Mercedes-Benz. GM's policy makers concluded that a luxury car with snappy Euro-styling would win back this important customer base.

The theory having been formulated, all that remained to be done was to actually design and make the car. The result was the Allanté, a posh coupe priced at more then $54,000. Allanté was launched in 1987 and sank without a trace almost immediately. The car would go out of production within a disappointingly short time.

For one time, while the Allanté may have emulated its European rivals in styling, it fell considerably short of them in power. The 170-horsepower engine just did not give the car the zip to go with the sleek lines.

The lines were a modern departure for Cadillac, but the body, handcrafted in Italy, turned out to be not especially well made. The car squeaked. The wind noise was loud. The roof leaked.

These problems did not appear like bolts from the blue after the Allanté's introduction. The quality control professionals were doing their job and pointing out the flaws. But the Allanté was more than just a car. It was the focal point of a carefully worked out strategy, which had evolved out of an important theory.

The strategy was geared to a kickoff date. GM had ballyhooed the car; the launching ceremonies had been planned, in their own way, as carefully as the car. The choice was delay the launch and fix the car or launch on time and sell the car warts and all.

GM launched according to schedule. The car, said *Business Week*, was "too small and expensive for core Cadillac buyers, but not really good enough to lure import buyers."

The Allanté had the potential to be a good car: they put in a 295-horsepower engine and an electronic transmission while pushing the price up to more than $60,000. But by this time the market had turned its back on Allanté.

General Motors brought the Allanté failure on itself. However, the notorious Case of the Exploding Trucks started with some problems affecting GM pickups, but was exacerbated when NBC's "Dateline" decided to run an exposé of GM.

The subject matter was dramatic: pickup trucks that burst into flames when hit from the side. There had been a spate of lawsuits against the big auto company. "Dateline" is one of the many magazine shows striving to match the long-running success of "60 Minutes," which has delighted millions over the years with the spectacle of some miscreant or other being confronted by Mike Wallace with the proof of his villainy and disintegrating into babbling confusion. But the most dramatic footage of all is found when the show can run an actual visual demonstration of the misdeed.

This is what "Dateline" decided to do. It wasn't enough to talk with the survivors of people who had been burned to death in the suspect vehicles. What would really be sensational would be to show one of the GM trucks actually blowing up right before the eyes of the audience. Think what that would do for ratings!

"Dateline" ran the story, and lo and behold, a GM pickup was struck amidships in a staged accident and exploded into a satisfying eruption of flame.

Then it came out. "Dateline"—perhaps not sure the truck would explode—had helped things along by strapping rockets to the fuel tanks. NBC had to abase itself before millions with an on-air apology. General Motors, which had been getting very bad press about its posture in the lawsuits, was transformed into a victim. NBC News, which produced the show, became the target of investigation. The president of NBC News resigned. "Dateline" found itself at the center of a scandal.

Obviously a lot of smart people had to be involved in putting the story on "Dateline's" agenda, planning the segment, and particularly in using rockets to blow up the truck while the audience was left to infer that the explosion was the result of the kind of accident that might take place on the road anytime.

What happened? At some point it became more important to provide a satisfying climax than to maintain integrity. After all, let's face it; the thrust of the "Dateline" segment was hardly likely to be that there was nothing to the lawsuits against GM, that the trucks were perfectly safe.

The people putting on the show had an objective—not the holding of a real test to gauge the riskiness of the truck, but rather a ratings-building conflagration. Once the group had locked onto that target, it looked for the best means of hitting it.

Slaves of System

The above examples of smart people collaborating to commit folly share two elements: goal and system.

Everybody has goals, of course. The Knights of the Round Table had a goal: the Holy Grail. (The Oxford scholar Benjamin Jowett was fond of asking, "After they found the Holy Grail, what were they going to do with it?") But King Arthur's knights did not have a system— they didn't band together to locate the Grail; each went off on his own or sometimes with another knight. If they had gotten together they might have found it faster and with less trouble, and kept Gala-had from getting all the credit.

Obviously not all collaborations involve smart people. The conspir-ators who smashed Nancy Kerrigan's knee had a Grail: Olympic gold and commercial loot. But they emphatically cannot be described as smart.

Most people of normal mental capacity don't spend all that much time on concept and system, because they lack the equipment to handle it. Smart people have the advantage of being able to deal with abstractions in a way that allows them to construct complex intellec-tual systems.

But at the same time, people of high intelligence run the risk of *be-ing trapped within the web of the systems their formidable minds have spun so skillfully.* The system takes over, develops a life of its own, enslaves its creators, blinds them to inconvenient realities, compels them to march in lockstep in the service of the system, long after the scheme has demonstrated glaring faults.

Smart individuals allow the end to dictate the means. Cyril Burt's concept of the identical twins who proved his theory of inherited intelligence got such a grip on his mind that he started to invent sets of twins. When a team of smart collaborators goes off the track, the shared folly feeds on itself. The team members reinforce one another. And they use the pressure of the group to keep members in line.

A diverse group, with each member free to voice opinions, may not always come up with the right answer—or even a good answer. Group dynamics presents some complex problems. However, the collective approach usually steers clear of extremes of folly, even if it misses the height of brilliance.

However, a group of highly intelligent people can, under certain circumstances, go careening off the track together.

Notes

1. *New York Times*, April 7, 1994, "Phone-Card Promotion May Be Promoting Fraud," by Stuart Elliott.
2. Gardner Murphy, Lois Barclay Murphy, and Theodore M. Newcomb, *Experimental Social Psychology* (New York: Harper & Brothers, 1937), pp. 734–735.
3. Richard S. Lazarus, *Emotion & Adaptation* (New York: Oxford University Press, 1991), pp. 374–375.
4. S. Schachter, "Deviation, Rejection and Communication," *Journal of Abnormal Psychology*, Vol. 46, 1951.
5. Doris Kearns, *Lyndon Johnson and the American Dream* (New York: Harper & Row, 1976), pp. 280–281.
6. Kearns, op. cit., pp. 323–324.
7. Anne Wilson Schaef and Diane Fassel, *The Addictive Organization* (New York: Harper & Row, 1988), p. 123.
8. *Wall Street Journal*, February 18, 1994, "Out of Control: Gitano Jeans' Fall Is Saga of Corruption and Mismanagement," by Teri Agins.

Part II.

HOW TO EQUIP AND USE YOUR OWN SMART SPA

We go to spas to keep our bodies fit. Or we build spas in our homes—pool, Jacuzzi, stair climber, weights, rowing machine, ski-walker.

Why not a spa for the mind?

Minds should be kept in tone as well as muscles. Intelligence carries within it a self-destructive potential, fostered by isolation and hubris. The concluding chapters of this book describe certain exercises that mitigate the main causes of SDIS and give the Superior Cognitive Intelligence Possessing Individual deeper self-insight, greater maturity, and a strong guidance system.

Your Mind Is Your Spa

We have been exploring the ways in which smart people use their own brainpower to hurt themselves. Luckily, smart people can use that same brainpower to furnish an inner spa, and to use that spa regularly to exercise intellectual muscles that aren't used enough; to enhance their self-insight; to build up their immunity to logic override; and to keep all aspects of their personalities growing at a healthy rate.

The spa is within your mind. In the pages that follow we suggest certain pieces of equipment and certain courses of exercise.

You will, of course, adapt the recommendations to fit your needs, situation, and individuality.

The important thing is to adopt the concept of the personal mind spa. You feel better physically after working out. There's more spring in your step. You react faster. You're brisk . . . up . . . motivated.

The smart spa does the same for you cognitively and emotionally. You read other people more acutely. You handle tough mental challenges better. You find your mind is more supple and durable, able to work longer without getting tired.

Most important, you strengthen the weak spots in your mental and emotional armor, build your resistance to error, and enhance your ability to make vital decisions and instant judgments in the confidence that you are not committing big mistakes.

You'll find a number of programs in the smart spa:

- *Self-Scoping*—how you see yourself, how others see you, bridging the gap
- *Growth Profile*—yardsticks of maturity
- *Guidance Control*—constructing and maintaining a values compass
- *Connectors*—continuing contact points with the real world
- *The Smart Relationship*—partnering for protection against SDIS

They're bracing exercises, easy but stimulating. They won't make you smarter—you're smart enough already. But they'll help to keep your intellect channeled to positive uses—and they'll protect you against the kind of disastrous dumbness that befalls only really smart people.

Chapter 10.

WHAT'S YOUR SDIS PROFILE?

SCIPIs—Superior Cognitive Intelligence Possessing Individuals—carry, concealed in their psyches, the potential for self-destruction. As one of this elite group you're among the designated Masters of the Universe, but that won't be much consolation if you screw up.

So let's not screw up. This is the point for you to start identifying your maximum points of vulnerability. Don't waste time wondering whether you harbor the SDIS virus. That's a given; it goes along with your IQ. Now's the time to consider the varieties of self-inflicted intellectual wounds we have been viewing in the SDIS laboratory, and to pinpoint those toward which you most incline.

We've seen a number of SDIS types.

Risk junkies take long chances for the sake of taking chances, or to prove that they are gutsier than the other guys, or just because they are bored. They're smarter and quicker than the people around them. Their agility keeps them balanced on a narrower and narrower limb as they edge ever farther outward. But when there is no limb at all, they crash.

Envelope busters go beyond pushing the envelope. The art of envelope pushing is to extend one's capabilities to the very limit of every nook and cranny of possibility—*without* puncturing it. Envelope busters always go too far.

Disconnectors lose touch with reality. Their brains enable them to reshape facts into a more pleasing configuration.

Entitlement freaks figure that because they want something they are entitled to have it. They use formidable ingenuity and acumen to gratify their wishes, by fair means or foul.

Self-sellers turn their persuasive powers inward, to convince themselves of things that they enjoy hearing. Their self-persuasion floods out their logical faculties.

Concept mavens develop ingenious theories and then apply those theories in the wrong places, using their formidable intellectual firepower to shoot down the objections of those who try to warn about the flaws.

These profiles, and others, are formed by a mix of hubris, narcissism, arrogance, and the need to fail—the cornerstones of intellectual self-destruction. SDIS operates in all areas of life—business decisions, career choices, money matters, relationships. Here are a few cases.

AT LAST, THE ANSWERS I WANT! Susan inspires the key management team of her company with her fervent desire to transcend the company's domestic markets and go global. She targets Eastern Europe—Poland, Russia, and other countries from the former Soviet Union. Before plunging ahead, Susan and her key aides agree that they had better take thorough research soundings. Proper market testing has been one of the hallmarks of the firm's success.

The company retains a well-known international market research firm. The researchers report that their project will take more time; it is hard to get reliable information in some of the potential markets; and, where information is available, it is hard to interpret it.

These are not answers that please Susan. She has laid out a timetable for penetration of the new target markets. She fires the market research firm and hires another group, a small, previously unknown firm that claims to specialize in Eastern Europe. Susan hires them on the basis of a snappy presentation and their promise to come back fast with the answers she wants.

And, lo and behold, they *do* come back fast—and with the desired answers. Waving away the reservations of the marketing director and others, Susan commits the company to full-scale entry into the market, staking the bulk of the firm's resources on the effort. The results are disastrous. Why didn't the research provide a warning? Because the fly-by-night firm that the CEO insisted on retaining faked the data.

But they did give her the answers she wanted.

TURNING WEAKNESS INTO DISASTER. Wilson had not fudged his résumé any more than people usually do when he got the job. There were a few soft spots in his background that he had covered. The Human Resource VP who interviewed him had not zeroed in on the weak spots—for example, the one where Wilson claimed to be doing consulting work for the Guatemalan government for a year.

The fact is that the HR manager, who had seen every form of deception, suspected that Wilson's background was not quite as he claimed in this respect. But Wilson had strengths that made him worth hiring, so the employer took a pass on the questionable claims.

But then, on the job, Wilson began to tout his experience in Central America, pushing himself forward as the ideal person to spearhead a new company effort in that part of the world. Wilson not only repeated the fallacious claims he had made, he elaborated on them, adding details that could be readily checked. The HR executive warned him, indirectly, about this. But by now Wilson felt he had to protect and enhance his reputation as a specialist.

He was not a specialist; his credentials were bogus; he was confronted, exposed, humiliated, and let go.

HE KNOWS I'M NOT LIKE THE OTHERS. Elizabeth was the first female senior account executive to go to work for Hambleton Associates, a small advertising agency in Englewood, Colorado, serving growing businesses in the Denver area. Jess Hambleton, the founder and head of the firm, was a charismatic leader, great at impressing clients, a popcorn machine of ideas, but not very good at following through and servicing accounts.

That was fine with Elizabeth. Meticulous attention to account service was her long suit. She thought she could learn a lot from Jess.

One thing she learned early was that Jess—a genial and generous man in most respects—had a coldblooded and primitive approach to women. He would, without any pretense, hire an attractive executive assistant with the understanding that an important part of the job was sleeping with him. At the same time, though, Jess implied that he was interested in a long-term relationship, probably marriage. He was a good-looking guy, with sophisticated tastes, money, and savoir-faire. When Elizabeth joined the firm, Jess was involved with Marci, a pretty but rather wide-eyed girl twenty years younger than the boss. Marci adored Jess. She was willing to do anything for him. He installed her in his condo as his consort.

Then, one day, Marci, pale and distraught, appeared at Elizabeth's door. Jess had tired of her, thrown her out, fired her. She was desolate. What could she do?

Elizabeth could offer little comfort.

Jess installed a new secretary, Dinah, if anything prettier and more innocent than Marci. The pattern played itself out again. Dinah was crowned Jess's queen, lifted to the top of the world. The people in the office watched, cynically, as the story unfolded. The guys who had been there a long time had seen it happen a number of times. Dinah was going to be chewed up and spat out.

Elizabeth didn't know how she felt. She would hate to see the girl hurt; but, after all, it was none of her business. Dinah was a grown-up. She should have her eyes wide open. It wasn't up to Elizabeth, as the only senior woman in the outfit, to play the role of Mother Superior. Besides, Elizabeth liked Jess. He was witty, he was fun, he was good at his job, and he dealt with Elizabeth as a professional equal.

Sure enough, one morning Dinah was gone, suddenly, dumped by the boss.

Who would be the next incumbent? Jess watchers joked about the "credentials" of the next executive assistant. Elizabeth herself joined in some of the comic speculation.

Amazingly, the new secretary was altogether different: Ruth, a hard-boiled veteran, totally unlike her predecessors in looks, temperament, and attitude, egregiously married and in no way a candidate for the post of inamorata.

Jess, over a drink with Elizabeth, said he had turned over a new leaf. He realized he had been irresponsible in hiring secretaries as mistresses. Ruth was a responsible choice; she could act as office manager, and the place would be more efficient.

Along with this revelation, Jess disclosed that he realized his succession of nubile companions had left him unfulfilled. Good in bed was not enough; there had to be a meeting of the minds. He needed to have a relationship with somebody to whom he could really talk.

Realizing with some surprise that Jess was putting the moves on her, Elizabeth was, at first, amused. She had heard some innovative lines, but nothing as smooth and seductive as this. Then she got to thinking. Why not? Of course, she would never consider moving in with Jess, playing the same role as the young secretaries; but why not go out with him, and see what developed? She was not involved with anyone at the moment, and Jess was attractive, polished, and able to afford the best in wining, dining, and entertainment.

Around the office, Elizabeth noted the knowing looks of her colleagues. She didn't care. Her relationship with Jess was a coming together of grown-ups. She was not making a total commitment, she was not moving in, it did not affect her career. And, besides, while by now sex was a fixture of the relationship, obviously there was more to it than that. Jess had been primitive and brutal in his dealings with the secretaries, and he was the first to admit it. But this was different.

Nevertheless, when Jess suggested that Elizabeth move in with him, she hesitated. Was it conceivable that she could go the way of Dinah and Marci and the others, chewed up and spat out? No way; she was no Dinah, no Marci.

Elizabeth moved in with Jess. She found herself in a deeper and stranger relationship by far than any she had ever experienced before. There were things about Jess she wanted to change. And she would change them. This time he was serious; it would not be long, Elizabeth was sure, before he told her he wanted to get married. They would run the firm together, as partners. The deal had its dangers; Elizabeth prided herself on being realistic. But on the whole, when it came she would be ready for it.

After five o'clock one evening, in the office, Elizabeth looked in Jess's door to see if he was ready to leave. He beckoned her in, said it had all been very nice, but now it was over. He handed her an envelope with her severance check, told her that her packed suitcases were in her car, downstairs in the office parking lot.

And that was it! Unbelievingly, Elizabeth heard herself pleading— for her place in his affection, for her career. He was cool, deft, and skillful; he had been through it all before.

Elizabeth found herself out in the cold—emotionally lacerated, humiliated, derided by her fellow professionals.

Confronted with all the evidence of Jess's pattern, she had focused on the illusory elements that seemed to her to indicate a change. She had performed prodigious feats of mental gymnastics to persuade herself that *this time, with her, it would be different.*

THE FINANCIAL BUNGEE JUMPER. Investment adviser Jeff was making a name for himself and a fortune for his clients through a shrewd mixture of sharp timing, understanding of his clients' needs, and well-thought-out portfolio mixes balancing aggressiveness with safe plays. Entrusted with his biggest opportunity by far, a large institution, Jeff abandoned the approach that had earned him his reputation. Instead he put his client, a staid old-line organization, into the cyclonic vortex of world currency speculation on a massive scale. One night Jeff guessed wrong, big time, on the Deutschemark. The portfolio imploded: so did Jeff's business, reputation, and future.

SHE'LL NEVER FIND OUT. Hensley is regarded by his fellow mathematicians as a genius. His formulations are renowned for their elegance and their bull's-eye applicability to the solution of problems. His family life is, most would assume, idyllic. He loves his wife, Frieda. Frieda is an exceptional person too—intelligent, humorous, attractive. Working as a team, they have written two best-selling books and are the stars of a popular and influential show on public television.

Hensley's love for Frieda transcends practicality, but even if he were not so deeply in love, it would make sense for him to maintain the relationship.

So why is the mathematician sleeping with one of his graduate students in the beach house he shares with his family? Hensley does not even particularly like the graduate student. Frieda, on her last visit to the beach house, has already noted some anomalies. It's only a matter of time until she finds out, especially since Hensley is spending the night with the student in the house just before Frieda is scheduled to arrive there early the next morning.

THEY ALL SEE IT THE SAME WAY I DO. Ken was walking on air when he went to Michigan City, Indiana, to take over as president of New Excelsior, Inc. Ken had been executive vice president for a large office furniture company in Chicago. When Tom Ferry, the board chairman of New Excelsior, hired Ken, Ferry had growled, "Never hired anybody from outside before. But I guess things change. We're into new lines and we need new thinking."

New Excelsior had pioneered the use of fiberglass in industrial applications: utilitarian structural members that offered few esthetic treats to the eye, but which stood up under wear for a long time.

Ken was intrigued by a possible big new market. This was a new industry for him; but he had put in some intensive time reading everything there was to read, talking to people, going to trade shows. He had learned that there was new machinery that could mold reinforced fiberglass into delicate and complex shapes, brilliantly colored. Ken's idea was to make a new line of products for commercial buildings and outdoor signs.

The company was closely held by the Ferry family. Luther Ferry, Tom's nephew, had been earmarked for the top job. But Luther, as sales manager, had allowed himself to grow fat and lazy. His idea of selling was schmoozing with clients and prospects over meals and drinks. Tom Ferry wanted something more dynamic.

Ken thought he would be at odds with Luther. But Luther could not have been more agreeable. Ken outlined his ideas for moving aggressively into the market for exterior architectural decoration. Luther said, "Gosh, do you think we can handle that, production-wise?" "No. Got to tool up," said Ken. "There's some programmed equipment they're developing in Germany. It will cost money, but I've already looked into that, we have the leverage with the bank. Of course it isn't just plant and equipment; the big change, frankly, has to be in our marketing." Ken braced for resistance, but Luther nodded.

"Guess we have to keep up with changing times. . . ."

Home free! Ken plunged ahead with his plans. The new machines were installed. Not all of the New Excelsior plant people were able to respond to retraining, so new talent was hired.

Luther's approach to selling—wining and dining construction engineers to get them to specify New Excelsior products—did not fit into Ken's plans. He held meetings, had four-color brochures printed, advertised in trade magazines.

One day, eighteen months after Ken had come on board, Tom Ferry said, "We're not moving as fast as I hoped."

"Takes time to establish credibility and penetrate," said Ken. But Ferry's real problem was that New Excelsior's bread-and-butter market—structural components—had fallen off.

Ken said, "Frankly, I'm glad you brought that up, Tom. I've been leaving that row to Luther to plow. And I'm afraid he hasn't been cutting it. Maybe it's time for us . . ."

Ken thought this was the time to consider putting poor Luther out to pasture. Instead, he learned, to his growing horror, Tom Ferry had mended fences with his nephew. Furthermore, the chairman was more inclined to cut back, revert to the methods that would secure the company's core business, and retrench severely on efforts to penetrate new markets.

That required the company to go in a new—or, rather, an old—direction. And to go in an old direction you call on an old steersman.

Good old boy Luther was in; Ken was out.

Ken had irised down so that the new market opportunity filled the entire lens. He had lost the surrounding context. He had disconnected from reality.

THE VICTORY CELEBRATION. A fledgling public relations firm had just landed its biggest account, a good-size bank. The client's top brass attended a little party at the agency's offices. George, the agency president, thrilled but exhausted, lifted his glass to the bank's chairman—who had not participated much in the negotiations. The agency president started to say what he liked about the client organization. Emboldened by the chairman's attention and stimulated by success and vodka, the agency chief then went on to what he did *not* like. His monologue grew more sweeping and expansive.

This kind of commentary had been a feature of the meetings leading up to the choice of the agency. The bank's president and marketing director had liked George's candor.

The monologue continued. The agency president went further than he had ever gone before; after all, they were all in the same boat now, right? But the chairman did not appreciate the frankness. George commented afterward, "I could see him icing up right in front of my eyes, but I couldn't stop myself. By the time I got finished I had blown the whole deal. It was like if you went onto the stage to accept the Nobel Prize and kicked the King of Sweden in the balls."

The bank reversed its decision and renewed the search, winding up with a bigger, more traditional agency. The man who threw it all away was forced to endure the reproaches of his colleagues and his own self-flagellation. One day, however, he said to a friend, "You know, we went bananas when we thought we won that account. But deep down, I guess I was wondering if we could really service the account. Sure, we're creative enough. But were we really ready to grow up and get gray hair and be a conventional agency? What would be the fun in that?"

He had his doubts. So, in the moment of triumph, he threw away a prize he wasn't sure he wanted to win.

BULLETPROOF. Here's another aftermath of victory.

Gavin was the youngest president in the history of his company. He had been cautious in dealing with the board of directors, a substantial number of whom mistrusted him because of his age and his pursuit of new ideas.

For more than a year Gavin had been working hard on a major expansion. His plan required considerable funding, union cooperation, and government assent, including regulatory changes by federal and state authorities. The "old fogies" muttered that Gavin would never achieve his pipe dream. He gritted his teeth, smiled, and forged ahead.

And at last he pulled it off! The last piece fell into place. Inflated with triumph, he faced the board and, for the first time, stopped treating them with kid gloves. "This is the way we're going to do it," he said. After all, they couldn't touch him now; he was bulletproof.

What Gavin overlooked was that his great accomplishment was only the first step. He had cleared the way for the expansion, but the dream was not yet a bottom line reality. Gavin knew the rest would be relatively easy. But the others did not know that. His cavalier treatment of the board turned just enough members against him to tip the balance. His wings were clipped, his scope reduced, his funding cut—and at last he was forced out.

THEY WORK FOR ME, DON'T THEY? Terry felt entitled to treat her underlings as a harem in just about every way *except* sexually. Sending people for coffee and Danish was just the beginning. Personal errands. Baby-sitting. Meetings that she did not feel like attending. Terry's haremizing extended to a wide range of areas. If somebody else had a rug, a chair, or a painting that she liked, she took it.

This continued right up to the point at which Terry's boss received a detailed documentation of her predations. Even though she was very good at what she did, she had to go.

DON'T TREAD ON MY IDEA! Austin scored impressive successes in a short time after he joined the international consulting firm of McClintock & Hodge. Austin's strength lay in his ability to grasp the essence of a client company's culture, possibilities, and problems, and then to devise the proper mix of management techniques—old and new—to achieve improvement.

Austin enjoyed the challenges of his work and the rewards of his success, but his restless intellect wanted something more. He wanted to be known as the creator of a major concept of corporate effectiveness. He read and attended seminars, studying various approaches.

And at last Austin developed his idea, which he called EpiCircle Management. He decided to try it out. McClintock & Hodge had won the choice assignment of working with one of the world's largest companies during a major reorganization. Austin headed up the team. To the astonishment of his colleagues, he insisted on introducing the EpiCircle concept as a major element of the reorganization.

His colleagues argued that this client—proud and tradition bound—was not the place to initiate something so radical. But Austin persisted; he was able to override objections with his armament of persuasive arguments.

EpiCircle Management was launched on its maiden voyage—and sank. The prescription did not work. The patient resisted. The client dropped McClintock & Hodge. And McClintock & Hodge dropped Austin.

FILTERED FEEDBACK. Andy had a great job—roaming the world in search of new theatrical properties that could be transformed into stage extravaganzas at a new theater in the middle of a burgeoning American city. In Italy, Andy found what he considered a gem: a highly successful musical production on a provincial stage that could be expanded and promoted into a hit. The show, called *I, Saviour*, had a religious theme. Andy did not set much store by religion, but he knew how to sell it.

The theater was supported by a variety of local businesses and institutions. Most of them had enough faith in Andy to accept his judgment almost without question. There were, however, a few warning voices raised about *I, Saviour*. One man said the subject matter might offend religious Jews. A woman commented that some Catholics might not be too happy about it either.

Andy had never considered either of these persons to be mental giants. He brushed their objections aside, noting that a few fringe objections would help to sell tickets.

But the opposition quickly swelled beyond the fringe. Established religious leaders from various sides entered the fray as rumors about *I, Saviour* spread. (The rumors were exaggerated; the play was nowhere near as lurid or blasphemous as some said. Andy had not bothered to set people straight; who cared what some superstitious nuts thought?)

Pickets . . . editorial denunciations . . . cancellations . . . uproar. *I Saviour* had to be canceled. Andy never recovered from the fiasco.

It was not that he had shunned all feedback. It was just that he accepted feedback only from those who met his intellectual standards.

WHEN YOU'RE ON A ROLL. Jennifer had worked hard to be promoted to senior vice president and division manager. She had also politicked hard. Her predecessor, Barry, was capable at the job, but had an unfortunate penchant for rubbing people the wrong way. This helped to keep people from giving him the credit he deserved.

Jennifer took advantage of Barry's unpopularity in her successful campaign for the job. Once in place, she determined that she would not fall victim to the same fate. She undertook a whirlwind campaign to upgrade the operation. She fell short in a few areas, but was largely successful. Her success led her to confront the CEO and say, "Being an unsung hero in this company doesn't get you anyplace. Barry was damn good; I think you and the senior policy group underestimated him. I don't want the same thing to happen to me."

The CEO looked at her wonderingly. "I didn't underestimate Barry, but I think you are badly underestimating me. Do you think it was invisible, the way you worked to undermine him?" Jennifer started to protest; she *had*, in fact, though her machinations were invisible.

"We knew what you were doing. We're not running a kindergarten. You're capable and you have a lot of promise, and when you damaged Barry enough we figured it was best all around to give you the job. It was up to Barry to take care of himself. But I guess because I didn't tell you I was wise to your act, you thought I was too dumb to have spotted it. You disappoint me, Jennifer. I'm afraid I have a whole different viewpoint on you."

Sketching Your Profile. Your perceptive faculties, when given the proper commands, may indicate a tendency that, unchecked, might lead on to trouble. You might be inordinately conscious of the perks enjoyed by others as compared to your own. You may have to suppress your frustration when you get answers you don't like. Your gambling impulse may push you toward the brink of wild risk taking—even though you have so far held back from taking the plunge.

Whatever your personal mix of SDIS elements, you can use some of the invigorating exercises in this book to build maturity in all areas of your personality and to keep you in touch with reality.

How Vulnerable Are You?

Do you think you're immune from self-destructive brain backlash? Try this little test. It's not a validated psychological instrument, but it is a useful indicator of your vulnerability to SDIS.

Take the test by yourself; don't share it. Be honest. Take the time to think about your answers.

The SDIS Challenge—A Self-Diagnostic Tool
Answer True, False, or Uncertain.

	True	False	Uncertain
1. Compared to others, I usually come out ahead	___	___	___
2. I love to take risks when the stakes are high	___	___	___
3. Most people like me	___	___	___
4. I know the right things to do, even when I don't do them	___	___	___
5. Nobody else can do the job as well as I can	___	___	___
6. Honest arrogance is better than dishonest humility	___	___	___
7. My mother/father treated me as special	___	___	___
8. When stimulated I can get by on less than five hours of sleep	___	___	___
9. I frequently challenge people in authority	___	___	___
10. I never get mad, I just get even	___	___	___
11. Nothing is accomplished without making waves	___	___	___
12. It's easy for me to see the shortcomings of others	___	___	___
13. I never forget a slight	___	___	___
14. If I'm in a jam I can always think or talk my way out	___	___	___
15. I can fake humility when I don't feel it	___	___	___
16. Thoughts of suicide have never crossed my mind	___	___	___
17. I don't worry about satisfying my partner sexually	___	___	___
18. I set impossible goals for myself	___	___	___
19. I never talk about my past with parents or relatives	___	___	___
20. People who talk about ethics don't live in the real world	___	___	___
21. I rarely explain or apologize	___	___	___
22. I don't trust anybody with my most intimate thoughts	___	___	___

What's Your SDIS Profile?

	True	False	Uncertain
23. When I'm on a roll I don't think about what can go wrong	___	___	___
24. I never feel guilty when I say no to somebody	___	___	___
25. Pressure always brings out the best in me	___	___	___
26. I feel my actions will always be vindicated	___	___	___
27. When making a speech I have difficulty sticking to the script	___	___	___
28. I rarely go back to where I used to live	___	___	___
29. I don't worry about the impression I make on others	___	___	___
30. Life is a series of achievable challenges	___	___	___
31. I'm confident of my sexual attraction and prowess	___	___	___
32. I never put off till tomorrow what I feel like doing today	___	___	___
33. Teachers and parents always forgave my little peccadilloes	___	___	___
34. I can accomplish anything, no matter what the odds	___	___	___
35. Even if I don't deserve praise I accept it	___	___	___
36. I rarely feel vulnerable	___	___	___
37. Other people's judgments don't count for much with me	___	___	___
38. I keep track of the praise and perks given to others	___	___	___
39. People who criticize me are usually jealous	___	___	___
40. I don't enjoy belonging to organized groups	___	___	___
41. Power is to be used, not shared	___	___	___
42. I remember grievances so I can even up the score	___	___	___
43. Pushing the envelope is always better than playing it safe	___	___	___
44. You can never have enough status or power	___	___	___

The SDIS Challenge—A Self-Diagnostic Tool (continued)

	True	False	Uncertain
45. I rarely think about religious or moral values	___	___	___
46. I am unique: the problems of others can't affect me	___	___	___
47. Criticism doesn't faze me	___	___	___
48. I'm entitled to everything I've got			
49. Risk takers live life more fully than others	___	___	___
50. I don't foresee any major problems in getting what I want	___	___	___
51. I rarely fail to achieve important goals	___	___	___
52. When I do something for somebody I expect to be rewarded	___	___	___
53. If the truth is embarrassing, I'm good at putting a spin on it	___	___	___
54. When you count on other people, they often let you down	___	___	___
55. Being late for appointments doesn't bother me	___	___	___
56. I resent it when people take issue with me	___	___	___
57. I often think about what I'm going to accomplish next	___	___	___
58. I never think about failure	___	___	___
59. I could get away with a lot more than I get away with now	___	___	___
60. Younger people don't appreciate what I've accomplished	___	___	___
61. I don't try to keep in touch with people from the past	___	___	___
62. Even when I'm on a roll I'm restless	___	___	___
63. People often disagree with me without justification	___	___	___
64. I get depressed after a victory	___	___	___

What's Your SDIS Profile?

	True	False	Uncertain
65. My fantasies are often acted out in reality	___	___	___
66. Sometimes the end justifies the means	___	___	___
67. I think "the masses are asses"	___	___	___
68. It annoys me when people I meet don't give me the proper respect	___	___	___
69. My highs are higher and my lows are lower than the norm	___	___	___
70. The accomplishments of famous people don't awe me	___	___	___

Add up your score. Give yourself a two for every TRUE, a one for every UNCERTAIN, and a zero for every FALSE.

Scores:

110–140 Your SDIS virus is far advanced; you're heading for a big self-induced problem.

80–110 You're vulnerable; take steps to increase feedback, self-awareness, and contact with the real world.

30–80 Your immunity is at a satisfactory level. Maintain it.

0–30 Maybe you're too modest and cautious; push the envelope a little more.

How to detect SDIS in Others

We developed the SDIS Challenge as a self-diagnostic tool. A human resource executive told us he uses adaptations of these questions in interviewing, to detect tendencies toward intellectual self-destructiveness.

We worked with other interviewers who find the questions useful in sizing up candidates.

So, if your work involves interviewing job candidates, we recommend that you select appropriate questions from the battery and add them to your repertoire. You'll develop greater insight into what makes people tick—and where they may go wrong.

Chapter 11.

THE FIRST JOB: AVOIDING THE "TOO-SMART" TRAP

Self-destructive Intelligence Syndrome usually strikes those who are in the full flower of their lives and careers. But it starts early. The hubris and isolation developed in smart youngsters through their school years can be a problem as soon as they venture out into the world.

This chapter focuses on the particular dangers of SDIS among young people.

The Cocoon

"You're too smart for your own good!"

Bright kids hear this admonition throughout their prepubescence. They stop hearing it when they get to college. In college, they find to their delight that there is no such thing as being *too smart for your own good*. The entire dynamic of higher education, it seems, is geared to megasmarts. Not just to the *use* of intelligence to learn, but (and this often seems more important) the *demonstration* of high intelligence.

And Then—REALITY!

The supersmart student emerges from the gates of academe with the notion (understandable in the circumstances) that the key to success is, invariably, the demonstration of brilliance.

Reality is a shocking shower of icy water.

The First Job: Avoiding the "Too-Smart" Trap

Take, as an example, Leanne. A few years ago recruiters would have been camped outside Leanne's dorm, besieging her with offers. Downsizing has changed all that. Leanne joins an army of rivals in looking for a good job.

Should this be all that tough? She has every reason to think not. She wiped out her rivals in school. She can wipe them out on the job.

Here is the first big miscalculation—or complex of related miscalculations—which beset so many of the youngest, best, and brightest. Leanne assumes (1) that sheer intelligence is the most important quality in doing a good job, (2) that the task of *getting hired* requires similar skills to those used in *doing the job*, and (3) that the job environment is basically similar to the school environment.

Wrong, on all three counts.

The Divergence of Brilliance and Logic

Up till now, for Leanne and her contemporaries, logic and brilliance have gone hand in hand. The *logic* of scholastic success was to deploy your brightness on every occasion. Sure, it was important to use your smarts, but it was even more important to display your smarts—against objective yardsticks, and in competition with other students.

Now comes the *first watershed*.

Brilliance and logic are no longer joined at the hip. Now, intelligence may point in one direction and logic in another. If you continue to act as if the urgings of brightness are the paramount, indeed, the *only*, drive, your wheels start coming off.

Tripping over Your Own Intellect

Here are some of the principal ways in which very bright graduates foul themselves up in their first job interviews.

1. Using School Achievement as the Golden Key. Academic accomplishment is something to be proud of. In school, it was the main prize. Now, however, it is just one club in the bag—an important club, a major weapon, but one that must be used in conjunction with the full panoply of other clubs to shoot par or below.

Innocent of awareness of this fact, the supersmart young person plays his or her transcript as if it were an ace. Calling attention, early in the interview, to high grades is frequently a losing tactic. For one thing, most businesses are run by B or C students. Certainly a lot of people who conduct the first screening interviews (and who thus cannot say the final yes but who can utter the definitive no) did not necessarily wind up at the head of the class.

Tip: Wait to be asked about your grades. Say, "I worked hard; I was lucky." This is, of course, untrue, and the interviewer knows it's not sincere; but it does signal that you don't think grades are the biggest of big deals.

2. Assuming That There Is a Right or Wrong Answer to Every Question. Interviewers sometimes entice applicants into pontificating about complex questions.

Q. How would you improve our marketing structure?

A. First I would eliminate all underperforming lines . . . (and on and on—a detailed and self-confident critique of everything the company is doing).

In the game-playing atmosphere of the classroom or the seminar room this is fine. There the rules resemble those of the formal debate. The actual content of what you say, or the amount of knowledge or experience you have to back it up, may be far less important than the power, panache, and imagination with which you present your case. Thus gifted debaters are indifferent to whether they are on the pro or con side of the question.

As we discuss elsewhere, some smart people never grow out of this stage—and it costs them. They use their brilliance to demolish the opposing arguments of not-as-smart and not-as-articulate people, whose only excuse for holding the opinions that they hold is that they happen to be right.

Job interviewers are not debating referees. They are the outriders of an organization that deals in practicalities, not pyrotechnics. They're leery about applicants who seem very sure of the answers without having all the facts.

Tip: Instead of giving flat solutions to complex questions, tell how you'd go about finding the answers. "First I'd want to get all the information available. . . ."

3. Scoring Points. Some of the most memorable triumphs in the classroom or seminar come through brilliant give-and-take exchanges with other students or instructors. This kind of verbal *mano-a-mano* may not have much to do with the actual subject. It is often a total digression, a side duel about semantics or attitudes or some point that is of the utmost triviality except that it triggers the exchange. When knighthood was in flower, pages—young persons in training to be knights—jousted or fought with one another as a matter of course, not because they were mad at one another but because it was part of growing up.

Brilliance is an asset in the interview—if it is used not as an end in itself but as a resource. Putting the other guy down for its own sake is, to put it mildly, unproductive when you're looking for a job.

Now, everybody knows this. But—and this applies universally, to all ages and situations—knowing something is one thing, acting on it is another. Irrelevant swordplay wearies interviewers rather than impressing them. And some of it is worse than wearying. Point scoring often consists in turning opposing arguments on their heads, jeering at absurdities, making the other guy look bad. Even human resource persons are human. While they try to be objective no matter what, they may well develop an unacknowledged bias against the candidate who puts them down.

Tip: Respond but avoid attack. If an interviewer says something you think is wrong, get on record: "I have a different idea about that. . . ." Wait to be invited to expand. If the interviewer seems to be welcoming, or even provoking, an exchange, use your adroitness to duck it gracefully rather than to plunge into a duel: "We could have a lively debate over that point. Could you spell out a little more why you feel as you do?"

4. Interviewing the Interviewer. Bright young people—particularly those who enjoyed a choice of colleges—can develop an unearned feeling of being sought after when they go looking for a job.

The job interview should, of course, be a two-way street. The applicant is there to find things out as well as to be evaluated.

But even though it's a two-way street, it's appropriate that more traffic move in one direction than in the other. The primary purpose is for the interviewer to ask questions of the interviewee. The interviewee's need to acquire information should take a lower priority. To acknowledge this unwritten rule is not to be a wimp; it is, simply, to respect the interviewer's time and the job the interviewer has to do.

Sometimes intelligent job seekers act as if they were doing the hiring. They take over the interview, asking penetrating questions about the company, its methods, its policies, its ethics, its future, its compensation practices, the benefits, the speed of advancement, and so on.

Smart people are curious. They're expected to ask questions. But when the job applicant takes over the interview, intellectual curiosity shades into arrogance. Most experienced interviewers can handle a certain amount of arrogance, but that doesn't mean they like it. A more serious problem for the interviewer—and, ultimately, for the interviewee—is that the interviewer's pattern is disrupted when the job seeker keeps breaking the flow with a lot of questions. Interviewers have a structured approach to their job. Their questions may seem random, but usually they are not. They represent an underlying plan. The interviewer needs to cover a list of subjects within a limited period of time. When the applicant grabs for the steering wheel, the session veers off the track. The interviewer has to make an effort to get it back on the track. If that effort is too great, well, there are always other applicants—maybe not as smart, but more interviewable.

Tip: Let yourself be interviewed. That's what you're there for. In due course the interviewer will signal that it's your turn. If not, wait until you've been asked the pertinent questions before embarking on a list of your own.

Or interject questions at appropriate times—but then let the other party set the pace again.

5. Missing the Road Signs. "I need a strategy for the interview," the job seeker tells himself. So he works up an effective method of presenting himself. When talking to the employer, he is eloquent about his ability to work on his own, come up with independent ideas, carry through projects without supervision or support.

The trouble is that the company places a far higher priority on team play than on individual effort among its newcomers.

The interviewer tries to help the job seeker by pointing this out. Most employment people will give hints to promising candidates. But this candidate—smart, articulate, and self-assured—is so intent on projecting lone-wolf resourcefulness that he misses the signals.

Interviewer: You'll be working alongside colleagues with a little more experience. At the same time your input and your fresh ideas will help to reach optimum solutions. . . .

Applicant: I look forward to that. I've learned that it isn't enough to come up with a good idea, you have to be able to sell it to those around you. . . .

Lynn Bignell, principal and cofounder of Gilbert Tweed Associates, Inc. (one of the first and most successful executive search firms run by women), remarks, "Some young candidates are very fluent, but they treat the interview like a solo rather than a duet. They don't give themselves a chance to find out what the interviewer wants to buy, so they sell the wrong thing."

If the job seeker is absolutely set on getting a go-it-alone job, and will not accept anything else, then the approach we've just described is not only candid but correct. However, in this case, as in so many other cases, the applicant was just trying to land a good job. The wrong-headed strategy, exacerbated by the failure to pick up the signals, was not based on principle. It was sheer expediency. It can be painful to see worthy candidates pass up jobs on principle. It's pathetic to see candidates blow the interviews through misbegotten expediency.

Tip: In preparing for the interview, formulate some good questions at the same time as you shape good answers. Such a question might be "Your company has a great reputation for teamwork. How do you balance teamwork against individual initiative?" This shows the interviewer that you've done research, that you want to find out what's important, and that you're interested in grasping the essence of the organization.

6. Dumbing Down. Some young job seekers flaunt their intelligence, to self-destructive effect. Some others go to the other extreme. Sensitive about looking like smart-asses, they play dumb.

As we said, scholastic accomplishment is not the golden key to being hired. However, modesty is one thing; self-denigration another. Some bright young people tell interviewers things like this: "Oh, I didn't have a clue about what was going on in that class. They must have graded on a really wacko curve for me to get an A." This is the kind of talk that smart, sensitive young people sometimes use to try to impress—or at least disarm—a bunch of jocks at a party. The interviewer knows it's phony.

Tip: Be yourself in everything you say. Never try to make yourself into something different, and especially don't try to make yourself look dumb. Your intelligence is a tremendous asset. The employer is looking for intelligence, but at the same time is looking for people who can apply their brains to furtherance of the company's interests. If you let yourself be perceived as dumb, you don't have a prayer.

7. Underestimating the Interviewer. Initial job interviews are typically conducted by lower-level people whose job it is to screen applicants down to a short list. Smart graduates can be misled into seeing the interviewer as a flunky.

The First Job: Avoiding the "Too-Smart" Trap

"I'm smarter than this guy." That's the thought that many young people have as they go into an interview. That's okay, even useful—up to a point. It quells the butterflies in the stomach, builds up the confidence. And it's probably true.

But whether or not the applicant is smarter than the interviewer is not the point. Yes, the job seeker has a higher IQ; but the interviewer has more savvy. And the interviewer holds the dominant position. You have to get past the lower-level people who can say no before you get to the guy who can say yes.

Giving interviewers their proper due means more than just being polite. Few sane people, of whatever age, are discourteous in job interviews. The problem comes when the applicant writes off the lower-level interrogator as having little on the ball, and therefore unqualified to make any meaningful evaluation. As a result, some bright applicants coast through the preliminary interview. They see it as a battle of wits. Since the other party does not seem equipped for an equal contest, why go all out?

Tip: Approach all interviewers as if they were CEOs. They represent the company. They have a job to do. Their job is to *screen*, to reduce the list of candidates to a manageable number. This is not quite the same thing as choosing the smartest applicants. Indeed, the screener may pass along to the higher-ups a mixed bag—some superbrains, some applicants most notable for their attractive personalities, some young people who meet other criteria.

Since screening at the preliminary level is more a matter of elimination than selection, interviewers may tend to look for "knockout" factors. For instance, some canny interviewers feign flunkydom. They act dull and insignificant to see how the candidate reacts.

Welcome to the Real World

Freud referred to the academic experience as meeting life in its most synthetic form. In school an answer is either right or wrong. In the real world of business, successful handling of challenges may depend on the *prima facie* assumption that there are no right or wrong answers.

A graduate's first employment interviews are the pressure lock within which one makes the transitional step between worlds. The people who may or may not hire you are not primarily interested in how smart you are. They want to know how you think, how you go about solving problems, how you adjust to changing situations, how you will fit in with those already on the payroll.

They assess candidates as functioning human beings, not walking transcripts or IQ scores. So the young applicant's best bet is to neither flaunt intelligence or hide it, but rather to put it to practical use in listening to the questions and answering in a way that gives the interviewer a well-rounded picture.

The best and brightest may come out of school with unbalanced psychic armament, like a boxer with a powerful left and a puny right or a painter whose superb ability to draw is linked to colorblindness. In the hothouse of academia, sheer brainpower flourishes while other attributes, like common sense, are left to atrophy. So it is not surprising when new graduates allow intelligence to trip them up in the interview. This is not *logic override* in the usual sense; there is not that much logic there to override.

Failed job interviews can be useful if the applicant is capable of self-analysis or gets some useful input. The experience may be an early warning of the danger of relying on sheer brainpower.

Smart Versus Smarts in the New Job

Job interviews offer ample opportunity to be too smart for your own good. The first job—especially the first weeks in the first job—contains dangerous pitfalls. Here is the point at which some extremely bright people have been trapped by their brilliance into doing some very dumb things. Here are a few examples.

Excessive Risk Taking. Daring is admired in school. Going out on a limb earns applause and wins academic recognition. A student who espouses a position that is basically ridiculous, arguing that position with resourcefulness and panache, looks good. It's a tightrope act performed without a net—but there's no need for a net, because there really isn't any danger of falling very far. It's risk taking without real risk. That can be seductive—and dangerous.

Say, for example, that a class has been divided into teams that constitute "businesses" competing with one another. The students we are talking about are the ones who always want to play the long shots, take the most extreme chances to win the mock business war. It's like selling all your other Monopoly holdings to put a hotel on Baltic Avenue; it looks screwy, but it might even work—and anyway, if it doesn't work, what difference does it make? You did something nobody else would do, and had fun doing it. And of course it's just play money.

If you're smart enough, you can bring off a surprising number of these schooldays long shots. Maybe your premise was unsound, but you carry the day through sheer audacity and surprise.

As Brendan Sexton, vice president of the Rockefeller Group, remarks, "It's all too short a step from knowing more than anybody else to thinking that you know *everything*."

As we discuss, the *risk junkie* is, unfortunately, an all-too-common figure. Risk junkies come in all ages, jobs, and genders. Newly fledged risk junkies come into their first jobs looking for a high-profile risk to take.

The idea seems to have a lot going for it. The academic achiever has taken a lot of bold chances and never even stumbled. Even when the risk turned out to be ill considered—for example, expending precious time in trying to invent the equivalent of the perpetual-motion machine—the risk taker comes out a winner, admired for imagination and flair and the nerve to take the risk. Sure, some fellow students may grumble enviously, but who cares?

So, from this ideal atmosphere in which you can take risks that have little downside, you move onto a board where they play with real money; where you need the cooperation, respect, and goodwill of your colleagues; and where the faculty, which reveled in the antics of the brightest undergraduates, has been replaced by policy-level executives fixated icily on the bottom line.

The fledgling risk taker has, like Alice, stepped through the looking glass. Heretofore, even when you lost the risk you were a winner. Here, even if you win you are apt to wind up a loser. Colleagues are alienated. Rivals are put on their guard. Bosses are wary; they are not comfortable with risk taking as performance art.

Using Risk Taking Flair Productively. Ann—risker par excellence while in school—gets the first assignment that allows her some latitude. As is her wont, she looks for a different way of doing it—especially a way that involves cutting corners, taking chances, sailing close to the wind.

However, instead of plunging into her high-risk act, she thinks through the steps she would take, and then goes to her boss.

"I'm ready to do the job according to the basic approach in the manual. But as I thought about it a couple of things occurred to me. What would happen if we tried to do it a different way?" And she outlines her approach, winding up, "If it works, we save time and money. I'm aware of the risks. . . ." She proceeds to enumerate the risks, then asks the boss's judgment.

Not as spectacular as if she took off on her own and scored an astounding success—or fell on her face. But it's a lot more constructive. For one thing, the idea might really be a loser, and here they are not playing with fake money. And for another thing, if it's a winner, Alice demonstrates that she's a team player.

Selective Listening. Kim was a leading student and a thoroughly nice person. In school, she did not snub or put down people of lower intellectual capacity. She made friends with people of all kinds and all IQs. Kids liked her. You could talk to Kim, even though she was obviously smarter. She wasn't arrogant, like some bright students.

What Kim was good at was looking attentive while not really listening. The apostle Paul wrote, "For ye suffer fools gladly, seeing ye yourselves are wise" (2 Corinthians 11:19). Kim suffered fools with abundant gladness. But she did not listen.

The First Job: Avoiding the "Too-Smart" Trap

Now Kim is out of school and in her first job. Being a likable and promising person, she is the recipient of a lot of what John F. Kennedy referred to as the "ultimate luxury"—*free advice*. One veteran manager in particular, George Carr, sits down with Kim and gives her a long and earnest lecture. She nods her head and smiles, but she does not take it very seriously. After all, George means well, but he is not an electric circus of intellect.

Kim is much more interested in the comments of the mercurial and sardonic Jerry Anderson. Jerry has some off-the-wall ideas and sour opinions, but he is undoubtedly bright.

BIG Mistake. Jerry Anderson's loose-cannon observations appeal to Kim's sense of humor and appreciation for sharp insights. That would be okay if she were just listening for entertainment. But Kim buys into Jerry's take on the company, its people, and its future. Jerry likes to shoot off conversational sparks for their own sake. He gets a kick out of impressing this smart young woman. His "insights" tend toward the extreme; they omit some essential truths about the organization and its culture.

And, when it comes time for Kim to make some significant choices, she is going to choose wrong, because she did not listen to the dull but sound words of George Carr, who may not be as bright as Kim or Jerry, but who knows things that are important to know.

Selective listening—with the selection made on the basis of perceived IQ—is a problem for people of all ages, on and off the job. James W. Wesley, Jr., president/CEO of Summit Communications, knows it well: "Smart people tend to surround themselves with other smart people. That's good—up to a point. But relying on brilliance to the exclusion of experience and common sense" leads to bad things.

It's an excellent idea to form, early in one's career, the habit of "scanner" listening—tuning in on *all* the wavelengths, absorbing *all* the messages and information available, collecting input from a wide range of sources and then subjecting it to analysis.

Using Brilliance to Conceal Problems. Nobody in school could top Richard in formal or informal debate. He could take a ludicrous proposition and argue it convincingly (and, just for the hell of it, that is what he often did).

When Richard moved into the world of work, his debating gift was put aside for a while. Then he got his first chance to make an important presentation. The presentation itself was well done; but where Richard really shone—and where he knew he would shine—was in the give-and-take following the formal presentation, when he fielded questions, comments, and criticisms. Several critics raised points that seemed to show up weaknesses in the proposal. However, Richard's command of impromptu argument swept these objections aside. The plan was approved without substantial change.

Alas, there *were* weaknesses in the proposal. The criticisms might have been considered more carefully—if only Richrad had been less devastating in demolishing opposing arguments. He would have done better to listen, evaluate, and revise, rather than to strike out reflexively to defend his argument. Richard was now in the real world, where the important thing was not to win the debate but to accept valid criticism and come up with the best possible plan. In school, the contest was over when the debate ended. On the job, after Richard's idea fell short, nobody said, "Yeah, but the important thing is what a great job he did at the meeting." They remembered that it was the young man's first project, and it flopped.

This case illustrates what one executive (John F. McGlynn, president, Technical Imaging Systems of Miles, Inc.) means when he talks about people who "not only rely too much upon intellect, but who use intellect as a mask." Here, Richard—without being aware of it—used his intelligence to mask the weaknesses of his proposal, instead of using the same intelligence to analyze and apply criticism.

Making the Brain a Tool Rather Than a Showpiece. Every graduate knows the move from student to job seeker and job holder is a major transition. Intellectual firepower is a great asset in finding and mastering the first job—but not if you shoot yourself in the foot.

Chapter 12.

SELF-SCOPING: THROUGH THE WINDOW

Alice started her second great adventure by stepping through the looking glass. An odd way to set off, perhaps, although some days it might seem no more difficult than getting to JFK or O'Hare or LAX through heavy traffic.

We'd like to send you on a trip. It's not a trip to exotic shores, although you may encounter things stranger than those you found on your last journeys to the Amazon rain forest or the South Seas islands or the fabled spires of Samarkand.

Maybe it's not so much a trip as a quest, or a mission. Your mission: to find the person who is about to screw up your life, to learn what you need to know about that person, and to do what has to be done to prevent that person from destroying your career, roiling your emotions, vilifying your name.

This person, of course, is yourself.

> The wise man knows that he has only one enemy: *himself.* This is an enemy difficult to ignore and full of cunning. It always seeks to loosen and lead one away from one's goal. It's an enemy never to be forgotten, but constantly outwitted.
>
> Ben Hecht

You will start by stepping not through the looking glass but rather through a window—what first looks like an ordinary four-pane window, like this:

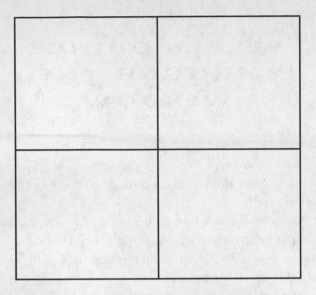

This is the outline of the Johari Window, a tool widely used in management training programs. Many executives who are counseled at BFS Psychological Associates (where the authors of this book work) go through the window frequently. The term *Johari* comes from the names of two psychologists, Joe Luft and Harry Ingham, who developed the tool.

The Johari Window consists of four panes of glass. The panes are given different designations in various adaptations of the technique. For example, it is used to help managers appraise their management styles. Here is how W. J. Reddin puts it in his book *Managerial Effectiveness.*[1]

Everything known and not known about ourselves can be put under one of four headings:

1. **What we know and others know (style awareness). (This is everyone's business.)**

2. **What others know and we do not know (style unawareness). (We must make this our business.)**

3. What we know and others do not know (personal history). (This is only our business.)

4. What we and others do not know (unconscious). (This is no one's business.)

The objective is to help managers improve their management styles. The first step is to give these managers a view of themselves in action. Let's face it: when we interact with other people, everybody else gets a better look at us in action than we get.

In our campaign to stamp out SDIS we will use all promising approaches. So we're going to take the four-pane Johari Window and apply a different set of meanings. The basic idea is the same as in management training: to help you get a better understanding of what you're really like, what impact you have on others, and what others think of you.

Maybe you're saying, "Who cares what others think of me?" If so, you fit right in among the hubrists. But you should care what others think about you—not necessarily because you give a damn, but rather because that knowledge is one step in a process that leads to your learning important things that will keep you from screwing up your life.

Anybody who knew Bill Casey would attest that he was one of the smartest people ever. William J. Casey was director of the Central Intelligence Agency, chairman of the SEC, adviser to presidents, and, once, a senior executive of Research Institute of America, where the authors of this book also worked.

Casey almost scuttled his career by refusing to put his extensive holdings into a blind trust when he went to the CIA. Casey's biographer writes, "Bill Casey was not a stupid man. So why the bullheadedness?"[2]

We suggest an answer. Bill Casey was tough. He was ready and willing to be ruthless in pursuit of a goal. But he had no intention of using his position to fatten his holdings—so how could anyone think otherwise? And why force him into a blind trust?

Very smart people can be utterly indifferent to what others think.

Get ready to set off on the journey inward, toward the core of your being. You're standing in front of our version of the Johari Window.

The first pane is *how you see yourself.* The second is *how others see you.* The third is your *idealized self-image.* The fourth represents the *gap between ideal and reality.*

How you see yourself	How others see you
Your idealized self-image	The GAP

Build up your immunity to the Self-Destructive Intelligence Syndrome by giving yourself a diagnostic examination. SCIPIs have a tendency to let the differentials represented by the panes of the window get too large. Driven by hubris, or narcissism, or the other elements we have been talking about, they permit the gap to grow so wide that it becomes a gaping area of vulnerability. They don't know themselves anymore, at least not their real selves. And self-ignorance makes them ignorant of others and of what is going on in the real world.

The questions which one asks oneself begin, at last, to illuminate the world, and become one's key to the experience of others.

James Baldwin, introduction, *Nobody Knows My Name*, 1961

Self-Scoping: Through the Window

Here's a simple exercise you can use to prepare for your trip. Think of several people. Your closest companion—spouse or partner. A friend. A professional acquaintance—boss, colleague, or assistant.

In the columns that follow you'll find a list of attributes. In the first column check the attribute that you feel is appropriate as applied to yourself. Then check the other columns on the basis of what you feel, in your gut, others think of you. Think a bit; don't make hasty assumptions about their opinions. Do your objective best to put down your best estimate of their view whether you possess that attribute.

Here's the list.

	Self	Companion	Friend	Colleague	Verdict
Kind					
Truthful					
Argumentative					
Tense					
Eager					
Generous					
Humble					
Firm					
Optimistic					
Egotistic					
Shrewd					
Good mixer					
Selfish					
Easily swayed					
Impulsive					
Talkative					
Confident					
Willing					
Touchy					
Sentimental					
Grouchy					
Aggressive					

	Self	Companion	Friend	Colleague	Verdict
Slow					
Reliable					
Aloof					
Efficient					
Tactful					
Fair					
Hostile					
Observant					
Stubborn					
Hotheaded					
Dreamer					

Objective Subjectivity

When the people we work with approach this task seriously they find themselves being more honest—and, maybe, more stringent—than they might have imagined that they would be. Sure, there may be a rare person who checks off all the good things about himself/herself and all the good opinions of others, without exception. But, while our typical subjects—successful executives and professionals—have very healthy egos indeed, they also have enough tough-minded shrewdness to understand their own weak points, even if they take pains to conceal them. And, once they put their minds to it, they can be pretty cool and objective in estimating what others really think about them, even when those others are very close.

But first you have to put your mind to it. In limbering up for your trip through the window, think about the person whom you like most in the world. You admire this person, maybe love him or her. But—does that admiration or love amount to blind, unquestioning adoration? Are you worshiping an idol? Do you think this other person is perfect?

Of course not. Even in our nearest and dearest we see imperfections. The essence of love or friendship is not blind adoration but rather affectionate acknowledgment and understanding of that person's faults. We don't harp on those faults. We overlook them, except when, in a helpful and understanding way, we offer constructive criticism. But we don't bestow perfection on those around us.

Curiously, though, even among very perceptive individuals it is easy to ignore the other side of that coin—the fact that our loved ones and close friends don't think we're perfect either. In fact, if you were a fly on the wall listening to a couple of your friends talk about you, you might be startled to hear some of their opinions.

By passing through the window you become that fly on the wall.

Prepare yourself by rating somebody you like very much. You'll find that you're very objective; that, no matter how close, you don't shrink from your opinions of them in certain categories. But while you might rate a treasured friend as argumentative, egotistic, and touchy, you still treasure that friend.

Do the Same Thing for Yourself

Okay. You've shown that you can be objective about your opinions of others. Now step through the window and evaluate yourself in the "Self" column. No false modesty, no excessive bravado. Just check the relevant attributes.

Now run down the next column, "Companion." Forget about what you think of yourself, or about what's fair or accurate. Check the words this other person would apply to you. You're not a mind reader. But you can make some reasoned guesses about what your companion or spouse thinks about you. Maybe he/she thinks you're argumentative. Never mind that you don't agree, that you only argue when you're in the right: check it off. And check off those words that describe your good qualities in the eyes of the other party. If the other person thinks you are kind, check it off, even if you don't exactly see yourself as brimming with the milk of human kindness.

Now look over your self-evaluation. Ideally, good and bad should be about evenly divided. If there are too many negatives—if you rarely checked the positive categories—you may be too hard on yourself. Or maybe you're just having a bad day. Try it again when you're feeling less down.

You didn't check every item (you couldn't have!). Add up the number of items you checked. The sum is a measure of your personal complexity. The more characteristics, the more elaborate the portrait.

Now compare the answers you checked for yourself and those you think would be checked by others. There will be differences. But there should be a basic personality core about which you and others agree.

What if there is no personality core? What if there are radical differences? Others are not seeing the real you. Why not?

Do they just misunderstand you? That's a facile assumption that some window gazers reach when the judgments of others seem to be considerably harsher than those appearing in the "Self" column. But that's a cop-out. You have to be ready to admit some weight to what they think.

Or you misunderstand what others think of you. If so, it's worth asking why.

Or you may be putting on a deliberate and successful performance—acting your way through life to fool others into thinking a certain way about you. If that's the case, it is also worth asking why. Why would an intelligent person put considerable mental and emotional resources into presenting a false picture to others?

What's That Face I See in the Window?

You may have found this exercise tough. Most people do, if they have given it their honest best. Let's consider that face you are beginning to see in the window.

Self-Scoping: Through the Window

> O wad some Pow'r the giftie gie us
> To see oursels as others see us!
> It wad frae mony a blunder free us,
> And foolish notion.
> > Robert Burns, "To a Louse"

There can be vast differences between how we see ourselves and how others see us. A says, "I'm good with people." B says, "What a bitch!" A says, "I'm too impulsive." B says, "It's like pulling teeth to get him to make up his mind."

Usually, though, the differences are not poles apart. They are expressed in terms of shadings, sometimes subtle shadings, of interpretation. A says, "I call 'em the way I see 'em." B says, "He goes out of his way to put you down." A says, "I'm stubborn." B says, "She sticks to her guns."

You're looking through the top two panes, first at how you see yourself, and, second, how others see you.

Now we come to the third pane: your idealized self-image. Idealized self-image is not the you of today. It is the you you would like to be, and are growing toward.

When we're children we immerse ourselves deeply in the world of idealized self-image, what we want to become. Kids find it easy to actually move into the fantasy world of the idealized self. They don't merely think about becoming actors or athletes or presidents: they become them. They can become anything they want, at an instant's notice. One day we were driving along a busy city street, saw a parking space, and pulled in. There, on the sidewalk, was a stocky five-year-old boy, standing with arms folded, erect, rigid.

"You can't park here!" he yelled.

"Why not?"

"Because," he announced, "I am a fire hydrant." This, at the moment, was his idealized self-image.

Another way of approaching the idea of idealized self-image is to ask the age-old question "What would you like to be when you grow up?"

Banish from your mind the notion that that question applies only to children. We should always be growing; when we stop, or when we think we've stopped, we're in trouble.

> Growth is the only evidence of life.
>> John Henry Newman, *Apologia pro Vita Sua*

The more gifted you are, the greater your responsibility to yourself and to the world to keep growing—growing taller, extending roots downward, growing outward into new dimensions. The greatest among us exemplify this in their lives. They pass through a series of idealized self-images, choosing the ways in which they will be truest to their talents. John F. Kennedy said to a gathering of Nobel Prize winners at the White House, "Never have so many great minds assembled under one roof—except when Thomas Jefferson dined alone." There are three things on Jefferson's tombstone: "Author of the Declaration of American Independence, of the Statute of Virginia for Religious Freedom, and Father of the University of Virginia." These are various idealized self-images chosen by Jefferson, the ones in which he took the most pride. He chose not to mention his two terms as president of the United States.

Jefferson happened to be better able than most of us to realize his ideal.

> The strongest principle of growth lies in human choice.
>> George Eliot, *Daniel Deronda*

Browsing Through the Gap

Now for the fourth pane. When the gap between idealized self-image and reality—as represented by what you think of yourself versus what others think of you—is too great, bad things happen. You act in ways that are inappropriate. You misread situations. You overreach—or you withdraw, shrink, fall into a depression. You try to do things that are beyond you. You make bad decisions.

In this context we are taking the view that others have of us as reality. Now we could get into an exquisite disquisition on the question "What is reality?" Let's not. Since we're talking about perception, let's stipulate that the inner image we have of ourselves is just that—an inner image, whereas what others think about us is practical reality. If it's not, it might as well be, because much of the course of our lives depends on the way others see us and the way in which our decisions react with those perceptions. Many of the stupidest things done by smart people happen because of the gap.

The adjustment of the gap between idealized self-image and reality is not a onetime calibration that we can hard-wire into our psyches. It's something we have to keep working at. This constant process of recycling of the self keeps us alive and moving ahead.

> One must be thrust out of a finished cycle in life, and that leap [is] the most difficult to make—to part with one's faith, one's love, when one would prefer to renew the faith and recreate the passion.
> Anaïs Nin, *The Diary of Anaïs Nin*, November 1932

The task is to keep reducing the gap, minimizing the difference.

Life is like clothing. Clothes never fit perfectly. Our bodies keep changing. Clothes need adjustment. George Bernard Shaw said, "My tailor is the only man who understands me, because he takes my measurements every time we meet."

A Tough Job, but Only You Can Do It

Real self-exploration is difficult and wrenching. It takes guts, strength of mind, and fortitude. When you step into the dark cavern of your mind you may find things that disappoint you or scare you. Not everything you find there will be pleasant, by any means.

That's the whole idea. The quest for self-knowledge is not a day at the beach. Sigmund Freud's pioneering journey into his own unconscious is one of the monumental feats of human experience. Hillary and Tenzing reached the peak of Everest, Amundsen reached the South Pole, Columbus sailed to the New World. They all had people with them. Freud made his journey alone; and he confronted mysteries, wonders, and monsters beyond the wildest imaginings.

Today we argue over many things about Freud—the genesis of his theories of childhood sexuality, the effectuality of his therapy, the cultural and gender bias implicit in his thinking. But it is hard to dispute his courage and his determination.

In your trip through the window we are not asking you to go anywhere near as deep as Freud. Nevertheless, you are venturing into the part of yourself that is ordinarily closed off to you, out of view. Others can see parts of it more clearly than you can. When you see yourself more clearly, you function better. You're able to focus more of your intellectual power on the solution of problems.

And, most important for our purposes, you're better protected against the Self-Destructive Intelligence Syndrome.

Smart people are often impatient people. They think faster than others. They sit, drumming their fingers, while their companions try to catch up.

Leave your impatience at the threshold. Self-insights rarely come in flashes of lightning. Few of us are like Archimedes, leaping out of the bathtub shouting "Eureka!" or Newton contemplating the apple. In Newton's shoes most of us would rub our heads, curse a little, and let it go at that. It would take a steady rain of apples to make us see the gravity of the situation.

One factor that impedes rapid breakthroughs in self-knowledge is our elaborate defense mechanisms. The idealized self-image is precious. It fights to preserve itself. The nearer you probe, the more it resists.

So insight comes in small increments. We never said it was going to be easy. It's what you get for being smart.

> We pay / a high price for being intelligent. Wisdom hurts.
> Euripides, *Electra*, 413 B.C. Translation by Emily Townsend Vermeule

Road Maps to the Interior

We recommend a couple of approaches to self-assessment. One is the *autobiographical method*. In this approach you go back into your past, looking for the critical incidents that have affected you. Take your father:

- **What was he like?**
- **How did you react to him?**
- **Did you resent his discipline?**
- **What hopes did he have for you?**
- **What dreams did you dream together?**

How about your mother? Did you get along well with her? Were you her favorite? Freud said, "I am great because I was my mother's favorite child," (Interesting, from the proponent of the Oedipus complex.) In considering certain examples of smart people doing dumb things—for example, General Douglas MacArthur—we have touched on the fascinating and only sketchily explored topic of the relationships of SCIPIs with their mothers and the possible influences of those relationships on outbreaks of SDIS.

Of course for a while there the mother influence was praised or blamed for pratically everything. One day, at a luncheon at Ohio State University, we heard the legendary football coach Woody Hayes say, "Our good quarterbacks have one thing in common. They all had wonderful relationships with their mothers."

What about the authority figures of your childhood—teachers, relatives, nannies? In our work with executives we have found something that, to us, is fascinating. The way executives use power often reflects the ways in which they were handled *when they were powerless*. If you have been handled erratically, you use power erratically. If you were handled compassionately, you respect power and use it with compassion.

Continue your journey into the past.

- **What successes in school made you happy?**
- **What were your biggest disappointments?**
- **Who were your friends? Did you have many friends?**
- **What experiences gave you the most satisfaction?**

Later in this book you'll find a supply of question checklists designed to help you to examine various aspects of yourself, your actions, and your relationships. These questions can be used in various ways. One way is as a guide in pursuing the biographical track to self-insight.

In wending your way through your own history, don't settle for just the dramatic easily recalled episodes. Look for the small details that your memory keeps sending to the surface every time you think of the past. Fish out and examine the bits of significant flotsam that appear and reappear, sometimes when you're nodding off to sleep or when you're just waking up. Then they disappear again, sucked down in the swirl as the tides of consciousness reestablish themselves.

Hints like this are markers for your journey. Enigmatic markers, not signposts. Not easy to understand. But worth trying to understand.

Look for the things that one might consider insignificant—but that keep recurring. *These are the things that have shaped you.*

Focusing on Today's Critical Happenings

There's another way in which you can look inside yourself. This method focuses not on the past but on today. It is the *critical incident method.*

Try this experiment. For a week, keep a record of the situations you encounter. Write it in a notebook. Dictate it onto tape. Set up a convenient computer file.

Keep notes throughout the day. Jot them in a pocket diary or on the back of an envelope. Record the situations you encounter—*and your reactions to them.* In this respect your record differs from the typical diary, which keeps track of events but doesn't usually record feelings.

Record your fleeting moments of anger, exhilaration, and frustration, and the events that immediately preceded them. You don't have to write volumes—just put down enough facts so that you can bring the events back to mind later. For this is not a journal to be read by others. It's a tool; its purpose is to trigger introspective thought. Typical entries might read:

Met Florence at the supermarket and she told me all about their trip to Greece. Felt depressed all day.

Jeff's car wouldn't start. I was able to show him how to clear a vapor lock. He looked at me as if I was a magician. I felt marvelous.

Ward took ten minutes to find the Bristol file. I blew up at him. Then I apologized, but I still felt like a heel.

We ate together in the Beige Banana, the little place we used to go to when we were first going out. The place seemed just the same. We talked and laughed just the way we used to. But something was missing.

Made the presentation. I was waiting for tough questions, at least from Franni and Cal. Nothing. God, what pushovers these people are!

Oscar held forth to the assembled crowd again, for about 20 minutes, telling us all what we knew already. Next time I'm going to show him up for the jerk that he is.

Do this until you have a variety of situations and reactions. It's important to record the reaction as well as the situation. For this purpose they work only as pairs.

Now sit down and review the critical incidents. Concentrate on the cases in which your reaction was stronger than usual. Don't "average." When they judge Olympic figure skaters they throw out the highest and the lowest mark. Here the highest and the lowest may be the most significant.

A particular reaction—rage or triumph or erotic arousal—may be rare, but that doesn't make it insignificant. It is the "rare" occurrences that shoot to the surface now and then to show us what is going on in the turbulence in the depths. A lot of people lose the value of this method by ignoring the "rare" extremes. They look back on a situation that ended in a big blow-up and dismiss it, saying, "That's not like me. I don't usually lose my temper."

Wrong. That is not only "like" you: it *is* you. The time that you got madder than you thought possible—or felt great for a seemingly trivial reason—often reveals more about you than normal behavior.

Look at these episodes in relation to one another and to other circumstances. You have an analytical mind. You probably have occasion, on and off the job, to study bits of data to find a pattern.

Look for patterns here.

- **What time of day did it happen? (Certain people have certain reactions at certain times. For example, for some the morning is a war zone.)**

- What kind of person was involved? Who brings out your neuroses?
- Who witnessed the episode?
- Where did it happen?

Ask yourself other questions, as if you were questioning somebody else to get all the facts about what really took place.

Now—*reverse the roles*. Go back and replay the incident on the screen of your mind—but this time cast yourself in the role of the other person. Does the story unfold in the same way? When you become the "jerk" who provoked an angry outburst, do you find that outburst justified to the same degree?

You can learn a lot about yourself by analyzing events and your reactions to them, and then putting yourself in the shoes of people to whom you react most strongly.

By using the autobiographical method and/or the critical incident method to examine your past and present with an eye toward what really happened and how you felt about it, you become better able to understand yourself.

Self-knowledge has a lot of obvious advantages. You can realize more of your potential. You achieve a greater measure of serenity when you have a better grasp of what lifts you to the heights and casts you into the depths. You can structure your relationships at work to achieve better results.

And you are better able to avoid the really dumb things that smart people do, because you know more about the intricate workings of that subtle, sophisticated mechanism that is the inner you, and you are thus attuned to the knocks and pings, the discordant notes that tell you something is going wrong. If, for example, you find that every time you have any kind of extended contact with a key colleague your blood boils, you should look ahead to the inevitable result if nothing is done to stop it: you are going to rip into the guy.

If that's not something you want to do—if it would be a mistake—then take practical steps to prevent it. Avoid him. If you can't avoid him, mutter mantras while he speaks. When you feel your needle going into the red, trigger your beeper and rush out to the phone. Do *something*.

That's the point of going through the window. When you see the gap, when you can gauge the ways in which your idealized self-image is out of synch with reality, you have the makings of a warning system that alerts you to *do something* before you make a fool of yourself and blow your opportunity, your job, your career, your reputation, your relationship, or your life.

Notes

1. W. J. Reddin, *Managerial Effectiveness* (New York: McGraw-Hill, 1970), pp. 147–148.
2. Joseph E. Persico, *Casey: The Lives and Secrets of William J. Casey from the OSS to the CIA* (New York: Viking, 1990), pp. 337–343.

Chapter 13.

ISN'T IT ABOUT TIME
YOU GREW UP?

SDIS is a childhood disease.

Oh, it strikes persons of all ages. But, however old they may be, the victims of self-destructive intelligence are, in one way or other, immature.

Brainpower can stunt your growth. A strong mind masks immaturity. Many SCIPIs go a long way and do astonishing things without ever growing up. Their overcompensating intellects make up for their immaturity. But finally that lack of maturity catches up with them. They hurt themselves badly by falling victim to one or another of the forms of the Feinberg Factor.

The same brainpower that militates against your growing up can be turned around to expedite the growth process. By becoming a more mature person you build up your immunity to logic override. You're more at peace; happier; better to be with; a worthier human being.

What Maturity Means

Psychiatrists and psychologists agree: our ability to make the most of our lives depends on our emotional maturity. Maturity is the *capacity to make constructive use of our inmost feelings.*

Some people fight their inmost feelings all their lives. They put up a great fight, but they pay a terrible price.

These days many people lose their jobs because the jobs are eliminated. However, when we consider just the cases where people are fired for cause, the causes—in four out of five cases—are largely based in emotional difficulties. Extrapolating, we can infer that when companies downsize, the persons who keep their jobs are apt to be those who are most free from emotional problems.

Emotional factors affect most of the other problems of our time—crime, delinquency, drugs, alcoholism, social conflict. In one way or other, each of these reflects failures in personal maturity.

The key to personal success is growth. That's what the psychologists say. Growth is interpreted in different ways. Some people act as if *growth* were a magic mantra. If you say it enough, you somehow achieve it. Others measure growth in titles, dollars, perks—the paraphernalia of promotion in their careers. This, we submit, is dangerous. Growth is not more windows in the office or a longer limo at the curb. Those who think it is are most vulnerable to explosive self-destructive mistakes.

Growth—the only true growth—is the progressive achievement of greater emotional maturity.

To become more mature, we must first know what mature people look like—not their physical appearance, but rather how they meet the challenges of work and life and how they view the world.

Let's take a psychological journey toward a definition of maturity for ourselves. We'll stop along the way to identify the landmarks of maturity. Once you can spot the landmarks, you're better able to map out your own road to satisfying growth.

How to Read This Part

The following few pages shouldn't be just a breezy superficial read.

We're asking you to contemplate your inner self. That's one of the most difficult things in the world to do. And it can be one of the most unpleasant. If you're willing to face the truth about yourself, good or bad, here's how to use this guide.

Read with two purposes: (a) to understand the ideas, and (b) to make the ideas a part of your personality (or, as we say at the psych shop, to *internalize* the ideas). To achieve both results, read more slowly than you usually do, sentence by sentence, asking:

- **Is this statement true of me?**
- **Did I reflect this quality in any situation during the past few days?**
- **Would others recognize this quality in me?**
- **If this desirable quality is not true of me, what can I do to make it true?**

Get into the act as you read. For example:
- **Highlight or underline the statements you think most relevant to you and your needs.**
- **When you come upon a sentence that seems especially applicable, read it aloud.**
- **Rephrase the sentences in your own words.**
- **When you've finished, reread the words you have marked.**

The beginning of wisdom is achieving an accurate *picture of yourself.* Bring that picture into focus.

Some Unpleasant Facts

Let's clear up some misconceptions about maturity.

Is it a Matter of Intelligence?

Maturity does not equate with intellect. In fact, as we have mentioned, a strong overcompensating intellect can impede growth. The most brilliant humans may be woefully immature in their emotions. Just look at Bobby Fischer.

Some of the smartest among us are like children

- In failing to control their feelings
- In their overpowering need for universal affection
- In the way they handle themselves and others
- In their response to frustration

The confusion between intelligence and emotional maturity stems in part from the fact that we speak about *mental* health when we mean *emotional* health. We're talking feeling, not intellect.

Are Mature People Always Happy?

Some people think maturity means happiness. Not so. Freud once said that he considered himself successful if he changed a patient's neurosis into "common unhappiness."

Becoming mature doesn't make you a flower or a vegetable. You have worries, conflicts, pain. Sometimes you blow your top—but the way you do it helps you stay healthy.

Nothing can make life completely free of pain. In some situations it is healthy to be angry, hostile, even depressed. Only a person who has barred all human feelings would be able to live through crises without emotions.

These days we're encouraged to aspire toward a pain-free ideal. Television commercials urge us to—at the first twinge of physical discomfort—rush to the drugstore and buy the latest remedy (STRONGEST MEDICINE YOU CAN BUY WITH OR WITHOUT A PRESCRIPTION! STARTS TO WORK EVEN BEFORE YOU TAKE IT!). We can be trapped into adopting the same approach to emotional pain. No amount of it, no matter how slight, is tolerable. Therefore it has to be stamped out—by taking something for it, by fleeing from it, by getting therapy.

In meeting the challenges of life, we all encounter fear, worry, envy, jealousy, hate, guilt. These emotions do not master the mature person, who takes the suffering as an inescapable facet of experience—part, as they say, of Life's Rich Pageant.

So: emotional maturity does *not* guarantee freedom from worry and difficulty. Emotional maturity is not measured in the way we avoid conflicts but rather by how we deal with them, and how we handle the pain. People who have matured view their difficulties as challenges, not disasters.

How Many of Us Are Mature?

There are many different degrees of maturity. By the strictest standards, most of us fall short of the ideal. So in a sense practically all of us are immature. (There is a kind of positive catch-22 aspect to it: recognizing that we are immature is a sign of maturity.)

So we're all in the same boat, sharing immaturity. That's no reason to despair. An ideal is a goal; its value is the effort it inspires. The practical test is not *what we are now* but *where we are going.* By realizing that we fall short of the ideal of absolute maturity we make real progress. By understanding the ways in which we are immature we make more progress. By taking positive steps to become more mature we grow. And by protecting ourselves against some of the most virulent effects of immaturity we can be happier and more productive.

A definition from Webster's helps to clarity the point: *Mature—to advance toward perfection.*

Note that the preposition is *toward,* not *to.* Perfection is out of reach. The ideal of life is to keep climbing toward it, though we can never touch it.

The Mature Personality

Let's be up front: the climb toward maturity is not a day at the beach. Psychological adjustment is won only through struggle. Some of the things we're talking about here seem hard. That's because they *are* hard. Dr. Lawrence Kubie said, "Psychological liberty means freedom . . . and like all forms of freedom it requires eternal vigilance. The struggle . . . is painful, and inner conflict is inevitable in life."

A brilliant intellect can be used for a time to protect the individual from the pain of struggle. But then the shield is pierced and reality comes flooding in. The individual is engulfed by problems without having developed the emotional maturity to deal with them. Far better to have used one's gifts to grow rather than using them as a shield for immaturity.

Winnowing down the voluminous observations by leading professionals, and guided by our interactions with many gifted individuals, we have arrived at *Six Basic Principles of Maturity*:

1. **Accept yourself**
2. **Accept others**
3. **Keep your sense of humor**
4. **Appreciate simple pleasures**
5. **Enjoy the present**
6. **Welcome work**

1. Accept Yourself

"Accept yourself" is the most important of the six principles—and the hardest to achieve.

Fundamental to mental health is the proposition that *people must accept themselves as they are and as what they are capable of becoming*. You're on the road to maturity if you can begin to appreciate yourself without trying to be what you cannot possibly be.

Immature people create idealized self-images that are fantasy visions, utterly at odds with reality. As we discuss, we all have an idealized self-image. The idea is to shrink the gap between the idealized self-image and reality, not by discarding our aspirations but by bringing them closer to realization.

Implicit in this concept, however, is that these aspirations are capable of realization. Some immature people set their sights on inappropriate goals and, worse, conduct themselves as if they have already attained those unreachable goals.

Emotional immaturity works in the opposite way on some other people. They simply give up on themselves, assuming the worst and assuming further that *the worst* is a permanent state.

Mature people are able to appraise themselves, sizing up the desirable traits and the bad ones. They understand themselves but they are not fixated on themselves. They're able to deal with the outside world because they're not constantly fighting inner battles. To a great extent, acceptance of self is a benefit of emotional health as well as a way of achieving it.

Some guidelines:

Your starting point is to know how you operate. Here the law of averages is on your side; everybody has strengths and weaknesses, likes and dislikes. Learn to know yours.

Be fair to yourself. When you look inward, acknowledge what you find. Take yourself in stride. Recognize your strengths without getting puffed up. Recognize your weaknesses without berating yourself. If you can accept and enjoy your victories, you won't suffer unduly from your defeats.

Take on the right challenges. You have to accept what you can't change, but when you find something that can—and should—be changed, don't duck the responsibility. One of the paramount keys to emotional health is to fight the battles that are worth winning and that you have a chance to win.

The writer Somerset Maugham provides us with a good example of success through ability to confront one's defects. Maugham had many battles to fight. He was scorned by the literati because his writing was too popular, too accessible to the multitudes. He lived under the agonizing necessity to conceal his homosexuality in a time when disclosure meant ostracism and, perhaps, prison.

Why Smart People Do Dumb Things

In his autobiography, *The Summing Up*, Maugham attributes his success to his ability to confront his defects and to make progress in the areas that were open to him without wasting his resources by hammering on doors that would be forever shut. He writes:

> I discovered my limitations and it seemed to me that the only sensible thing was to aim at what excellence I could *within* them. I knew that I had no lyrical quality. I had a small vocabulary, and no efforts that I could make to enlarge it much availed me. I had little gift of metaphor; the original and striking simile never occurred to me. Poetic flights and the great imaginative sweep were beyond my powers. . . . I was tired of trying to do what did not come easily to me.
>
> On the other hand, I had an acute power of observation and it seemed to me that I could see a great many things that other people missed. I could put down in clear terms what I saw. I had a logical sense, and if no great feeling for the richness and strangeness of words, at all events a lively appreciation of their sound. I knew that I should never write as well as I could wish, but I thought with pains *I could arrive at writing as well as my natural defects allowed.*

Maugham is talking about the craft of writing, but his observations apply in the wider sphere to the craft of living.

It's easy to admit our strengths—it's tough to tell ourselves what our weaknesses are. But self-acceptance involves both.

If you're like most people, here are the realities that you will find hardest to accept about yourself:

- **You have experienced failures because of your own deficiencies**
- **There are some situations in your life that you handle badly**
- **You're not happy with the place you now occupy in the world**
- **You still have adolescent dreams that you have not yet given up**

To be mature you must be willing to come to grips with your faults. As Saint Augustine put it, (in *De Ascensione*) "We make a ladder of our vices, if we trample these same underfoot." By doing so we each develop our own unique personality, not a superbeing, free of faults, but rather with our own special combination of virtues and faults.

What a liberating moment, to be able to acknowledge—and, beyond acknowledging, to *celebrate*—our own flawed uniqueness!

The philosopher Martin Buber tells us to actualize our "unique, unprecedented, and never-recurring potentialities, and not the repetition of something that another, and be it even the greatest, has already achieved. . . . The same idea was expressed with even greater pregnancy by Rabbi Zusya when he said: 'In the world to come, I shall not be asked, Why were you not Moses? I shall be asked, Why were you not Zusya?' "

2. Accept Others

Only if you accept yourself with all your faults can you accept others in spite of their deficiencies.

We see, over and over again, very smart people making calamitous mistakes because they don't seem to understand some basic things about dealing with others. They're arrogant, or indifferent, or manipulative, or vindictive. This is not a matter of intellect. Your relations with other people are a basic test of your maturity. If you don't get along well with others it's not because you're not smart enough, or because you're smart and they're dumb. It's because you still need to grow up in some vital centers of your being.

Yes, you deal with people who can drive you crazy. The brighter you are, the more impatient you can become with people who are careless, lazy, conceited, wrongheaded, or just plain dumb. The way you react to their faults is not a judgment on them but on yourself.

Angry people who make you angry reduce you to their level. People who heal your anger with a soft answer raise you to their level.

We all, from time to time, react badly to someone else's deficiency.

It's important to understand why we do so. We may kid ourselves into believing that it's because of the other person's lack of logic, but that's a self-snow-job. If only logic were involved we would respond with logic, rather than with emotion. In such a case the real reason for our anger is that the other person's fault is a threat to us because it makes us doubt ourselves. Our own insecurity has been triggered.

When we know ourselves better we eliminate those "insecurity buttons." We understand that we are not perfect, and we accept the lack of perfection of others. Note that acceptance of others does not mean yielding to their follies. This is a problem that comes up with highly intelligent people. Sensitive to the point of shame about their superiority, they "dumb down" in order to be accepted. Some smart people develop the instinct of dumbing down in childhood. School-mates and playmates can be very cruel indeed to those who are different, and high intelligence makes you different. It's understandable that you might soft-pedal your smarts as a kid to get along; when you continue to do so as a grown-up you are doing something stupid and self-destructive.

Acceptance of others helps you to recognize and deal with their faults. If you are tolerant of their faults you will have no sense of guilt in trying to help them correct their errors. You can criticize constructively, knowing in your heart you have no desire to injure. This can be an all-important key to successful management.

When you accept others with all of their faults, you have the right to expect them to accept you with all of your faults. You don't have to dumb down or give in to their whims in order to make them like you. Mature people don't constantly require the approval of others in order to respect themselves.

A strong intellect can, for a long time, mask the need of its possessor for interactive relationships with others. Sometimes very smart people carry on surface relationships that are simply masterful jobs of acting, good enough to persuade even the actors themselves. This works all right for a while—but finally we all need real connections with other human beings. But we shy away from forming those connections; we don't know how. Or we're scared.

One of the advantages flowing from an acceptance of others is that *you stop being frightened at the idea of depending on others.*

Barbra Streisand has it right: people *need* people. No matter how smart we are, our cognitive power can carry us only so far. We cannot shoulder the responsibility for all of life's multitudinous tasks.

Once we admit to ourselves that we need others, we can accept them and start depending on them without a feeling of anxiety. We can recognize our need for their affection, approval, and appreciation without fear, guilt, or shame.

But when you acknowledge your need for others you can't let the pendulum swing too far in the other direction. It happens. A hard-driving executive, who has never allowed affection or friendship to divert him from his upward drive, reaches the top, relaxes for a moment, and collapses into a ludicrous infatuation that lures him to destruction.

Dependency is uncharted territory for the person who has stood alone. There are pitfalls—going overboard, forming relationships with the wrong people, abdicating one's independence completely, laying oneself open to being hurt. How can we establish a healthy level of dependency—enough, but not too much?

Remember, too, that we are talking here about SCIPIs—persons with exceptional mental resources. They need people—but, frankly, their needs are different from those of more everyday attainments.

Here are the salient characteristics of mature dependency for individuals possessing superior cognitive intelligence:

- *It is occasional, not full time.* SCIPIs lean on others only in times of real need. Dependency is not their normal way of life. Knowing themselves, they pick and choose relationships that will enlist the aid of others to compensate for their weaknesses. They remain independent in the area of their strengths.

• *It is realistic.* Mature dependency is selective—directed only toward those who are (a) able and (b) willing to fulfill our needs. If these two tests are not met, the mature person does not pursue the relationship. Scarlett O'Hara pursued a neurotically immature attachment to Ashley Wilkes, who shrank from her advances, and who, if he had not shrunk, was totally inadequate to the task of giving Scarlett what she needed. When others are able to provide the requisite relationship, but don't want to, mature people don't feel rejected, as Scarlett O'Hara did. They understand that "No, thanks" is not necessarily a personal judgment.

• *It is reciprocal.* The traffic must move both ways. Mature people create relationships that not only allow them to be dependent, but also call upon them to be depended upon.

Reciprocity is an absolute in the mature relationship. We don't have to follow our partners around, opening doors for them. But when they need us, we have to be there. Our reliability doesn't have to be obvious. In *Moby Dick,* all the members of the ship's company (and a ship is a metaphor for interdependence) are more or less immature, including Captain Ahab, who turns his burning gift for command upon the pursuit of a whale. The one exception is the first mate, Starbuck, the one real grown-up on the *Pequod.* Starbuck is reserved, taciturn, careful. But when he is needed, he comes through. Melville tells us that Starbuck's courage was a staple of the ship, like bread or beef, never to be wasted, but always in store when required.

Suppose the other party in the relationship never seems to need you? That's not a complete relationship or a fully satisfying one. You grow by giving of yourself as well as by taking from others. Taking and giving are two sides of the same emotional coin—one can't exist without the other. The mature person is capable of both.

When two people are able to maintain a close relationship based on *mutual dependency* there are no losses—only gains for both.

Healthy dependency often depends on confidentiality. That is one of the primary benefits. The chance to confide in another human being permits you to unload feelings that, if bottled up inside, could get distorted.

The ability to share attitudes is a great privilege, valuable professionally as well as personally. Within the confidential cloister of your relationship you can trot out your weirdest and most off-the-wall notions, your most extreme opinions, the prejudices you would not want anyone else to know about.

One of the curious and precious things about the confidential, mature relationship is the fact that you will get at least as much—and maybe more—out of what you have to say as from the advice you receive from the other party.

Note that the mature person is *selectively* confidential. Some people rush headlong into confidentiality with everyone. You may have run into such folks. You meet them at the hors d'oeuvres table and five minutes later you are hearing the excruciating details of their dreams, their finances, their digestion, and their sex lives, as you look around wildly for somebody to rescue you.

We extend confidentiality along a continuum. With some we exchange the time of day. With others we discuss our feelings about our jobs. With a select few we exchange the intimate confidences of our personal life.

3. Keep Your Sense of Humor

"Laugh and be well," said the English poet Matthew Green. The mature person acts on the advice.

A sense of humor is an important adjunct of maturity. But there is a world of difference between immature humor and mature humor. Drift into a bar across the street from the advertising agency, or the insurance company, or the architect's office, or the computer firm, or any kind of business at all. From one corner you hear snorts of shrill laughter. People are vying to put each other down and to rip those who are not present, especially their bosses. Over in this other corner things are quieter. There are smiles, though, and an occasional laugh. Here people are carrying on exchanges that contain occasional observations on life, on fortune, and on the foibles of the speakers themselves.

Mature persons don't often joke at the expense of other people. Nor do they find it hilarious when other people are hurt, or made to look silly or inferior, or derided because of appearance or handicaps or misfortunes. These days we have seen a kind of apotheosis of imma-ture humor: Howard Stern; Rush Limbaugh, who is a kind of Liberace of the far right; even David Letterman, a sophisticated comedian who makes it with immature stuff because that's what works.

Let's make a distinction here. Juvenile humor—jeering, in-your-face, dirty—is often *very funny*. We the authors enjoy it as much as anyone else. But it's shtick, not substance.

Emotionally healthy people like their own personal humor to be good-humored. On the whole that's not only the healthiest but also the most productive kind of humor for business and personal rela-tionships. Your humor reflects your attitudes toward people. The ma-ture person uses humor not as a bludgeoning hammer but rather as a plane to shave off rough edges. Here Abraham Lincoln was a master. Typically, one day he was visited by a delegation of irate citizens who had come to criticize him vociferously about something or other. Lin-coln suggested to them, "Suppose all the property you were worth was in gold and you had put it in the hands of Blondin [the world-famous French tightrope walker] to carry across the Niagara River on a rope. Would you shake the cable or keep shouting at him, 'Blondin, stand up a little straighter—Blondin, stoop a little more?' No, you would hold your breath as well as your tongue, and keep your hands off until he was safely over."

Tact is another way by which mature persons show their basic respect for others. Henry Clay was noted for his skill with the tactful, humorous compliment. He was asked by a lady, "Don't you remember my name?" Clay replied, "No, for when we met long ago, I was sure your beauty and accomplishment would very soon compel you to change it."

You could not get away with it today, but it sure worked for Henry Clay.

4. Appreciate Simple Pleasures

Emotionally healthy people are not constantly seeking unusual kicks—helicopter skiing from 12,000 feet, exotic places, exotic drugs, exotic sex.

Mature people have their own special tastes, of course. Some like to walk in the woods. Some like to be around little kids. Some enjoy watching a ball game, while others get the same thrill from a book. Some are never happier than when learning new things—a language, a woodworking skill or sewing stitch, a computer program. Some derive equal enjoyment from teaching what they know to others. The capacity to get excited over things even when they seem ordinary to others—this is a sign of a healthy personality.

Nor are mature people bored by repetition. Some folks are enslaved by the cult of the new. Mature people continue to enjoy the things that are valuable to them no matter how often repeated. Repetition, to them, is a joy, not a drag. They are not like the wife whose husband complained that she never said she loved him, and who answered, "I told you I loved you the day we got engaged, and you know I never go back on my word." Good things, like good dishes, can be savored again and again.

Mature people enjoy the simple pleasures, knowing that through them they achieve success as one philosopher defines it:

To laugh often and love much;

to win the respect of intelligent persons and the affection of children;

to earn the approbation of honest critics and endure the betrayal of false friends;

to appreciate beauty;

to find the best in others;

to give oneself

to leave the world a bit better, whether by a healthy child, a garden patch or a redeemed social condition;

to have played and laughed with enthusiasm and sung with exultation;

to know even one life has breathed easier because you have lived—*this is to have succeeded.*

5. Enjoy the Present

Maturity means knowing how to make the most of *today*. Emotional grown-ups don't live on an expectancy basis. They plan for the future, but they know they must also live in the present. The mature person realizes that the best insurance for tomorrow is the effective use of today.

Too much joy goes down the drain because smart people waste their intelligence by kicking themselves about what has gone past or worrying about the future.

Monsignor William T. Greene of Saint Patrick's Cathedral in New York observed that each day should be lived as it if were "all time and eternity." This view of living, he said, kills morbid regrets over the past and morbid worry over the future. In the process, you do not disregard the future; each day is set in harmony with the days to come.

Immature people lack a good grip on the future. Some have a great fear of the future. Others act, as the saying has it, as if there were "no tomorrow." Emotionally healthy individuals know there is a tomorrow.

They automatically crank that knowledge into their handling of today. They acknowledge that, while we can provide for tomorrow, we cannot altogether foresee it or control it. So they do not allow the uncertainties of tomorrow to interfere with their enjoyment of today.

Mature people handle uncertainty with aplomb. They are not frustrated by being left in doubt. They can tolerate the ambiguous. Intolerance of ambiguity leads smart people to do foolish things as they try to abolish uncertainty from their lives. The unknown does not frighten them. They don't cling to the familiar. They are willing to venture into new projects and new places.

One interesting current approach to eliminating uncertainty from life is by the construction of systems. If your system is sophisticated enough you are immune to the vicissitudes that beset ordinary mortals. Gamblers with systems are beloved by casino operators, who lure system players with "comps"—free meals, drinks, rooms, and so on. This is, of course, because nobody has ever devised a system that can actually beat the house at roulette, blackjack, or craps. But this does not stop a lot of smart people from trying.

They try in Wall Street, too. Early in April 1994 the newspapers reported[1] that David J. Askin, a hot fund manager, had lost more than $500 million, which had been invested in his two funds, Granite Capital and Granite Partners. The investors included blue chip corporations, wealthy families, and pension funds. As the *Times* reported, the funds "promised investors 15 percent annual returns with low risk, and over the last two years they had successfully delivered such returns."

Without going into too much detail, it seems the essence of Askin's approach was "a low-risk approach to investing in bonds backed by home mortgages." David Askin, described as "articulate, arrogant, brainy and egotistical . . . had parlayed his years of experience in finance into a theory about how a small corner of the financial markets behaves. Perhaps, it would seem in retrospect, he came to believe too fiercely in his theory that he could invest money so cleverly that it would bring a handsome return with only a smidgen of risk. Perhaps he thought he had the perfect riskless system."

In looking at David Askin's case we note the words "a theory about how a small corner of the financial markets behaves." This is what we might call the Closed System Fallacy. If that small corner were altogether insulated from the larger world perhaps the theory would work, returning 15 percent perpetually. But *the system—ANY system—is almost never closed.* The world comes flooding over the gunwales.

There are no magic formulas to stamp out ambiguity. The uncertainty principle pervades life, moment to moment. Revel in the variety; look forward to the surprises that each new moment brings.

6. Welcome Work

Emotionally healthy persons know how to enjoy the experience of work—that is, work in all its aspects, the "Mickey Mouse" along with the momentous, the nitty-gritty as well as the big picture.

Appreciation of work is a hallmark of mature people—bankers, scholars, builders, researchers, and so on. Immature people are constantly fighting certain aspects of their work. They resent routine reports, or meetings, or correspondence. They allow these annoyances to grate on their nerves continually. Satisfaction in doing a good job is blocked out by the dust speck in the eye of resentment over trivia.

You enjoy your work thoroughly once you stop fighting parts of it. The parts are necessary. Routine is susceptible to skillful handling as are big decisions. Mature people develop—and enjoy—what Thorstein Veblen called "the instinct of workmanship." Oliver Wendell Holmes talked about pride in one's work: "To hammer out as compact and as solid a piece of work as one can, to try to make it first rate"—this is a goal of all mature people.

Isn't It About Time You Grew Up?

A One-Day Test of Your Maturity Quotient

How grown up are you?

Try this experiment. Set aside a day that you expect to be normal. Not too much pressure—and not too little.

Now make up your mind that you are going, on this chosen day, to aim at achieving four acts of maturity:

1. *Give more than you usually do, and enjoy it.* Be a spendthrift with time, energy, ideas, comfort—whatever people reasonably ask of you. For example:

  • **When anybody asks for five minutes of your time, decide that he/she can have ten**

  • **When somebody asks how long a project will take, don't give an off-the-cuff or "political" answer—give it some real thought**

  • **When you're tempted to put off an unpleasant task, make that a reason for doing it immediately**

2. *Try to understand instead of condemning.* On this day, as on others, things will go wrong. Welcome the mishap as a chance to test your maturity. Look for causes, not scapegoats. Find out *why* it went wrong.

3. *Increase your contact with people, and keep it pleasant.* Combine pleasure—a laugh, a casual remark, a wisecrack, a question about personal well-being (ask "How's it going?" and really listen to the answer)—with business and the everyday transactions of life. Don't just look like you are listening—really listen. When you find something to praise, praise it.

4. *Show flexibility.* Look for opportunities to change your mind. Explore different approaches to familiar jobs. Give serious consideration to suggestions. Pay double attention to criticisms.

Shoot for these four goals all day. Then, when you get home, check out how you feel. Are you more relaxed? Do you feel better about yourself, about other people? Did you accomplish as much, or more, with less effort?

Try it and see. You may find that these principles are worth following every day. After all, *every day of your life is really an experiment in maturity.*

Growth Checklist

By answering the questions below you can get some idea of your growth during the past year—in your working life and in your personal life. Whenever the answer is yes, check the appropriate box.

In judging your own responses, remember the first principle of maturity: *Accept yourself!* The number of checks you make is not significant. What does count is the quality of progress you have made in *areas that you yourself select* as important to your life.

Check off the list. Put it aside. Then, in six months, check it again.

	In the past year	In your work	In your personal life
1. Did you take training or instruction to further your progress?	_____	_____	_____
2. Did you step up your reading?	_____	_____	_____
3. Did you increase your participation in group activities?	_____	_____	_____
4. Did you improve your ability to handle routine and repetitive activities?	_____	_____	_____
5. Did you at any time review what you are doing, asking which activities should continue, which should be dropped?	_____	_____	_____

	In the past year	In your work	In your personal life
6. Did you find it easier to deal with people?			
7. Did you have fewer emotional flare-ups?			
8. Did you get greater enjoyment out of periods of relaxation and recreation?			
9. Did you devote more time to thinking about why others behave as they do?			
10. Were you more likely to concentrate on one activity until it was complete?			
11. Did you devote more time to helping others solve their problems?			
12. Did you get greater satisfaction out of helping others?			
13. Did you improve any of your skills?			
14. Did you develop any new talents?			
15. Did you come up with any new conclusions about yourself, your personality, your habits?			
16. Did you seek more varied activities?			
17. Did you develop new friendships?			
18. Did you find yourself making more independent decisions?			
19. Was it easier to live with problems that had no immediate solutions?			

	In the past year	In your work	In your personal life
20. Did you change some of your opinions and feelings about things?	_____	_____	_____
21. Did you show a willingness to open yourself to new experiences?	_____	_____	_____
22. Did you gain a clearer conviction and/or a better understanding of the basic truths (religion, philosophy) in which you believe?	_____	_____	_____

Notes

1. *New York Times*, April 5, 1994, "Fund Manager Caught Short by Crude and Brutal Market," by Saul Hansell.

Chapter 14.

GUIDANCE CONTROL—
CALIBRATING YOUR
INNER COMPASS

They're testing a new guidance system for drivers. Your car is hooked up by radio to an electronic nerve center. At this headquarters, an operator watches as tiny dots of light move around on a large grid map of the surrounding area. Your car is one of those little dots. As you move along a street, stop at a light, turn a corner, the blip of light moves, stops, turns on the map. Whether or not you know where you are, the operator is aware of your exact location.

So you get lost. Instead of looking for a gas station or pulling up and asking some dubious-looking louts on the corner, you just ask for help from HQ. The operator knows where you're going and where you are. A confident voice in your ear says, "You're now on Prince Avenue. Proceed two blocks until you come to a traffic light. That's Princess Street. Turn right. Go four blocks until you come to a stop sign. This is Elm Street. Turn left on Elm. Your destination is the King Building, number 314, which is the fourth building on your left from the corner. . . ."

It's a pilot program. No doubt, one fine day, the whole process will be automated. As you drive, you can check your position, destination, and proper course at any given time. And, beyond that, the time will come when you get into your vehicle, punch in your destination, and sit back while you are transported automatically.

We all lose our way now and then, and not just on the road. That's okay; we don't stay lost for long. Our guidance system kicks in. Some of us communicate with an operator at headquarters. We pray to be shown the way. Others of us lack the consolation of a formal religion and a definable God to whom we pray and who leads us along the path of life He has chosen for us. But that doesn't mean we lack a guidance system.

Healthy mature people, whatever their degree of religious belief or lack of it, have a set of values. For many, their values are inherited, passed down the generations. Others grow to adulthood wearing certain beliefs, like clothes, and then discard those beliefs for new ones.

You don't need a religious creed to have a healthy set of values. How should people act when they honestly find no ultimate meaning to existence, and no predetermined values laid down for us by a Higher Authority? It's a vital question—because our values are the components of the guidance system that will lead us through the minefields of self-destruction.

The existentialist approach to life, delineated by Jean-Paul Sartre, says that the human mind is incapable of discerning any meaning in existence. (This is not the same as saying that there is no meaning—just that it will always remain a mystery to us.)

The meaninglessness of existence might lead to despair; for many, unfortunately, it does—not a sudden gush of despair, but a slow, creeping despair that wastes away one's inner fiber. The existentialists and similar thinkers say that, in the absence of a morality handed down to us from heaven, we must create our own morality.

Perhaps the most important element in this earthling-created morality is honesty with oneself. This is not a passive morality, a set of values that we give lip service to, but which we don't try to exemplify, saying, "What's the use?" Sartre said that we have a responsibility to ourselves and to the other men and women with whom we share the planet to espouse values, make those values into a cause when appropriate, and advance that cause, fighting for it when necessary. The proper position for the human being is that of being *engaged*—actively engaged in the shaping of one's life.

Albert Camus agreed with Sartre about some things and disagreed about others. Camus accepted the burden of living life without an ultimate meaning or purpose. Nevertheless, says Camus, we can live with dignity when we face our condition and try our best to find and live by such human values as individual freedom, intercommunication, and love.

In a way, says Camus, in *The Myth of Sisyphus* (1942), our existence is like that of the mythical king Sisyphus, condemned forever to push a huge rock to the top of a hill, only to see it roll back down again. But that is not a reason for despair. Even within the Sisyphusean limitations of our lives, we are capable of grandeur, nobility, accomplishment, joy. The last words of Camus's essay, (in Justin O'Brien's translation, Knopf, 1964, p. 123) are:

The struggle itself toward the heights is enough to fill a man's heart. One must imagine Sisyphus happy.

Do-It-Yourself Kit for a Compass

Everybody needs values—not as vague abstractions, but rather because they are of great pragmatic use in living a happy and productive life, getting ahead, attaining our goals, and steering clear of the pitfalls of self-destructive intelligence.

The smarter you are, the more necessary it may be for you to build a guidance system into your makeup. Values are the microchips and transducers of the system.

A. H. Maslow popularized the term *self-actualization*. Self-actualizing people are the doers and achievers, the people who achieve the harmony of psychic wholeness. Maslow identifies various qualities in the self-actualizers: detachment, autonomy, problem centering, spontaneity, interpersonal relations. Maslow finds that a strong set of values is essential.

These are not hand-me-down values: "The topmost portion of the value system of the self-actualizing person is entirely unique and idiosyncratic-character-structure-expressive."[1] When you think about it, it's obvious. No two people are exactly alike, so no two value systems can be exactly alike. People may "buy the whole nine yards," conforming to what their parents said, or what a religious leader says, or to some other set of values. But since we cannot know every nook and cranny of another's mind—no matter how close we are—we're bound to adapt what we receive, even if we don't want to.

So Who Needs Values?

Nowadays "values" gets misused a lot. "Family values" is a political buzz term. It's a useful term, connoting a general set of viewpoints on questions ranging from prayer in schools and pro-life versus pro-choice to taxation and the death penalty. But the term is misleading. It's even more misleading when the implication is that values are things that "good" people have in abundance, whereas "bad" people lack values. Conversely, there are those who scorn "values" as outmoded encumbrances that just hold us back when we are fighting to survive in a dog-eat-dog world. Thus the person who refuses to cheat on a test is deemed to have values, whereas the cheater does not.

Let's clear that up. Both cheater and non-cheater have values. They're different, that's all.

Then there is the common comparison between *absolute* values against *relative* values. "Relativism" has become a bad word. A person who is accused of having relative values is somehow designated as being of lower worth or moral character than the person who espouses "eternal" values.

Since values are the main components of our guidance systems, it's important to establish a good working definition of the term.

For openers, all living creatures have values. The psychologist Charles Morris[2] observes that there are "operative" values—the behaviors of organisms as they show preference for one objective as against another. Carl Rogers, commenting on Morris's statement, says the "lowly earthworm, selecting the smooth arm of a Y maze rather than the arm that is paved with sandpaper, is giving an indication of an operative value."[3]

Since human beings are not earthworms, we go about the job of establishing values a little differently. We conceptualize; we envision values in terms of symbols or generalities ("Honesty is the best policy").

A "value" is a control device that guides the behavior of the individual in filling a need. Needs, or "objects," vary. One of the abiding psychological works tells us, "The *value world* of a given organism is the *world of objects to which it is fixated*."[4] The earthworm's object is to keep moving along the smoothest path. The tiger's object is to nourish itself with meat. The concertgoer's object is to get pleasure from listening to Stravinsky or Springsteen.

The *values* we live by—whether they are deliberately thought out or automatic—are the internal controls that guide us toward our objectives, toward the fulfillment of our needs. The needs of lower organisms don't change much. Humans adopt or discard values as their situations change.

Back to the standard work: "For our purpose, a value is thus simply the maintenance of a set toward the attainment of a goal. . . ."

At any given time we are a seething mass of values. Those values may come into conflict. An eminent political consultant has, as an important value, the election of the candidates who hire him. He has a concomitant value—to be recognized as a leader in his profession so that he will be hired by other candidates.

If those were the only values at work, then the consultant would not, a few days after a tremendous victory, tell the media that he won by cheating. There is another value at work here. Making a rival feel bad? Looking like a tough guy? Exposing the prevalent corruption of politics?

We don't know. What we do know is that, in that case, and in a multitude of cases of smart people going off the rails, it is not so much a matter of the value system failing as it is a matter of other, hidden values taking over. When you see the dreaded computer virus spreading across your screen, it's not that there is no program at work, it is that another, malignant program is taking over.

As we work to upgrade and overhaul our guidance system, the components we deal with are values.

Some cynical, hard-boiled people are surprised when we bring up the topic of their values. They don't think they have any. They're like Molière's Monsieur Jourdain, the title character in *Le Bourgeois Gentilhomme*, who reacts with astonishment when he learns that he has been talking prose all his life and never knew it.

We all have values. They guide the flow of our decisions, small and large, as we move through the day. Trouble is, we don't always know what mix of values is driving us at a given time.

Revaluing Yourself

If your guidance system is working properly, you do the right thing instinctively without having to stop and think. If his system had been in good working order, Ed Rollins would not have had to ask himself, before facing the media, "Shall I tell these guys I stole the election by paying off the opposition?" Nor, if their inner compasses had been calibrated properly, would Hillary Rodham Clinton and Stew Leonard and Stephen Chao and all the other smart screwups have had to carry on interior debates. They would know *instinctively* the way to go to avoid self-destroying mistakes.

To tune up your guidance system, look over the following eleven life goals. Most of us are guided by a mix of goals, with one goal dominant and several subordinate.

1. Leadership. Running things. Organizing. Controlling other people. Calling the shots.

2. Expertness. Authority on special subjects, respected by other experts. Reaching high levels of skill and accomplishment.

3. Fame. Being well-known, even notorious. Recognition, awards, status.

4. Service. To contribute to the well-being and improvement of others. To lighten burdens, to help those who need help.

5. Wealth. Amassing a lot of money and a big estate.

6. Independence. Feeling free of outer pressures and inner compulsions; being able to make one's own decisions.

7. Affection. Sharing companionship, friends, partners, family.

8. Security. Stability in life, a steady job, dependable sources of financial support.

9. Self-realization. Optimizing personal development, achieving personal best. Achieving one's maximum creative potential.

10. Duty. Total dedication to worthy principles. Submersion in service to persons and/or ideals.

11. Pleasure. Enjoying happiness, having the good things in life.

These are the components of human guidance systems. Your system has at its core a mix of these motivations. When you know your dominant life goal, and the two or three collateral life goals that make up your motivating cluster, you have a better working understanding of yourself. And you are better equipped to frustrate the gremlin who lurks within your intellectual circuitry, scheming to impel you to make a fool of yourself.

Compatible Life Goals

Some goals nest together nicely. Effective *leadership* draws *wealth* and *prestige* in its wake. *Independence* is a fertile culture for *self-realization*.

Incompatibilities

If your highest goal is *affection*, you may not be able to exercise all-out *leadership*. If you try to balance *service*, *duty*, and *wealth* as equivalent goals you are likely to fail.

Excesses

Anything carried to excess is harmful. That goes for life goals. In *Death of a Salesman*, Willy Loman's burning dream was not just to be liked, but *well* liked, and it drove him to destruction.

Defining Goals in Your Own Terms

Goals are not abstractions. It's vapid to pursue some big word like *duty* without figuring out what it means in your life. We asked a great musician—an instrumentalist and arranger—how he defined *independence*. He said, "When you sit at the piano and strike three bars for love and one for dinner, you're all right. I was striking three bars for dinner, so I quit."

Rank Your Goals

What's your dominant goal? You may not have thought in terms of life goals, at least not in a long time. Or you may assume you know your dominant motivating ideal, but you may be wrong.

The idea of this exercise is to enable you to lift the hood and get to know your guidance system. For openers, you need to reexamine three basic questions:

- **Who am I?**
- **What do I want?**
- **What price will I pay?**

Here's a checklist that will help.

Who . . . What . . . How Much?
- If you could have any job in the world, what would it be?
- What do you enjoy most in your leisure time?
- Who or what has the greatest emotional hold on you?
- Who or what irritates you the most?
- How important is it for you to win?
- How intelligent are you compared to most people you know?
- Do you enjoy power?
- What do you worry about the most?
- If a genie could give you anything you wished, what would it be?

Let these questions lead to other questions. Think about what you like, what you dislike, what you want. That means, what you *really* want—not what you think you're supposed to want, or what other people expect you to want, or what you used to think you wanted. We're talking *now.*

When you've thought about who you are and what you want, turn to the life goals. Which is most important to you? And how much are you willing to pay to achieve it? A bodybuilder who wants to be the strongest man in the world doses himself with steroids until he is a monstrosity. Some people take emotional steroids. In pursuit, say, of unlimited wealth, they ruthlessly trample over affection, self-realization, even pleasure. All well and good—if that's the goal you really want, and the price you're willing to pay for it.

Identify Your Current Constellation of Goals

Figure out, to the best of your ability, the dominant life goal and the two or three collateral goals that drive you. They are your guidance system. If, say, your dominant goal is *fame,* then, when faced with a choice between achieving good results quietly and making a big splash, you will plunge in for the big splash, even if it's the shallow end of the pool.

If your guidance system is accurate—if the goals that drive it are the valid goals for you—then your inner compass will keep guiding you in the right direction, though you may stray from course once in a while.

Review your goals periodically. When your life situation changes, your goals should change appropriately. When you have two kids and a mortgage, *security* grows in importance relative to your other goals—though it need not drive them out. The idea is to realize that you have a guidance system, to make sure it isn't guiding you in the wrong direction, and to review important options in the light of your values.

Chats with David Letterman

A man we know—a dyed-in-the-wool SCIPI—loused up his life on several occasions by making spectacularly bad choices. Now, faced with important challenges, he talks them over, in his imagination, with a devil's advocate. To add realism and punch, he imagines the devil's advocate to be a real person—someone who will jeer, scold, and shame him if he's about to do something really dumb.

Typically, he "talks over" a big career move with David Letterman:

DL: Let me get this straight. You spend twenty years with big corporations. And now you're gonna run your own little company?

OUR FRIEND: That's right.

DL: Get your own coffee? Stamp your own letters? Remember to turn off the lights at night?

OF: Yeah. What do you think?

DL: I think you're NUTS! The first day, you'll never get out of the men's room. You'll be standing in there waiting for somebody to hand you a towel!

Tune up your value guidance system. Tighten the connections, clean the terminals. Get it in good working order, and then let it do its job of steering you clear of the rocky reefs of intellectual self-destruction.

Notes

1. A. H. Maslow, "Self-Actualization: A Study in Psychological Health," in *Symposia on Topical Issues*, vol. I, W. Wolff, ed. (New York: Grune and Stratton, 1950).
2. C. W. Morris, *Varieties of Human Value* (Chicago University Press, 1956).
3. Carl B. Rogers, "Toward a Modern Approach to Values: the Valuing Process in the Mature Person," *Journal of Abnormal and Social Psychology*, vol. LXVIII (1964).
4. Gardner Murphy, Lois Barclay Murphy, and Theodore M. Newcomb, *Experimental Social Psychology* (New York: Harper & Brothers, 1931), pp. 198–199.

Chapter 15.

CONNECTORS: CONTACT POINTS WITH REALITY

Your mind keeps pulling you away from contact with reality. You tend to disconnect. In your cocoon of intellectual isolation, you grow careless. You can do anything. Nothing can hurt you.

You're riding for a fall. The further you have withdrawn from reality, the greater the damage that fall will do.

Build connectives into your everyday life. Here are some examples.

Roots Retrieval. At least once a year author Feinberg and his brother, a surgeon, drive to the Bronx to see the neighborhood and the house in which they grew up. It's a largely Hispanic neighborhood now, poor; it was poor when the Feinberg family was struggling to make it there.

Sara Meléndez heads the Independent Sector, the largest philanthropic coalition in the United States. Meléndez is Puerto Rican. She worked her way through Brooklyn College. She raised a family in the Brownsville section of Brooklyn. Her younger sister, Rebecca, gave her "a small silver model of the old-fashioned sewing machine with treadle" that their mother used as a seamstress. Sara Meléndez said, "It came with a message: 'You've come a long way, baby! But don't ever forget where you came from.' "[1]

Cary Grant, born in Bristol, England, as Archibald Leach, wanted to keep remembering his early struggles; he named his dog Archie Leach.

Cut a plant off from its roots and it dies. Your background is an essential part of you. Replenish your feeling for it. Revisit the place you came from or a place like it. Remember what it was like. Take an objective look at what it's like now.

Connectors: Contact Points with Reality

You exist not just in the current moment but as the result of a process, a step along a continuum. To more truly gauge where you are now and where you're headed, look back to where you've come from.

Mirror, Mirror. Meshaulam Riklis, the merger and acquisitions tycoon and art connoisseur, looks at his face to keep his feet on the ground. Every day, while shaving, Riklis looks into his mirror and asks, "Who's the best?"

"You are," comes the answer. This reply satisfied the wicked queen in Snow White, but it does not satisfy Riklis. "Who says so?"

"Your public relations man says so."

Riklis nods and says, "I'm paying him to say so." He's able to proceed on his day with a sense of humor and perspective about himself.

Listening for the Metamessage. One of the dangerous drawbacks of being smarter than other people is that you don't listen to what they're saying. It's trite. It misses the point. You've thought of it already.

You're wasting a great gift. You may not be the Amazing Kreskin, but your intelligence gives you the power to read minds.

At least once a day, when you're forced to hear something uninteresting, make it interesting by listening, not to the words, but to the *metamessage*.

Samuel I. Hayakawa—scholar, university president, U.S. senator—defines the metamessage as "a message *about* the message ... the most important pieces of social information that we have about each other are not messages so much as they are metamessages."

As people talk banalities, they are really expressing some of their hopes, fears, feelings about you. Some occasions, like cocktail parties, are primarily for the exchange of metamessages. So listen. Ask yourself, "What is he/she really saying?"

You will be exercising a useful intellectual muscle. You will make boring conversations infinitely more interesting. And you will be making connection with the real world.

Self-Questioning. The eminent executive search consultant Gerry

Roche, chairman of the board of Heidrick & Struggles, told us that when the great titans of industry relax with him, one-on-one, they often manifest a high degree of insecurity, asking, "How did I get here?"

We all have questions like that. We use our agile minds to deflect them, thinking of something else.

It's not a bad idea to sit down alone with yourself—say, once a week—and contemplate the toughest questions you can:

- **How did I get here?**
- **Do I really deserve to be here?**
- **What do I fear the most?**

The answers won't come easily, if at all. If your mind does produce some pat answers, it's giving you a snow job. The point is to bring before your mental gaze, front and center, the ephemeral nature of success, the caprice of fortune, and the fallibility of all humanity, you included.

Formulate Mental Mantras. We can keep ourselves from doing dumb things with pertinent slogans. A smart, but sometimes overly intense, financial manager stops himself by flashing on his mind screen the simple warning "Don't get compulsive, Jimmy."

Great thinkers of the past provide us with valuable intellectual bumper stickers. For example, we've discussed the tendency of smart persons to overintellectualize, making things more complicated than they need to be.

Listen to Occam's razor, the dictum of the fourteenth-century philosopher William of Occam, who said, *Entia non sunt multiplicanda praetor,* which of course means "Entities should not be proliferated needlessly." A more commonplace and useful version: "Always pick the simplest answer."

Get a (Second) Life. Amusements and hobbies may not be enough to keep your intellect fit. The writer Peter Drucker urges that gifted people develop avocations that use elements of skill not used in their everyday work. The involvement should be serious, and it should be subject to the judgment of peers. Sometimes the alternate career is light-years removed from the first career. As Drucker comments, Field Marshal Sir Archibald Wavell, leader of British armies in World War II, was a good minor poet, respected by other poets and academicians. Inevitably this brings to mind the great American poet Wallace Stevens, who had a successful career as a lawyer and insurance executive in Hartford, Connecticut. They say that at Stevens's funeral in 1955, some of his insurance colleagues were astonished to learn that he had been a world-renowned poet, and some of the leading lights of the world of literature and poetry were amazed to learn of his insurance work.

You're not likely to astound the world with your second career. That's not the idea. The idea is to do something that you and others respect, that extends your intellect, and that gives you a satisfying feeling of accomplishment. The range is vast, from politics to petit point; the goal is to be as good as you can be.

Temper Expertise with Feedback. Experts can get so caught up in their specialties that they lose contact with common sense. Here's one example. In 1993 the American Jewish Committee commissioned the respected Roper organization to conduct a poll. One finding was shocking: the poll results appeared to show that one out of five Americans doubted that the Holocaust ever happened.

Now it turns out that the poll was flawed by the wording of a key question. The polling experts worked long and hard to construct a "neutral, value-free" query. Here's what they came up with: Does it seem possible or does it seem impossible to you that the Nazi extermination of the Jews never happened?

Huh? How could they have expected people to understand this? The pollster Burns W. Roper said, "We never should have approved the question, and we certainly never should have written it."[2]

To the experts, immersed in their discipline, the wording of the question was the solution to a professional problem. If they had listened to feedback from nonexperts they would have realized that it was gibberish.

Slowtime. Our world moves faster and faster, and our minds with it. Today, thanks to the beeper, the portable phone, the modem and the fax, there is never any downtime for the brain.

We pay a price for all this instantaneousness. Smart people get ahead in the environment of speed because they think faster than others. But, paradoxically, if you think fast enough for long enough, it's as if you stop thinking altogether.

Give yourself some *slowtime*—time away from instantaneousness. Spend the moments before going to sleep not with TV or a fast-moving magazine article, but with a big, leisurely novel: *Middlemarch . . . Washington Square . . . Death Comes for the Archbishop . . . War and Peace.*

Great, solid books impose their own, slower time on you. It's not that they are dull; far from it. They scroll before our eyes the rich multifariousness of existence. But they do it on their own terms. They will not be hurried.

Your form of *slowtime* needn't be a book. Go for a weekend to someplace where there is "absolutely nothing to do."

Build some slowtime into your fast-track life.

Become Part of an Ethical Community. One valuable way to renew and refresh your contact with the world, and to put your view of yourself into perspective, is to become part of a community that is devoted to an ideal.

Religion is an obvious choice. Even for nonbelievers, there are rich rewards in familiarity with the concepts and tenets of religion. You don't have to be an observant Jew to respond to the Haggadah read at the Passover Seder, when it talks about how people "can be enslaved to themselves. When they let emotion sway them to their hurt, when they permit harmful habits to tyrannize them—they are slaves. When laziness or cowardice keeps them from doing what they know to be the right, when ignorance blinds them so that, like Samson, they can only turn round in meaningless drudgery—they are slaves.

When envy, bitterness and jealousy sour their joys and darken the brightness of their contentment—they are slaves to themselves and shackled by the chains of their own forging."

Sampling the Bible, the Talmud, the Koran, the book of Mormon—and other religious texts—is a nourishing experience.

Or your ethical community may be more secular, devoted to the earth and its creatures, or to the contemplation of history, or to the pursuit of philosophy. Being a part of such a community is a *connective*.

Revaluing. Periodically store people go through the place looking at the stock and changing the prices.

Sit down with yourself and hold a revaluation inventory. What do you believe that you did not believe before? What do you no longer believe? What opinions are less important than before? Which have become more important?

What's your bottom line? Think of the position from which *you will not be dislodged*, no matter what. Loyalty to a friend. A promise. A debt of honor. A principle you will not give up, no matter what you're offered, no matter what price you have to pay.

If, in your revaluing process, you discover that you have *no* bottom line—that there is no principle on which you are willing to stand, come hell or high water—then it's time to take another look at the meaning of your existence.

"It Seemed Like a Smart Idea at the Time." People who make a fair share of mistakes are always reviewing their reasons for doing something, because they're not sure of themselves. Those who "never" make a mistake never look back.

That, in itself, is a mistake. Circumstances change. The factors that made your decision right yesterday may have altered by today. Insecure people have their own problems, but at least they take another look at the premises on which they are acting.

From time to time, revisit the launch point of an important course on which you have embarked. Evaluate the factors afresh, not as they were then, but as they are now. This kind of review may save you from having to say, "But it seemed like a smart idea at the time."

Stay Aware of the Syndrome. Once you begin thinking in terms of self-destructive Intelligence Syndrome you see it everywhere. When you read the papers and see, for example, that some of the country's biggest corporations and financial institutions gave millions to a guy who promised a 15 percent return with hardly any risk, stop for a moment and speculate on what happened.

The talk and tabloid TV shows do not teem with great intelligence, but you will nevertheless find smart people doing dumb things. The news broadcasts are a rich storehouse of smart stupidity.

Some of the best entertainment shows are built around the idea of intelligent people committing idiocies. Jerry Seinfeld and his buddies are a seething mass of self-destructive intellect, smart people forever lousing themselves up *because* they are so smart.

You find the syndrome in outstanding movies, like *Howards End, The Remains of the Day,* and any number of Woody Allen films. (While you're at it, think about what happened to Woody Allen.) Certain great classics of the screen focus totally on smart people doing dumb things. Take the enduring *All About Eve.* It's worthwhile for those interested in SDIS to rent the film. In it, bright, successful persons swirl around each other, using their cleverness to commit blunders that devastate their own lives and the lives of others. Only one character, the critic Addison De Witt (played by George Sanders) *knows* he is betraying his intelligence by doing something fatally stupid. But he does it anyway.

And, as you look around you and see smart people doing dumb things, ask yourself, *"How do I know something like this can't happen to me?"*

Hi Mom, Hi Dad. In gatherings involving parents, siblings, other relatives, many of us tend to switch off most of our lobes and make the right smiling responses without really listening. That's a waste. Observing—and thinking about—your closest kin can be instructive.

You know, of course, that your relations with your parents have contributed substantially to making you the person that you are. Think about how a sheltering relationship with a parent may have enhanced a tendency in you toward superiority, intellectual arrogance, and rash self-confidence.

Look at your siblings for hints of such relationships and influences. Look at your relatives for traces of tendencies that you might be harboring, all unknowing, in your own makeup.

Notes

1. *New York Times*, May 20, 1994, "Philanthropic Coalition Names a New President," by Kathleen Teltsch.
2. *New York Times*, May 20, 1994, "Pollster Finds Error in Holocaust Doubts," by John Kifner.

Chapter 16.

THE SMART RELATIONSHIP

Hubris and isolation accompany intelligence and accomplishment. If you're smart and successful, you are prey to these dangers. And you don't see them as dangers. Your brains enable you to avoid most of the pitfalls of life; you think fast, you process information efficiently, you sense implications. But the inner encroachments of self-destructive intelligence mask themselves from you. Your intellect is working to keep you from seeing what is happening to you.

Narcissism is a nasty word. We would all instinctively reject the notion that we are narcissists. But it comes with the territory. In a talk he gave to a group of executives the psychologist Aaron Stern said that "success, by definition, breeds narcissism." Moreover, the society in which we flourish celebrates narcissism.

Horatio Alger Is Dead

Decades ago our society idealized the dedication of one's gifts to step-by-step climbing of life's ladder through loyalty, hard work, frugality, and so on. Today's ideal is the stunning one-shot—the dedication of brilliance to the big score.

This profound change in our outlook is, we submit, neither good nor bad in itself. (We're not writing a morality tract.) It just *is*. Billy Joel's message differs radically from Horatio Alger's. It would be idle to deny that success breeds narcissism, enhances our natural hubris, and walls us off from the realities.

That's dangerous.

One danger of the feeling of extreme isolation is despair. Today we are seeing an extreme and tragic manifestation of despair in the self-immolating behavior of many homosexuals. When the ghastly reality of AIDS hit home, perceptive members of the gay community did the common-sense thing and changed their sexual habits.

But now a growing number have resumed the high-risk activities that they know to be ultimately fatal. This is logic override to a massive degree. The folly is, to the functioning mind, undeniable. It takes a special effort of intelligence to construct a system of denial.

Suicidal behavior is the absolute outer limit of the kind of risk addiction that overwhelms so many smart people.

The Computer Is a Downer

Our world promotes isolation as well as hubris. Impersonality is the essence of our way of life. The computer is the central symbol of this development. E-mail is the antithesis of personal contact. Technology has rescued us from many of the inconveniences that used to beset our lives. At the same time technology is cutting us off from human interaction.

In his talk, Aaron Stern said, "Stress increases geometrically with impersonality." In electricity, a static charge builds up in one terminal when communication with another terminal is blocked. When the charge becomes overwhelming, it rips out in a lightning bolt. Stress is the charge built up by lack of communication between humans. You don't cure stress by jogging; you cure it by opening up channels along with the charge can flow.

With some people, such channels run in only one direction. Certain personality types relieve stress by laying it off on others, without reciprocation. ("I don't get ulcers, I give 'em!") Such devices do relieve stress, at least for a time. But they are not relationships. To function best in the world, and to fend off the inroads of self-destructive intelligence, we need special kinds of relationships.

Make Yourself Useful, Eros

We end, appropriately, With Love.

The person to whom you are closest should be your strongest ally in keeping your intellect on track, and pulling you back from the brink of folly. A loving relationship should be a critical relationship—critical in the sense of evaluation, analysis, and judgment. And the loving relationship is a two-way street. Each party helps the other. The help consists of what is *needed*, not what is wanted.

People who really love each other frequently fail to help each other because of misplaced ideas of what love is all about. If love is doing what pleases the other person, moment to moment, then of course there isn't any place for the kind of mutual help we advocate.

That, however, is not what love is. A deeply committed relationship between two people should be a *smart* relationship, in which each uses intelligence to help the other.

This assumes that the parties are essentially on a par intellectually. You may hook up with somebody who is a lot dumber than you are, and you might make it work, but it will not be the kind of relationship we're talking about here. When there is a great gulf in intelligence between the parties, then the attraction is based on something else.

Usually sex. But it is usually more complicated than those three little letters imply. From the point of view of the smarter party, is the relationship cemented solely by the pleasures of intercourse? To what extent does domination come into play? Or trophy collecting? Or personal abasement? In Somerset Maugham's *Of Human Bondage*, the sensitive, talented Philip Carey is brought low by his obsessive affair with the sluttish Mildred, who brings nothing to the intellectual table.

The most satisfying, viable relationships for smart people are with other smart people. Sure, there are frictions . . . arguments . . . ego clashes. But living together successfully must involve a meeting of minds as well as body parts.

Furthermore, from our point of view, smart people should get together with other smart people because they can strengthen each other in immunity to SDIS. This may seem somewhat pragmatic—but, after all, what good is love if it doesn't have some practical aspects?

Love is not an excuse for not telling helpful and cautionary truths. It is an opportunity to use the channels opened by caring and affection to beam messages that keep the other person's inner compass in working order.

The Suspect "Strategy of Six"

A woman whose job gives her a good vantage point on women in business says, "Entrepreneurism among women is a strong growth sector. Many women are deciding against the corporate route. Partly this is because of the 'glass ceiling.' But it's also because women don't want to repeat the mistakes made by their male counterparts. They resist getting involved with the kinds of bureaucracies that have grown up in corporations."

However, says this observer, women in business are fragmenting their personal lives by adopting the "Strategy of Six":
   • A younger man to take to Club Med
   • A companion for the theater, concerts, art shows, and so on
   • A man to take home on family occasions
   • Someone to "hang out" with; perhaps a gay friend
   • A man for out of town
   • An international lover

"You never develop the personal side of your life with this strategy," says our observer. Worse yet, you have no one with whom you can have a *smart relationship.*

High Points of the Smart Relationship

Here's how smart people in love can keep each other from doing dumb things.

In-house Consultation. Businesses benefit from consultants. You can do the same. Use your partner as a consultant—on business, on career decisions, on lifestyle. While your partner may not have credentials as a therapist or management consultant, he/she makes up for it by knowing you far better than such third parties. And vice versa. You perform the same service for her/him.

Make the sessions calm, semiformal. Lay out the facts. Use Q and A. Reason together to narrow down the possible courses of action. Agree on what is to be done and the timetable for doing it.

Besides getting advice that takes into account exactly who you are and what you want, you will save a lot of money.

Hi-Lo Alarm Service. Your needle is starting to edge up into the red or slump down toward zero. You're getting a little manic or you're sliding slowly toward depression.

You can't tell. But your partner can. And you can detect the same signs in your partner.

Some partners just grit their teeth and try to ignore the highs or lows in the other person. Some try the placatory approach, being nice, saying the right things. Some react in exasperation: "For God's sake snap out of it!"

There's a better way. Talk about it. When you detect hi-lo danger signals, sit down and discuss it. The way to do it is to focus on the facts. Don't say, "Last night you acted like a maniac!" Instead, say, "When Roberta got started about law and order, you really showed up the logical flaws in her argument. She looked like a dope. Usually you don't pay her any attention, like the rest of us. What made you go after her this time?"

Quiet Repose. Sometimes just sitting quietly is the most soul-nourishing—and intellect-healing—thing we can do. The frantic pace of life today doesn't lend itself to quiet time. Even people who are very close to one another feel that silence is like dead air on a talk show, a vacuum that must be filled.

Your relationship is not a talk show. In fact, the moments that test the true quality of the relationship are the quiet moments.

The Smiling Mirror of Reality. When the French actor Jean Carmet died in April 1994, someone suggested to a friend that Carmet was so well liked by ordinary people because he "was one of them."

"No," said the friend, "actually he was different, an extraordinary person. He reflected people back to themselves—but with a funny face."

People who love each other can hold up the mirror of reality, helping each other to fill the gap between self-image and the perceptions of others. This can be done as a kind of instant replay ("Now let's loom at the play from another angle") in which something that one party did is run endlessly and critically on a screen.

It's better if the reflection has a "funny face." Use warmth and humor to help your partner see himself/herself in the mirror, in a pleasant but nevertheless realistic way. And in turn allow your partner to hold up the mirror. Really *look* at what the mirror displays. It is you, reflected in loving eyes.

Sounding Boards. Just listening can be the most important thing one partner does for another at a given moment.

Partner A says, with some emphasis, "Let me tell you what I have in mind." A proceeds to describe an off-the-wall course of action that is certain to arouse alarm and disapproval in B. A is waiting for a sharp rejoinder, ready to rip into a heated argument. But B just listens.

A feels frustrated at first, but then subsides. A begins to pick holes in the plan, without B getting into the action. In the end A has talked himself/herself out of it.

Partner B has performed the great service of being the perfect sounding board—intelligent, understanding, sympathetic, quiet—getting the point but not picking a fight over it. It takes a smart person to play this role, even though it's a relatively silent one. A would not talk the same way to a dummy.

Compass Checking. We've discussed the importance of personal goals and values, and how they give us our compass bearings in times of confusion, when we're straying off course. You can check your own compass. You can check your partner's compass. And you should encourage your partner to check out your own compass by, from time to time, reminding you of the things you think are important:

"Sure you can shake everybody up by saying you rigged the election, but what happens tomorrow?"

"There's more money in our pockets if we skim a little on the taxes, but can you imagine what they'll say about us if it comes out?"

"You can get away with it. I'll help you if you want. Just let me ask this. How will you feel about yourself a week from today?"

Clear-Channel Communication. Overall, the smart relationship rides on constant, candid communication. Nothing to needlessly hurt the other one, but nothing held back if it will help. The communication need not be verbal. When two people are close, a look or a gesture may be enough to flash a message:

"How far do you want to push this?"

"Do you need to prove something to yourself? To me? To whom?"

"*I love you*—and I see you starting to hurt yourself. Let me help."

Omnia vincit amor is a deathless line, but Virgil was using poetic license. Love does not conquer all; sometimes it conquers just the lover. But in a truly loving relationship between two people of intelligence and accomplishment, the parties bring their brains to bear on saving not only themselves but their partners from self-destructive folly.

Considering what can happen to strong intellects when they run amok, this may be the greatest gift that love can bring.

Staving Off Inmania

Nobody likes criticism. We've discussed the case of Bobby Ray Inman, whose insulation from criticism lured him into high-profile dumbness.

Are you shielding yourself from criticism to an excessive extent? "Of course not," you say. Of course you'd say that; *you are the last to know.* Your brain has constructed a defense mechanism that screens out the criticism and keeps you from knowing that there is any criticism to be screened out.

A word about defense mechanisms—we often find that people connect the concept of defense mechanisms with weakness. Wrong. Defense mechanisms are necessary to human functioning. They are positive initiatives taken by the personality to make a stronger whole. A youngster who is not good at sports studies hard and becomes a star student.

In healthy doses, we blot out a painful episode by forgetting; thus we are able to carry on. (Note that "forgetting" is not the same as never being conscious of the episode at all.) When pride and memory conflict, pride tends to win. Typically, a student fails a school examination and gets sick. Later, he remembers that he got sick *first*, and thus flunked the exam. In unhealthy degrees, the forgetting is carried to such degrees that a deeper withdrawal results. If the withdrawal amounts to a complete loss of contact with reality, then we have true mental illness.

But those are extreme cases. We all have defense mechanisms. The healthy psyche maintains defenses that operate in moderation. For example, it screens out the heaviest impact of criticism, turns down the volume on strident criticism, and filters out harsh and unremitting attack. But it does not lift us above criticism, nor does it transform us into creatures about whom nobody ever says a bad thing. Who, after all, attains to that state? There are even those who knock Mother Teresa.

The screening out of *all* criticism is a defense mechanism run wild; call it *inmania*. Inmania hurts in two ways:

- **The inmaniac, oblivious of criticism that might be helpful, blunders unguided into a morass**
- **When a small dart of criticism does at last penetrate the shield, it hits with the impact of a rocket shell**

Instead of a screening mechanism—or of a wide-angle antenna that leaves us open to all criticism—we need a *scanner*. The electronic scanner enables its operator to surf through the wavelengths, sampling what is being broadcast. The psychic scanner gives us a sampling of what is thought and said about us at any given time. It is an invaluable check of the width of the gap between self-image and public perception.

And of course one of the insidious qualities of inmania is that people don't realize they have it.

> ## Are You an Inmaniac?
> Do people usually approve of you?
> When was the last time somebody criticized you?
> Did you get the import of the criticism or just the fact that it was made?
> Did you resent it?
> When was the last time you changed something about yourself because of what someone said?
> Are your critics motivated by envy, spite, or some other base motive?
> Are those who praise you objective and judicious observers?
> Do you know what people think of you?
> Are you reluctant to criticize others?
> Do people benefit from perceptive criticism?
> Might you be better off if you tuned in to criticism?

The Nitpicking Partner as a Career Plus

One of the best safeguards against inmania is to have, close to you, a person who has your welfare at heart, who knows you well, whose judgment you trust, and to whom you will listen.

From time immemorial the nitpicking mate (traditionally depicted as a nagging wife) has been a figure of fun. Those of us who have reached a certain age grew up with the characters, Jiggs and Maggie, from the comic strip, "Bringing Up Father"—Jiggs's joie de vivre is always being rebuked by Maggie's carping. In *The Odd Couple*, Felix filled the role of nagger, constantly lamenting Oscar's relaxed lifestyle.

The folklore is that we resent and reject critical commentary by those closest to us, and that we are right to do so; and of course many of us act this way. But the *healthiest relationships involve mutual criticism; and there are pivotal times when the critical role of one partner can save the other partner from disaster.*

My wife, Gloria (says author Feinberg), is my best critic. I came back from a Washington seminar comprising senators, representatives, and cabinet members and said, "I listened to those fellows and I tell you I am as bright as they are," to which she replied, "That's the trouble with the United States."

Constructive criticism between partners needs ground rules to work. The particular ground rules within a relationship depend on the personalities of the people involved, the sensitivities on either side, and the good will of the parties. Certain general principles apply.

Watch the Timing. Partner A comes home after a wretched day and complains "You know what that SOB said about me? That I'm sloppy!" Partner B says, "Maybe he's right." And the battle erupts.

Preparation for companionable criticism need not be as elaborate as that of a gaggle of diplomats arguing over the shape of the table before getting down to discussions, but it merits some thought. Mornings, when both parties are fresh, may be the optimum time for some (with the added advantage that there is a time limit, since both parties have to go off to their respective occupations). Or maybe it's in the evening, after a good dinner and a decent wine.

Consent Between Adults. We acknowledge that sexual intercourse should be agreed on by both people, and that it should be preceded by a pleasant buildup. Abruptness is analogous to rape.

A little foreplay is essential in criticism, too. First, Party A should determine that Party B is willing and able to listen. This is not a matter of asking a question like "I have some suggestions that will help you shape up; do you want to hear them now?" The universal impulse is to answer, "Mañana!"

The conjugal critic has to be a little more direct: "There's something I want to talk with you about; this is a good time, right?"

Facts, Not Accusations. "You're always . . ." These two words, which start out many critical observations, carry the ring of doom for the effectiveness of the criticism and, eventually, of the relationship itself. When a critic begins with *you*, the connotation is that of a personal attack rather than a judicious comment. And the *always* is typical of the kind of exaggeration that marks critical exchange among people who are close to each other and who, in spite of the tenor of the remarks, like each other.

Criticism fails when it attacks the ego rather than the behavior.

But let's face it; it is unreal to expect a person close to you to always deliver criticism couched in language suitable to a brief submitted to the Supreme Court. When someone cares about you they are anguished when they see you doing something harmful to yourself; they speak emphatically, even passionately. The emphasis grows out of affection, not dislike.

So the critic should be as cool and objective as possible. And the person being criticized should be willing to make allowances.

Use Humor Carefully. The conceited husband says, after giving a speech, "I brought the house down!" His wife replies, "So do termites." Not a bad one-liner. But conjugal criticism is not a sitcom. Smart people are often witty people, and wit can be pointed, even cruel. The exchange of genial insults is often a staple of a healthy, easy-going relationship. However, the combination of the mock insult with the sincere criticism is a dangerous mixture.

A better way of using wit in criticism lies in the third-party approach. Snappy partners often amuse each other by satirizing others: colleagues, friends, relatives, and so on. Not necessarily the most noble of pastimes, but one that is basically harmless. So a useful lead-in to the critique is to choose an appropriate target:

"God, did you hear Jerry going on about his trip to Sri Lanka?"

"Yeah. Whatever anybody says about a vacation, he has to top it. If you tell him you're going to Saturn he'll tell you about his tour of Pluto."

"He gets caught up in how great the trip was, and he doesn't realize how boring it is for everybody else. We all do that, in a way. Even you, the other day, when . . ."

Cast the First Stone at Yourself. A variation of the previous ploy is the self-critical approach.

"I really blew it today; held forth at the meeting for ten minutes on what I'd do to solve the problems over in Financial, with poor Steve sitting there listening to me, and probably thinking, 'Easy for him, he doesn't have to cope with what I have to cope with.' Happens to all of us, I guess. Didn't you do kind of the same thing that time when . . ."

Be Calm and Straightforward. When the way has been cleared, make the criticism clearly and unambiguously. Don't sugarcoat it with a lot of half-baked praise: "You're the greatest person in dealing with people I ever met, but . . ." Don't throw in gobs of smarmy reassurance: "I wouldn't say these things if I didn't have your best interests at heart." (It should be obvious that the speaker has the other party's best interests at heart; otherwise the relationship is in trouble.) Don't use yourself as a shining example: "Don't you remember how I dealt with that?"

Just lay it on the line.

Keep Criticism Current. Often when we get angry, the past is brought out like an old duffle bag full of grievances that we carry around forever. We hurl out old indictments and air old wounds from long ago. All criticism should be in the present tense.

Don't store up criticism in a duffle bag, in which it will fester until it becomes toxic, and perhaps, explosive. Keep it current, and keep it timely.

Observe the Statute of Recriminations. No matter how close the relationship, when A is criticizing B, the best moment for B comes when the critical session ends. (Unless, of course, the underlying theme of the relationship is some variant of sadomasochism, which, unfortunately, is not all that infrequent.)

Once the criticism has been made, there should be a definite conclusion: "Okay. End of critique. Let's go out for Chinese."

Partnerships for Protection and Survival. The person closest to you should be an important asset in keeping your intelligence on a positive course. Two people who are close to each other should, when necessary, deflate each other's pride and open each other's eyes to what's really going on. Anti-SDIS maintenance and therapy can be one of the most important things we do for those we love.

If one party rejects all comment and criticism, the relationship is not as close as it should be. If both parties join to feed each other's hubristic follies and to build a wall of isolation around themselves, then both will run into problems.

Grow Up, Listen Up, Get with It

Your intelligence has gotten you far. As we've tried to demonstrate, it can also be your enemy.

Knowing about the problem is a long stride toward preventing it. We suggest, further, that you build for yourself a set of intellectual exercises. We've suggested a series of them. After all, John Elway works out to strengthen his arm; Whitney Houston vocalizes the scales. Your brain is your most important tool. Keep it in shape.

The greatest dangers posed by superior intelligence are lack of emotional growth in certain areas, overweening pride, and isolation from reality. Check your maturity. Listen—*really* listen—to other people. Get involved in the world with all of its rough edges and coarse spots. Learn to appreciate people (and there are a lot of them) who are not blessed with your intellectual attainment. And stretch your intellectual muscles by finding worthy tasks for your brain.

Smart people do dumb things, sometimes, because their brains betray them. Be kind to your intelligence. Keep it in shape; and it will remain faithful, doing what you need it to do without having it lay traps for you.

And when you do that, why, there's no downside to being smart!

INDEX

Index

Index

Index

in politicians, 74, 121, 123–24, 127, 130, 133–35
to the property of others, 134, 172–73
public exposure vs., 134–36
rationalizations in, 119, 133–34
in religious leaders, 121–22
to sexual relationships, 21, 33, 119–27
to taking advantage of one's position, 133–34
underlying feelings of inferiority in, 126, 134
entrepreneurs, 18, 27, 33–34, 37, 38, 43–44, 152–55
envelope busters, 32, 163
"Equity" computer program, 18, 34, 44
Erdman, Robert M., 65–67
ethical community, participation in, 248–49
Euripides, 205
exhibitionism, 75, 125
existentialism, 234–35
expertise:
    fallacy of, 147, 150
    feedback needed by, 247–48
    as life goal, 239
extramarital affairs, 41, 48–49, 89, 168–69

failure, unconscious need for, see unconscious need to fail
fame, as life goal, 239, 242
"family values," 236
Fancher, Raymond, 47
Fassel, Diane, 151–52, 153
Fazzini, Dan, 125–26
fear of success, 112
Federal Bureau of Investigation (FBI), 38–40
feedback, 173–74

needed by expertise, 247–48
    see also criticism
Feinberg, Gloria, 261
Feinberg, Harvey, 116
Feinberg, Wilfred, 64
"Feinberg Factor," 28, 211
Festinger, Leon, 145
feudalism, 120
finances, 93–94, 168, 227–28
    sense of entitlement in, 127–34, 135
    see also taxes
first job, 180–92
    concealing problems in, 191–92
    risk junkies in, 188–90
    selective listening in, 190–91
    see also job interviews
Fischer, Bobby, 213
Fisher, Bernard, 47–48
folie à deux, 146
followership, 121–22
foot fetishism, 41
Ford Motor Company, 137, 148
France, 92, 96, 116, 135
    Socialist party financial scandal in, 135
Frankfurter, Felix, 61
Franklin, Benjamin, 53
fraud, scientific, 45–48
Freud, Sigmund, 114, 187, 204, 205, 214
Friedman, Stanley, 133–34

General Electric (GE), 131
General Motors (GM), 99, 129, 155–58
    Allanté automobile of, 156
    exploding trucks produced by, 156–58
Germany, 79–82, 91, 92, 116
Gerstner, Louis, 36
Gibraltar Amusements Ltd., 65–67

Index

Index

Index

Index

Pericles, 52, 89
perks, 75, 76, 98, 121, 136
  excessive demands for, 21–22, 27
  reduction of, 135
Perlman, Barry, 70
Perot, Ross, 105
Persia, 54
Peters, Tom, 18, 34, 44
Philby, Kim, 132
phone calls, *see* telephone calls
PIN (Personal Identification Number)
  numbers, 23–24, 140–42
Pissarro, Camille, 111
Pittsburgh, University of, 47
pleasures, 127
  as life goal, 239
  simple, mature appreciation of,
    225–26
Plutarch, 53, 54, 55
Pointillism, 111
politic, definition of, 117
political campaigns, 17, 29, 31,
    237–39
  issues in, 84, 89–90, 93–95
politicians, 17, 32–33, 41, 48–51,
    77–84, 85–95, 245, 261
  British, 18, 42, 92–95, 135, 149
  cover-ups attempted by, 20, 33,
    88–91
  enemies made by, 117–18
  feelings of omnipotence in, 78
  group folly of, 147–51
  intolerant of criticism, 84, 101–8
  isolation of, 97
  media coverage of, 20, 22, 42,
    48–49, 73–74, 79–82, 86, 93–94,
    101–5, 106, 117, 135
  mistakes of others repeated by, 20,
    86–91
  Officeholder's Afflatus in, 84
  public relations managers of,
    79–83

sense of entitlement in, 73–74, 121,
    123–24, 127, 130, 133–35
  superior moral stance taken by,
    93–95
  unconscious need to fail in, 50–51,
    73, 108, 116–18
polls, opinion, 247–48
power, 78, 125, 136, 119
  childhood experience of, 206
  misuse of, 124, 134
pressure-for-results, 131
Priam, King of Troy, 52
pride, 72, 259
  "downplaying" of, 83
  group, 57–58
  overweening, 56, 57, 265
  see also hubris
primus inter pares ("first among
    equals"), principle of, 145
Princeton Associates, 147
public relations managers, 79–83
public television executives, 128–30
Publilius Syrus, 54, 102

race, intelligence and, 45
racist remarks, 27
Rain (Colton and Randolph), 122
rape, 33, 119–20
Raskin, Robert, 125–26
rationalizations, 29, 41, 43, 119,
    133–34, 139
Reagan, Nancy, 79, 81
Reagan, Ronald, 34, 44, 101, 102
  Bitburg cemetery visited by, 79–82,
    91
real estate developers, 152–53
reality blindness, 32–33, 159
  see also connectors with reality; dis-
    connection from reality
reciprocity, mutual, 222
Reddin, W. J., 194
Reedy, George, 151

Index

Index

Self-Destructive Intelligence Syndrome (*cont.*)
self-diagnostic test for, 175–79; *see also* self-assessment
types of, 163–64
in young people, 180–92
self-esteem, 76
self-image, 107, 257
idealized, 196, 201–2, 205, 210, 216
self-justification, 146–47
self-persuasion, 164
self-questioning, 245–46
self-realization, as life goal, 239, 240
Sequoia, 73–74
service, as life goal, 239, 240
Sessions, William, 38
Seurat, Georges, 111
Sexton, Brendan, 98, 151, 189
sexual compulsions, 116–17
sexual harassment, 19, 42, 121, 124
sexual relationships, 38–43
compulsive, 116–17
extramarital, 41, 48–49, 89, 168–69
homosexual, 50, 217, 253
mistakes of others repeated in, 165–68
obsessive, 21, 38–41, 42, 254
sense of entitlement in, 21, 33, 119–27
in tutorial relationships, 41–43
Shakespeare, William, 114
Shaw, George Bernard, 203–4
Shea, William A., 58–59
Shoemaker, Willie, 113
"shoulder surfers," 140
Silverman, Joy, 38–40
Simpson, O. J., 95
Sirius, 57
"60 Minutes," 157
Skinner, Thomas, 130
slowtime, 248
Socrates, 52

sodium amytal, psychiatric use of, 119–20
Solarz, Stephen J., 117–18
sounding board, acting as, 257–58
Sparta, 53–54, 55
Spectrum Information Technologies, 36–38
spies, 132
hubris in, 71
moles, 132, 142–43
stalkers, 21, 38–40, 133
Stanford-Binet intelligence test, 11
Stern, Aaron, 74, 76, 252, 253
Stern, Howard, 224
Stevens, Wallace, 247
"Strategy of Six," 255
Streisand, Barbra, 221
stress, 253
"suffering fools gladly," 117–18, 190–91
suicide, 11, 61–65, 95, 135
Summing Up, The (Maugham), 218
Summit Communications, 191
Sun, 93
Superior Cognitive Intelligence Possessing Individuals (SCIPIs), 26–27, 163
Swaggart, Jimmy, 122
Sweeney, Dennis, 50–51
Swift, Jonathan, 104, 121
systems:
construction of, 227–28
intellectual, 158–59

tact, 224–25
Tallent, Norman, 75
taxes, 135
evasion of, 18, 19, 34, 44, 131
failure to file, 61–65
Taylor, Maxwell, 148–49
teachers, 19, 42
Tec, Leon, 112

Index

ABOUT THE AUTHORS

Mortimer R. Feinberg combines an academic career with his role as a consultant and confidential counselor to management.

Dr. Feinberg is a consultant for Fortune 500 companies and the U.S. government. He is Professor Emeritus, Baruch College, City University of New York. His academic posts include those of Professor of Psychology, Chairman of the Psychology Department, and Assistant Dean at Baruch College. He travels 150,000 miles a year to lecture in the United States and other parts of the world, including China, South Africa, the United Kingdom, Germany, Turkey, and Greece. In 1985, Dr. Feinberg was one of the first industrial psychologists to speak before the Chinese Management Association in Beijing. He is a continuing resource of the Young President's Organization, and has served as principal lecturer at the American Management Association.

After serving as Chief Psychologist at the Research Institute of America, Dr. Feinberg founded and became Chairman of the Board of BFS Psychological Associates, an organization specializing in the application of practical psychology to the solution of business problems.

Dr. Feinberg is the author of many articles in general publications and professional journals. He is frequently quoted in prominent newspapers, and he appears often on television. He is a regular columnist for the *Wall Street Journal's Manager's Journal*. He is the author or co-author of a number of books, including *Effective Psychology for Managers* (Prentice-Hall, 1965), *The New Psychology for Managing People* (Prentice-Hall, 1975), *Leavetaking* (Simon & Schuster, 1978), and *Corporate Bigamy* (William Morrow, 1980). He lives with his wife, Gloria, in Cortlandt Manor, New York.

John J. Tarrant is a writer and consultant. He is the author or co-author of more than a dozen books, including *Power Public Relations* (NTC Business Books, 1992), *Business Writing with Style* (John Wiley, 1991), *Stalking the Headhunter* (Bantam, 1986), *Perks and Parachutes* (Simon & Schuster, 1985), *Career Stages* (Putnam, 1983), and *Drucker: The Man Who Invented the Corporate Society* (Cahners, 1976). Tarrant collaborated with Dr. Feinberg on *The New Psychology for Managing People* and *Leavetaking*. Tarrant's articles have appeared in various magazines, including *New York*, *Smithsonian*, *Cosmopolitan*, *Family Circle*, and *Nation's Business*.

John J. Tarrant and Mortimer Feinberg first worked together when Tarrant was Director of Management Programs at Research Institute of America. He was Director of Training for Benton & Bowles, the advertising agency. As an associate of BFS Psychological Associates he handles a variety of consulting assignments. Tarrant lives with his wife, Dorothy, in Westport, Connecticut.